A Life in Balkan Archaeology

John Chapman

OXBOW | books
Oxford & Philadelphia

Published in the United Kingdom in 2021 by
OXBOW BOOKS
The Old Music Hall, 106-108 Cowley Road, Oxford, OX4 1JE

and in the United States by
OXBOW BOOKS
1950 Lawrence Road, Havertown, PA 19083

Paperback Edition: ISBN 978-1-78925-729-8
Digital Edition: ISBN 978-1-78925-730-4 (epub)

A CIP record for this book is available from the British Library

Library of Congress Control Number: 2021943927

Printed in the United Kingdom by Short Run Press

Typeset in India by Lapiz Digital Services, Chennai.

For a complete list of Oxbow titles, please contact:

UNITED KINGDOM
Oxbow Books
Telephone (01865) 241249
Email: oxbow@oxbowbooks.com
www.oxbowbooks.com

UNITED STATES OF AMERICA
Oxbow Books
Telephone (610) 853-9131, Fax (610) 853-9146
Email: queries@casemateacademic.com
www.casemateacademic.com/oxbow

Oxbow Books is part of the Casemate Group

Front cover: Cheile Turzii gorge, Transylvania (author's photo)
Back cover: Right: Experimental house-burning, Nebelivka village, May 2015 (author's photo, Nebelivka Project); Left: The limestone pillars of the Pobiti Kamuni Mesolithic landscape (author's photo)

Ultimately, his paintings are encounters with the absence of certain individuals, the poignant frailty of relationships being an abiding concern. People come and go, their presence illuminates a moment, and their departing leaves a void. Some leave, never to return. Memory, however, brings them back.
– Paul Moorhouse and William Boyd on Howard Hodgkin exhibition in the National Portrait Gallery (Guardian Reviews, 11/03/2017)

Zaludo raboti, zaludo ne stoï
– 'Work in vain but do nothing in vain': Bulgarian proverb: translated by B. Gaydarska

Writing a memoir (Copyright: Tom Gauld)

This memoir is dedicated to my daughter Eleanor, whose childhood was partly shaped by archaeological trips to Dalmatia and Hungary

Contents

Acknowledgements

In one of her 'The joy of small things' columns for the Guardian Weekend magazine (10/04/21), Hannah Jane Parkinson observed that, in opposition to the trope of the toiling writer in a solitary study, writing books is actually a 'team sport'. This could not be more true of a memoir, for the range of people contributing to the work covers my entire lifetime. Most of the *dramatis personae* to whom I am indebted are mentioned in the various chapters, so I shall not repeat their names. Those family members and friends kind enough to read chapters and offer comments are: Laci Bartosiewicz, Paul Bland, Duncan Brown, Marga Díaz-Andreu, Stašo Forenbaher, Anthony Harding, Andy Jones, Bill Kataky, Kristian Kristiansen, Cătălin Lăzar, Predrag Novaković, Chris Scarre, Boyan Vassilev, John Watson and Alasdair Whittle. I am very grateful to them all. Thanks, too, to Louise Martin, for taking many photos of the London Institute of Archaeology and Gordon Square as they are today.

The four people who have made the greatest impact on my life and career remain in my thoughts every day: my father, Charles, who introduced me to historical sites and Greek prehistory; my mother, Freda, whose artistic nature helped me to appreciate the lovelier things of life; my university lecturer, John Nandris, whose love of the Balkans inspired me to return again and again; and my wife Bisserka, whose unsparing, razor-sharp comments have improved my writing more than she could ever have hoped. I cannot thank my Quartet enough.

List of figures

List of plates

Image credits

Any images not listed are the author's own.

Frontispiece: Tom Gauld, Guardian *Weekend* magazine, 17/04/2021, p. 26; Fig. 1: Devonport High School for Boys; Fig. 2: Photo, p. 51, in Woods, S. H. (1988) *Dartmoor Stone*, Exeter, Devon Books; Fig. 3: Frontispiece, in Strong, D. E. (ed.) (1973) *Archaeological Theory and Practice*, London, Seminar Press (photo by Richard Hubbard); Fig. 4: photo by Louise Martin; Fig. 8: Babić, S. & Tomović, M. (1996) *Milutin Garašanin. Razgovori o arheologiji*, Beograd, 3T, Foto album; Fig. 10: Carlisle City Museum; Fig. 11: Harlow Museum; Fig. 15: photo provided by Pál Raczky; Fig. 18: Gaydarska, B., Chapman, J., Raduntcheva, A. & Koleva, B. (2007) The *chaîne opératoire* approach to prehistoric figurines: an example from Dolnoslav, Bulgaria, in C. Renfrew & I. Morley (eds), *Image and Imagination, a Global Prehistory of Figurative Representation*, Cambridge, McDonald Institute, fig. 13.1; Fig. 22: lithograph from Felix Kanitz (1875–79) *Donau-Bulgarien und der Balkan*, Leipzig, Hermann Fries, republished in www.stara-sofia.com; Fig. 27: watercolour by Noel Blake (1978).

Plate 2: photo provided by John Nandris; Plate 18: Bökönyi, S. (1988) Von kupferzeitlichen Schafen und Pferden, in Lichardus (eds), *Macht, Herrschaft und Gold*, Saarbrücken, Moderne Galerie des Saarland-Museums, abb. 81; Plate 19: Chapman, J. (2010) Houses, households, villages and proto-cities in Southeastern Europe, in D. W. Anthony with J. Y. Chi (eds), *The Lost World of Old Europe. The Danube valley, 5000–3500 BC*, New York, Institute for the Study of the Ancient World, p. 74; Plate 21: European Association of Archaeologists; Plate 22: Elin Dahl (main photo) and European Association of Archaeologists (inset); Plate 26: University College London; Plate 28: University of Alba Iulia, *per* Professor Mihai Gligor.

Preface

Like a good single malt, the idea of writing an extended life-story has been maturing slowly over the last decade or more. There was once a decent number of members of the 'Balkan Prehistorians Club' – researchers into ABC prehistory (Aegean–Balkan–Carpathian), who knew each other, even if they usually disagreed violently with each other's conclusions. The list of members has recently gone into free-fall, whether through proximate retirement or the ultimate variety. Each passing makes one re-assess one's place in the Club and the contributions of each person. A memoir helps to put these good folk into context.

The second impulse came from teaching my special subjects on ABC prehistory to generations of hard-pressed Durham students. Each time I felt the class needed cheering up, I told them a story about a Balkan researcher, which usually had the desired effect (at least for a few minutes). But I never had a positive answer to my question after each story – 'Have you come across this person in your reading on ABC prehistory?' Although lack of reading was the obvious reason, even the one student in 50 who had downloaded the reading list still had no idea of the *persona* of the member of the Club. I began to suspect that, if someone did not publish these stories soon, they would disappear into the prehistoric fog.

A framework for the memoir could have utilised one of the main archaeological dimensions of variability – space or time. But pulling together all of the stories about Kosova or Moldova seemed faintly absurd – although not as absurd as all of the stories from the mid-1980s. In the end, I settled for the main stages of my life, whether as an undergraduate, a teacher in Durham or a specific research project. One consequence is that tales of my time at Newcastle and Durham Universities can be read relatively independently of the main research projects I was working on at the time. I wonder why that may be ...?

The format for the memoir also took time to emerge. I did not want this memoir to be an investigation into my research contributions – surely a less biased researcher can be found for that (perhaps my wife?). So I did not want a book heavy with footnotes, though there are enough details about how the 'fragmentation premise' came about to offer partial satisfaction to historians of archaeology. Instead, I hit on the setting of the warm, comfortable back room of a Durham pub (a snug, as it is called in the DisUnited Kingdom), in which people swap stories on a winter's night. There is only one chapter not really suited to a snug: Chapter 7, which is a historical-plus-autobiographical account of the emergence of the Third Balkan War of the 1980s–90s. But one exception can surely be made.

I should dearly like to meet the designer of the fridge magnet who has been quoted by Tom Robbins: 'People write memoirs because they lack the imagination to make things up.' In the weird world of ABC prehistory, there is absolutely no need to make things up – you just have to keep a straight face long enough to record your impressions. I hope you find these impressions worth reading.

John Chapman, Durham, 21st May 2021

Chapter 1

Growing up

I was born in 1951 in Plymouth, Devon – a city locally known as *Costa Geriatrica,* the place to which people would retire. But my father Charles had been offered a teaching job there just after the Second World War, so he moved from North Yorkshire with my mother Freda in 1946. I was one of the Baby Boomers who were to rejuvenate Plymouth over the next two decades.

It was a long time later that I found out from my mum and dad that I was not their first child – nor even their second. Food rationing was still in place and Freda's diet was probably not too great. She was also small and not strong, so all these disadvantages came together to produce one miscarriage after another. I was in adulthood by the time I found out that I had had two sisters who never survived. So for both parents and Mum in particular, I was a miracle baby – third time lucky, the survivor of the family – and I was treasured as an only child and exceedingly spoilt brat. One thing I never wanted for was love.

When I was three, we moved into a house with its own front and back gardens in a district called Peverell. My parents named this house 'Farndale' after the North York Moors valley where they went courting. Plymouth's lack of heavy industry meant that the fresh air and the parks were great for kids growing up. I would walk through the park to my local primary school, first with my mum and later on my own. I would play in the park and take my puppy, called Jenny Lou, for walks there. The front garden had enough grass to make a tiny one-hole mini-golf course and the path at the back of the house was just wide enough to form a cricket 'pitch'. There were raspberry and redcurrant bushes and on one side of the house was a pear tree that regularly produced two pears a year (to be enjoyed only if picked before the local children spotted them).

There were only three incidents that I remember from my primary school days which broke the unending pleasure of growing up in a loving family. The first was the time when I had to go into hospital for the first time since birth for a minor adenoids operation. In those days, hospital visits were strictly monitored and neither parent came to see me for three days. When the time came to go home, I sat on the steps of the hospital, crying, till my parents arrived and calmed me down. Abandonment in practice.

The next incident was when I was walking to school one day through the park and I hadn't realised that my young puppy, Jenny Lou, was following me, even when I crossed the main road. I didn't see the motorbike hitting Jenny Lou – all I knew was that she was dead and that the motorcyclist hadn't even stopped. Mum collected Jenny Lou's remains and took her back home. I was seven years old and absolutely heartbroken. Unfortunately, my parents decided that it was probably better not to buy another dog, which would only lead to more heartbreak, so I stayed without a pet for the rest of my childhood.

The third incident happened at school one summer when I was playing with some friends in the afternoon break. We were all sitting on top of a high wall, larking around, and I fell off and landed on my head. There was a lot of blood but I wasn't badly hurt – it just looked serious. The school called my mum immediately and she ran over to the headmaster's office – doubtless getting a real shock at seeing the bloodied bandages wrapped round my head. But what happened soon after was that my eyesight deteriorated and I had to wear National Health Service 'pebble' glasses. This was a social disaster that made life in class really tough. At that time, I was only the second person in the class of 30 to have glasses and so I became known as 'four eyes' and 'goggle eyes' for the rest of primary school. I think it was only in my 30s or even later that I realised that my fall off the wall may well have been connected to my need for glasses.

An early experience of religion managed to put me off for some time but not alienate me completely. Although they were not deep believers, Mum and Dad thought that a religious education was an essential part of my cultural upbringing, so they took me to a Church of England Sunday School at Emmanuel Parish Church. The young ones would sit in on the first part of Morning Service before processing over to the Sunday School. On my first visit, I came into the Sunday School to see rows of small chairs facing a trestle table covered by a blue cloth with two yellow initials – 'J. C.' As the children filed into the room, they put small coins on the yellow letters. I made the obvious assumption that the money was meant for me, not Jesus Christ, and began to collect all the coins assiduously. I was very surprised that the priest stopped my collection and insisted I replaced all the coins on the letters. It was not a good start to my relationship with God.

The junior school I went to was only a short distance from my primary school. Since everyone in my class moved to the junior school at the same time, it didn't really seem like a new school at all and things went on in very much the same manner as before, except with more music and drama. I loved singing in choirs and small groups and I also enjoyed playing the recorder a lot. Starting from the descant recorder, I progressed to the treble recorder and even the tenor recorder, testing the patience of my parents enormously with my lengthy practice.

The other novelty provided at junior school was drama – especially the chance to appear in the school play. In my final year, I was cast in the school play as the Wild Rider. I had only one entry – at a certain moment late on in the play, I would appear stage left on my hobby horse, ride twice around the assembled cast and end up standing in front of everyone and singing my Wild Rider song. This went well in rehearsals; however, on first night, when I circled the cast for the second time and came to take my position in front of the group, I slid across the floor and fell off the stage, landing on top of a cellist. The cello came off worse than I did, since I recovered sufficiently to sing my Wild Rider song before leaving the stage. I suspect this put an early end to my drama career, since I was never invited to take part in a school play again.

The 11+ exam that people sat in those days was a two-hour test taken in our junior school. I didn't do any particular preparation for this but I knew that the day of the test was important. Maybe a year and a half or two years before, my Bristol grandmother, Emily Phippen, had come to live with us in Plymouth and taken over the large spare bedroom and she would come down every morning for breakfast with us around 8 o'clock. On the day of the 11+, she didn't come down for breakfast and I asked my parents about this. They said that Grandma was resting and that she didn't feel like getting up. Having other things on my mind, I was satisfied with this reply and went off and sat the 11+ exam. Grandma didn't come down for lunch either and my parents said, 'no, she's still not well and best not to see her since she's probably sleeping'. I never saw her again. In fact, she died in the night before the exam and was lying there dead as I walked round the house. I can understand that my parents didn't want to disturb me on the day of the 11+ exam but I wonder why they didn't explain later. Ten days later, my parents told me that they had to go away for the weekend and that I couldn't come. They said that everything was arranged that I could stay with the neighbours – a nice couple called Fred and Kathleen Pittaway. The Pittaways took me in and gave me some dinner and I had an exciting night sleeping in a strange bed. They looked after me the whole of Saturday but it was on the Sunday morning that I distinguished myself. The Pittaways asked me what I would like for breakfast and, with a straight face, I said that I usually had a dozen sausages on a Sunday and was amazed that they complied with this request. I probably didn't have a very heavy lunch before my parents came back on the Sunday afternoon and life resumed. Not as normal, perhaps, because Grandma was not there. Eventually, Mum and Dad must have told me that Grandma wasn't coming back. It was, again, not till much later in life that I realised that my parents had gone away that weekend to North Yorkshire for the funeral of my grandmother, which was held in her home village of Kirkleatham.

Later on in the summer, we got back the results of the 11+ exam and I had passed, so I was eligible to go to one of the four grammar schools in Plymouth. Since my dad taught at one of them, I didn't want to go there; since the second one was a predominantly Roman Catholic school, Mum and Dad didn't want to send me there; and since the third school was regarded as snobbish, they didn't want me to go there either. This left Devonport High School for Boys as the only option. This was perfectly fine for me, since a lot of my friends from junior school were going there as well. DHS was the brother school to Devonport High School for Girls, which was actually closer than my primary school to our house and whose girls in their green and white uniforms I had become used to seeing over the last five years. The boys' school was indeed in Devonport. I had to get the morning school bus there, then I'd have a sandwich lunch (not daring to risk the appalling school meals) and, after school, I walked back through Devonport and Central Park.

The school itself was set within an enormous granite stone wall, which seemed to me at least 20 ft high (in fact, it was probably 5 m high) and went around the entire school, with only two entrances: a small side gate that was closed most of the time and the main gate, which led to two drives – one to the left going to DHS and the other to the right going to Tamar Secondary Modern school (a school for pupils who'd almost passed the 11+ exam). The whole complex (Fig. 1) was originally part of Her Majesty's Devonport Dockyard, built in the early 19th century and the grim,

Fig. 1. Colonnade, Devonport High School for Boys, Plymouth

grey, granite walls dominated all places in the school. They were solid, unforgiving and bleak, like the walls around Dartmoor Prison.

I suppose everyone has got memories of their most favourite and least favourite teachers. The headmaster, Mr Cresswell, was an extremely remote, God-like figure, tall, upright, with grey slicked-back hair, a yellowing skin and tortoiseshell-framed glasses. His only human touch was to be hypocritical over smoking and so any boy who was caught smoking on school premises would be sent for retribution to the headmaster's office and Mr Cresswell would cane the boy while smoking a cigarette at the same time. Although he taught French very little, he set high standards and, when we were in Sixth Form, had a long list of general books we should read if we wanted to try for the Oxbridge entrance exam. I remember two of the books that he talked about, which I read only much later, written by the American anthropologist Margaret Mead, *Coming of Age in Samoa* and *Growing Up in New Guinea*.

Two of my maths teachers who made a big impression were Mr Way and Mr Warne. 'Whipper' Way merited his nickname because he was prone to punishing interruptions by beating the boy on the hand with what he called his 'Cat of three tails' – a small leather strap like the Scottish tawse. 'Whipper' Way was medium-height and wore tortoiseshell-framed spectacles, with short brown hair and tweed jackets. He was not a nice man but he had one enduring trait. He was ambidextrous, so that, if there was a long formula to write out on the blackboard, he would start by writing with chalk with his left hand and halfway through the formula he would take the chalk in his right hand and continued writing as if nothing happened. He was first and foremost a disciplinarian whom we feared rather than loved.

The other maths teacher who took over from Fourth Form upwards was Mr Warne, nicknamed 'Tubby' because, although he was a rugby player in his youth, he had put on weight since then. He was tall with an oval face, little hair left and heavily built – more a prop-forward than a fly-half. He took over my maths teaching just as it became too complicated for me. He had the endearing trait of teaching probability with the use of poker dice, which we all enjoyed a great deal. But when it came to algebra and calculus, Mr Warne's teaching lost me, so I gave up on higher maths.

There were two classics teachers: a Welshman – 'Taffy' Radler – who could never keep classroom order at all. He had tufts of black hair around a soft face with black-rimmed spectacles and wore check shirts with nice suits. He was always making absurd statements, like 'those three at the back make a right pair' and, whenever interrupted, 'every time I open my mouth, some fool speaks'. He was hopeless but very lovable – the polar opposite of the Greek and Latin teacher, Mr Nicholas, who was so hated he didn't even have a nickname. He was small, with a round face, also Welsh and played rugby as scrum-half or fly-half. He had as high a set of standards for us as did Mr Cresswell and expected us to have read all of Shakespeare's plays and sonnets by the age of 16 (which none of us managed). He was a hard man and made the teaching of Greek so unpleasant that most pupils gave it up as soon as they could. I struck a deal with my father, who was also a classics teacher, that if I studied Latin to A-level, I could give up Greek after two years. Mr Nicholas was the teacher who warned me off archaeology, saying that I would never find a job in it. I remain grateful to him for making me determined to do exactly that.

Another teacher with extremely high standards but who loved his pupils was Mr Whitfield, nicknamed 'Elmer', who taught English, poetry and drama and produced all the school plays. He was small, with little remaining hair and a boot-shaped face that could turn red or even bright purple when he became emotional (often the case). He never really appreciated my lack of talent at his subject until Sixth Form, when I contributed to various productions in youth groups, which, out of interest, he came to see. He was one of the most enthusiastic teachers in the school and inspired several of the brightest pupils, such as Philip Evans and Richard Foster, to read English at University.

The last language teacher to make an impact on me was my German teacher, Mr Hopford. He made the same impact on all of us – a quiet man who could never keep discipline in the classroom, daydreamed his way through life and was constantly forgetful. Mr Hopford sometimes came to school wearing one black shoe and one brown shoe and, when challenged to explain, said that, ever since the Second World War, he had dressed in blackout and sometimes mistook his shoes. The school's favourite Hopford story concerned his driving into the centre of Plymouth one Saturday morning to do some shopping. When he had bought what he wanted, Mr Hopford could not remember where he had parked his car and phoned the police to report it stolen. After lunch, he drove his wife's car into town to look for the first car, forgot where he parked the second car and reported that stolen too. None of us could imagine how Mrs Hopford could live with such a man!

I suffered from having two history teachers, neither of whom were great guns. Mr Vanstone was a tragic case. At the start of his career, he was apparently a wonderful, outgoing teacher. Soon after he joined the school, he took part in the annual staff–school cricket match as a fast bowler but one day he let slip a bouncer, which hit the school cricket captain on the head and killed him. Mr Vanstone never recovered from this catastrophe and went into a psychological shell for the rest of his life. Each day – summer or winter – he would ride to school on his Lambretta, wrapped in three of four layers of clothing (this was especially weird in summer) to protect him from the memory of this awful event. We were sad that he had lost the qualities as a teacher that he once had. The second history teacher was Mr Evans, nicknamed 'Mousey' – a small man with little hair left bar two great sideburns and small glasses, and a smart line in tweed jackets. He was just about to retire, so he was living on his past glories, coasting along and not preparing us for very much history. Partly thanks to my inherent laziness and partly thanks to these two teachers, I did pretty badly in history A-level.

Another great Welsh rugby-playing staff member was the PE teacher, Mr Wilf Nash, who played at No. 8 for Pontypool (or conceivably Pontypridd), was lean and tough as old boots and with more lines on his face than a 1950s TV set. He too set high sporting standards and ran the school rugby teams with iron discipline. His main contact with me was during cross-country runs, when he would howl across the school field, 'Come on, Chapman – go like a stag!' Not my style, really. We were amazed to learn that, within six months of retirement, the ultra-fit Wilf Nash had dropped dead of a heart attack. This gave us pause for thought, since it happened in the same summer that one of our classmates, Bart Ireland, out hunting with another friend, Bimbo Harris, had accidentally shot and killed him by catching the trigger of the rifle in barbed wire. This gave us a new perspective on mortality.

The star of all the DHS teachers for me was someone who arrived when I was in my fifth year. Trevor Farrow was fresh out of the Royal Academy of Music in Manchester and he knew about pop music. What's more, he actually loved Beatles songs and had heard them live in Liverpool. He was wonderfully advanced compared to our previous music teachers and even got the school choir to sing pop songs in school assemblies, which must have devastated a lot of the older teachers. We got on like a house on fire; by then, my clarinet playing was pretty good and so he would accompany me on the great clarinet sonatas – the two Brahms and the Poulenc – in school concerts. Once, we played the first two movements of the Mozart clarinet concerto at a school concert. I enjoyed playing music with him so much that I stayed on in the 3rd-year Sixth Form, partly to take part in Cambridge entrance exams in the first term but mainly to study A-level music in one year with Trevor Farrow. I had a wonderful year, played a lot of music and listened to even more and even managed to squeak through my A-level music exams. Mr Farrow was much more fun than the conductor of the Plymouth Youth Orchestra, which my parents thought would be a good idea for me to join. I played second clarinet for three years but Mr Phillips, the music master in the snobbish grammar school in Plymouth, was a serious conductor, dedicated to maintaining high standards. But playing in an orchestra was good for my musical and social skills, which I took with me off to University.

Perhaps the most painful experience I had suffered at DHS involved my first experience of public speaking. In our English class, we were asked to prepare a 10-minute talk about our favourite book at the time. I was reading Eric Kästner's *Emil and the Detectives* and I put together a short talk that I thought I'd prepared well. When the time came to talk, I totally froze and uttered gibberish for three minutes before sitting down in total embarrassment. Unfortunately, nobody talked to me about this and I was too embarrassed to talk to my parents about it. If someone had tried to explain that this wasn't the end of public speaking but just the beginning, I could have overcome the problem much sooner. When I was in Sixth Form, with the opportunity to join the school Debating Society, the memories of that English talk five years ago were so strong that I didn't dare to join the Society. This would have been one of the most useful things I could have done before going to university.

One of the formative experiences of my childhood was joining the Scouts, first as a Wolf Cub, then as a Boy Scout and later as a Senior Scout. This was almost inevitable since my father was a Scout leader in his school, later City Commissioner for Plymouth and later still County Commissioner for Devon. So there was really no question about whether I was going to be in the Scouts. My father helped me socially by choosing a Scout group from the part of Plymouth where he was headmaster in a rough, tough secondary school. Quite a few of the other scouts in the 21st Plymouth group knew my father and therefore thought this was a great opportunity to take their feelings about their headmaster out on me. I did not appreciate what my father did to me but eventually it was good that I got away from meeting only grammar-school kids like myself and it helped me understand other kinds of kids – particularly working-class kids from poor families who had very different interests and different approaches to life from mine and my friends. Nonetheless, it was a real struggle for me, especially for the first two years of scout camps, when I was the youngest in the patrol of six and was picked on to wash the dishes and clean up the frying pan. Although I was never actively bullied, I was certainly put in my place and it took me a while to get used to that. At the same time, the Scouts were fun and it helped me to learn how to live away from my parents, especially in summer camp for two to three weeks, and get out into the countryside and enjoy outdoor life.

When I was 16, I progressed into the Senior Scouts. In our group, we had a Senior Scout leader called Brian Dyer. Bri Dyer was the ideal sort of leader: he kept us within the bounds but otherwise let us do pretty much what we wanted. The Senior Scout group was small and four of us bonded into an action team – Shreddie Everett, Martin Pearce, Ian Young and myself. Ian had joined as a new member from Saltash, and I tried to make him feel as welcome as possible: I had experienced how hard it can be for newcomers to join an established group. We planned our own programme: if we wanted to join a night hike on Dartmoor, we would join it; if we wanted to enter a weekend First Aid competition on Dartmoor, we would do that too. Bri Dyer supported us in all of these activities, including a one-week camping trip to the Black Mountains and the Brecon Beacons. One winter, my dad drove the four of us to Bonehill Farm, just above Widecombe-on-the-Moor for a camping trip from 27th December to 1st January. My dad knew the farmer, Mr Peters, so there was never a danger that we should fall into hard times, even when the wind destroyed our tent on the second night. But it was Bri Dyer who made all these things possible without any interference and in this he was a great leader. This was the first time that I experienced the male bonding between blokes who are exploring life. I really enjoyed those times when we became like brothers – Dartmoor Musketeers.

By the age of 14, I was starting to get my parents to take me out regularly onto Dartmoor and when the school rambling club didn't walk – perhaps two or three weekends a month – I would pester my mum to accompany me on walks across the moors, forcing her to struggle up as many tors as possible in a day. Dartmoor slowly became more than familiar – the place I really loved to walk over more than any other. Although seemingly bleak and featureless, with hardly any trees and covered with extensive blanket bog, Dartmoor's scenery is broken up by its many tors – granite rock formations each of which has a distinctive appearance, which, with time, you can recognise (Fig. 27). I slowly got to know and appreciate Dartmoor tors very well and could navigate across most of the north moor without a map. One particular feature of the tors were the rock basins that the rain had eroded into the top of the granite formations on most tors. I suppose the first 'scientific' report based on my original research was a report I wrote about the rock basins of Dartmoor, based on visits to perhaps 130 or more tors and measurements of maybe 200 rock basins. I still have another 20 tors to visit and I don't know how many more rock basins to record.

The other thing that I noticed on Dartmoor – one could hardly miss them - were the archaeological remains (Fig. 2). I found out from reading William Crossing's *Guide to Dartmoor* that these were largely Bronze Age monuments, whether hut-circles or enclosures, stone circles or stone rows. It is interesting that I didn't make these monuments the primary focus of any walk but, if there was a stone circle on the route I was planning, I most certainly visited it.

Our Senior Scout group made one small contribution to Dartmoor life. When we were walking the Moor, there were five letterboxes established at places that were out-of-the-way and hard to reach. The most famous one was at Cranmere Pool, with others at High Willhays, Fur Tor, Crow Tor and – at the time the only one on the south

Fig. 2. Downtor stone row, Dartmoor

moor – Ducks' Pool. The tradition was that a visitor would leave a postcard (with a stamp!) in the metal box to be collected and posted by the next visitor. Our Scout Group added a sixth letterbox at a tinners' hut on Fish Lake on the south-east part of the moor, which was not so often visited. We visited the tinners' hut regularly to see how many visitors had made it. Much later, in the 2000s, there was a craze about putting stamps in many different places on the moor, with over a hundred tors having their own stamps. Walkers would make a fetish of collecting as many stamps as they could on a single day. But at the time we added the Fish Lake stamp, it was only the sixth and we thought it was a positive thing to do.

I was in Sixth Form when I had the opportunity to go on an archaeological excavation for the very first time. Of the four medieval border castles protecting Dartmoor, the eastern castle is at Gidleigh, near Chagford. My father knew the owner, Geoffrey Hands, who was interested in seeing if there were any medieval deposits preserved in the main cobbled yard. So in the summer of 1967, I went there for a two-week excavation, staying in the castle and meeting Geoffrey Hands' daughter Jessica, who dramatically improved the quality of the stay in Gidleigh Castle. Even though I was the only digger, the daily programme was carefully structured, with a good breakfast at 8 am and digging from 9 am to 1 pm, a lunch hour and digging from 2 pm to 5 pm. I soon realised that a medieval cobbled yard floor was not very productive – in the two weeks, I found one medieval potsherd – but great for developing wrist-strength. The Gidleigh dig was one of the most artefact-free digs I would ever go on in my life and, if it were not for the company of Jessie Hands, I think I might have given up after a week. This made me realise that medieval archaeology was not something I really wanted to study.

The other family events that made a real difference to my interest in the past were our holidays. One of the first history holidays was in 1965 – a tour of Welsh castles. We visited all of the major castles from Conway in the north to Caernarvon in the south, with Harlech being the most dramatic monument in a stunning landscape. One thing I noticed concerned our base – a bed and breakfast in the small tourist town of Colwyn Bay on the North Coast. It was not that I was unhappy about the holiday, yet, for some reason, I could never settle in Colwyn Bay. It took me a long time to realise that the *Axis Mundi* of Colwyn Bay was all wrong. In Plymouth, where I grew up, the sea was on the south side of the town and that set your life-compass. It was hardly Colwyn Bay's fault that the sea was on the north side of town and that is what made the place all wrong for me. Much later, it occurred to me Colwyn Bay was a great example of how 'natural' features can have a strong impact on how you perceive a place where you lived or even visited.

The two holidays that made the greatest difference to my love of the past were two trips to Greece in 1967 and 1968. In the summer of 1967, my parents and I went with our Bristol relatives George and Christine on a holiday around Mainland Greece. Although I had encountered the Minoans and the Mycenaeans from the books of

Leonard Cottrell, these holidays became a personal introduction to the Aegean Bronze Age. Visiting these amazing sites was pivotal to me becoming an archaeologist.

We travelled to Greece in a curious way that probably cannot happen now – the Motorail.[1] We put our car on a train at Waterloo Station and slept on the train until we arrived next morning at Bolzano in north Italy. Here, we unloaded the car and drove south. Our main stop that day was Ravenna, replete with Byzantine basilicas; we then drove down to Ancona, where we took the ferry to Patras in the Peloponnese. After, we drove to Athens to see the great Classical sites, soon returning to the Peloponnese, where we spent two days in a small campsite on the shores of the Corinthian Gulf. Our first climb was the ascent of the Acrocorinth – the great hilltop ritual centre above the town of Corinth. So as not to disturb the other campers, we pushed our car out of the campsite at 3 or 4 am without turning the engine on. We then drove to the foot of the Acrocorinth and started the steep climb. We managed to reach the top for an unforgettable scene – the sun rising over Corinth, setting fire to the marble and limestone buildings.

Later, we drove to Mycenae, where it was amazing that we were able to pitch our tents in the courtyard of the taverna, *La Belle Hélène*, where Heinrich Schliemann had stayed during his excavations there. This very personal connection to Schliemann made our walk around Mycenae really special; seeing the Lion Gate, the Grave Circles, the Treasury of Atreus and the acropolis palace was truly memorable (Plate 1).

From Mycenae, we drove across the Argive Plain to what was perhaps the most impressive Mycenaean site of all – Tiryns. The remains of the palace were far more concentrated than at Mycenae and the size of the amazing Cyclopean walls put even the Treasury of Atreus into perspective. We walked around the site twice – first on the outside of the walls and then on the inside. We walked in and out of the little Postern Gate and got a feeling for defensive architecture at its most dramatic in the Aegean Bronze Age.

For a budding prehistorian, it was a disappointment to move out of the Mycenean heartland and drive northwards to Delphi. Although the Delphic Oracle was mysterious and the race-track impressive, the Mycenaean bug had bitten me and nothing could overshadow the Lion Gate and the Cyclopean walls of Tiryns. Then we moved north to Thermopylae, now a dilapidated village set next to the gorge where the famous battle took place between the Greek city-states and the Persians led by Xerxes in 480 BC. It was intriguing to see the setting for the battle but Thermopylae had been poisoned by the fumes of its famous sulphurous spring. The fumes made the hotel where we stayed really unpleasant, with the most unfriendly staff we had encountered in Greece, who clearly didn't like living in smelly rooms and serving smelly food. We left as soon as possible next morning. We drove across the Plain of Thessaly to the early Christian site of Meteora, with monasteries perched on top of vast cliffs. Unfortunately, we were not taken up to the churches in a net – the

[1] Motorail services connect parts of Continental Europe but not from the UK.

classic way to visit. We were running out of time and had to drive back south and across the Peloponnese. We barely had time to enjoy the Classical temple of Olympia before rushing back to Patras to take the ferry back to Ancona. This holiday brought the Mycenaean world to life for me and left me with bright new perspectives on a Europe more than 3,000 years ago, which stirred me more than any other monuments I had yet seen.

My parents were clever enough to follow this holiday up with a trip to Crete in Easter 1968 to discover the Minoans. We flew to Athens and then on to Heraklion in a small and very scary plane with twin engines precariously mounted on its wings. There seemed no way that this plane could achieve lift-off or ever reach the centre of the Aegean Sea. Yet, as predicted, we arrived in Heraklion, where my dad tried his much-practised trick of going to the dirtiest restaurant in the main street to find the best food and speaking his schoolmaster's version of Ancient Greek to the waiters. It was a great start to our Cretan visit to go into this restaurant, pointing to what you wanted to eat and having it served up within five minutes.

Knossos was a 15-minute bus ride from the centre of Heraklion and we reached there in time for the first guided tour. Who could dispute Arthur Evans' decision to restore the palace? It was impossible not to marvel at the reconstructions – especially the Grand Staircase. Something I could never have expected occurred at Knossos – painted frescoes that eclipsed even the finest Mycenaean architecture.

Our most challenging walk was the descent of the Gorge of Samaria from the centre of Crete to the South Aegean Sea. For this, we took a bus to Chania, the largest town in Western Crete, and another bus across the Omalos Plateau. Our late afternoon bus was soon in the clouds and gave up at Lakkoi, a village on the northern edge of the plateau. This left us with a long walk across the plateau and, with directions from the local bus driver, we started off in the thick fog, with a visibility of maybe 10 m. After two hours' walk, we came upon a little cluster of houses, which was the first settlement we had seen on the plateau – the hamlet of Samaria. This looked promising, especially since there was a *kafeneion* sign on one of the houses. We stopped there and asked if we could get anything to eat and, more importantly, if there was a room for the night. The owner of the *kafeneion* looked dubious at this prospect but took us out of the cafe, up an outside staircase, into a room which might have been under an active sprinkler system, how damp it was. The walls were streaming with water, the bedclothes were damp, the pillows were damp – everything about the room was soaking wet but it was the only place he had, so we gratefully accepted his offer. Luckily, we all had sleeping bags and slept inside them after a basic but very welcome meal. By the morning, the mist had lifted and so we set off for what turned out to be only a short walk of 15 minutes to the top of the Samaria Gorge. The descent through the gorge was one of the most spectacular treks in Crete in the 1960s. The only way down was a steep, narrow path sometimes marked with low green railings to stop walkers falling down into the gorge. We zigzagged our way down the path into the gorge, which took most of the morning on a bright, sunny day in which very little sun made it into the gorge. It was a peaceful walk in the most beautiful surroundings, with no one else on the track. Eventually, we reached the level of the river, which started off as a stream but slowly gained in size and pace. After a further two hours, we came to the rocky part of the gorge, where the path narrowed until it was blocked on both sides by 50 m high crags with a narrow, bubbling stream. Further down, the path disappeared completely, the rocks came in and the only way through was to wade through the river for 100 m or so. Although we were wet up to our thighs, we kept our supplies dry. It was a magical moment when we came out of the gorge to see the southern sea for the first time. That night, we camped on the beach beside the wine-dark sea, near the village of Aghia Roumeli. Next morning, according to a tradition that I'd read about, a fisherman from the next village along the coast to the east would come with his boat to collect anyone who'd walked down the gorge the previous day. We were the only customers for the trip to Chora Sfakion. During the long wait for the Heraklion bus, we strolled around the village and came to learn more about this remote spot.

Chora Sfakion was one of the very last villages to fall to the Ottoman invaders of Crete in AD 1669. There was no obvious way into the village from the north and the village was well defended on the seaward side. But the village was betrayed by a family who let the Turks know of the secret back entrance into the village. The Turks soon finished off the rest of the villagers and, as a reward, granted the treacherous family a small island 100 m from the shoreline. Several centuries later, this family still owned the offshore island. In the 1960s, this family had a problematic uncle called Giorgios, who simply loved his ouzo. Nothing the family tried could wean the uncle off his liquor, so they hit on a plan to give Giorgios bread, water, cheese and olives and leave him on the family island for three days to dry out. After much protestation, Uncle Giorgios was bundled into a boat with his provisions, rowed to the island and left for three days. The family were convinced that this plan would work and so they did not worry until the fourth morning, when they returned to the island. There was Giorgios, completely drunk and singing loudly. How on earth was this possible? Giorgios was still alert enough to be able to point across at a barrel that lay on the shore – a barrel of red wine that had floated across the Mediterranean from Africa and ended up on Giorgios' island. At this point, the family gave up all attempts to save Giorgios' liver and he drank himself into oblivion over the next few years.

The next day, we took the bus from Heraklion to the Palace of Phaestos, sitting snugly on a low hill on the north side of the plain of the Mesara. We had arrived on the Orthodox Good Friday and could only explore the palace, which was officially closed for the entire weekend, when the guards had gone home. The elegance of the Grand Staircase and the Central Court at Phaestos more than made up for the lack of Arthurian colours. On Easter Saturday, we discovered the fragrance of the Mediterranean in a short walk from Phaestos to the Minoan Villa of Aghia Triadha. This miraculous walk across the hills brought a new and bitter smell, with every step crushing herbs as we went to the villa – a minor gem with a wonderful panorama to the Bay of Mesara.

My father knew that there would be a series of Easter processions across the plain of the Mesara that evening. We climbed up the side of Phaestos hill to get a panoramic view over the plain. Just before midnight, tiny lights started to appear in each of the Mesara villages and processions made their way to the central village to arrive at midnight – the start of the holiest day of the Orthodox calendar. This was a fitting end to our short stay at Phaestos.

We were amazed to discover that there was a bus back to Hieraklion on Easter Sunday, which we leapt aboard. We then went further to Mallia, arriving there on Easter Sunday afternoon. In our travel bag, we had a secret weapon – an amazing guidebook to Crete, which featured in the section on Mallia a photo of an old man and his daughter picking grapes in the *Pension Lapithes*. When we arrived in Mallia at the bus station, we asked for the *Pension*. The bus driver directed us to the *Pension*, where, amazingly, the old man in the photo was there in the front garden. My father re-engaged with his Ancient Greek and tried to explain to the old man how his photo was in a book we had brought all the way from England. The old man ran off with the book inside the house, to emerge with his daughter – also in the photo – who spoke English. The Lapithes family welcomed us with open arms, brought us a late lunch and insisted that we shared an Easter Monday lunch with them and their extended family. The centrepiece of the feast was a spit-roasted lamb and unbelievable quantities (for a Sixth-Former) of ouzo and retsina. We stayed with the Lapithes family for two days, which gave us enough time to explore the Minoan palace. So in this fantastic Eastertide, we lost a guidebook but gained great friends.

Our next bus trip after the town of Agios Nikolaos was to the easternmost town on Crete – Sitia – and then on to the recently discovered Minoan palace of Kato Zakro. We found a taxi driver who agreed, for a trifle, to take us there and back with an hour to look at the palace. Astonishingly, we were the only visitors to an almost completely excavated Minoan Palace, so this visit was unique for our entire trip. On the way back, the taxi driver's attention was unequally divided between the appalling road and the football commentary on a World Cup Qualifier between Greece and Bulgaria. The score remained 0–0 up to the 87th minute, when Greece scored. The screams of delight and roars of approval from the crowd were matched by the taxi driver, who was so overjoyed by the goal that he almost drove off the road into a ravine!

One of our most dramatic walking trips was from Ayios Nikolaos up into the hills to the Dark Age hilltop site of Lato – a brilliant choice of a fortress on twin peaks with a great view to Ayios Nikolaos. The path to the fortress was also lovely in the early spring freshness, especially near a small Byzantine chapel. Unusually, Mum was feeling a bit tired and didn't want to walk up the hill to Lato, so she sat down near the chapel and started to sketch it with pencils. One of the most lovely recollections I have of that entire holiday was Mum's sketching. I only wish that she had found a way to develop her talent. If she'd had encouragement from family and friends, she would probably have been a good artist.

After seeing the completely excavated Minoan town of Gournia and the windmills of the Plain of Lasithi, we took the last bus to Heraklion, for the last supper and overnight stay of our holiday. After this trip, nothing was going to stop me becoming an Aegean archaeologist!

I had decided to stay in school for a third year in the Sixth Form to sit the Cambridge entrance exam in the autumn and then remain to complete an A-level music course. The advice from my school against studying archaeology at university persuaded me to divide my university entrance application (the UCCA form) between history and archaeology. Because Cambridge had to be in top place on the UCCA form, and because my father had been to Peterhouse, I applied for Peterhouse. I went there for a history interview before the written exam but, by the end of the interview, I knew that I was not going to study history at Peterhouse. Unfortunately, neither Dad nor the school had warned me that Peterhouse was famous for its right-wing views. Two old historians took a particularly personal delight in chopping a young, left-leaning candidate into small pieces with their infinitely superior knowledge of 18th- and 19th-century history. This interview was such a humiliating experience that it took me many years to recover from, leaving me with a long-term inferiority complex about Oxbridge students.

When I went to the Institute of Archaeology in London for interview, I was astonished that the expected ordeal never materialised. It was clear that the Institute wanted to accept me and only one demanding question came up, from the Registrar Mr Edward Pyddoke. He asked me how I would cope with the everyday things that prehistorians studied – the grotty pottery and chipped stone – when all I was interested in was Minoan frescoes. I gave a confident reply that I would be happy to learn all about them, get to know them and understand them. This answer seemed to satisfy Mr Pyddoke and Professor John D. Evans and I was not at all surprised that I soon received an offer of a place at the Institute. Shortly after my rejection from Cambridge, I was accepted as a student at the Institute.

Chapter 2

Undergraduate days

I started my undergraduate life in the University of London at that small independent college, the Institute of Archaeology, in 1969. I missed 1968 – the Great Year of Protest – by one year: some may say the story of my life. This was the first time in Western Europe when there was a chance that protesting workers and intellectuals/students could combine forces to overthrow the *status quo*. Even though I didn't paint the LSE Senior Common Room walls red or go over to Paris to join in the street *manifestations*, there were still big demonstrations in Trafalgar Square in 1969 and 1970 – especially the two great South African apartheid demonstrations. After those, I could never really trust the police, especially the mounted police who rode straight at demonstrators and injured some of my friends. There was another reason I could never really trust the police after this year. Several of my friends and I joined a homeless food run on Friday evenings, when we would go around in a van with a jorum of hot soup and lots of sandwiches for rough sleepers. In one of the regular stops – the Arches underneath Waterloo Bridge before they were gentrified – we arrived to find the pavement and the rough sleepers and all their belongings soaked through. They told us that the police had hosed the area down to try to clear the Arches. Who can trust the police after such behaviour?

This was an optimistic time when progressive politics was afoot, with the Labour Government led by Harold Wilson and later by Jim Callahan. It was also a time when the Irish Troubles had very much arrived in London, with IRA acts against the Government and the people beginning in 1970. What was troubling were the squad cars with armed officers in Euston Square, underlining the menace and the tension in the city. But there was also a feeling of social change, with feminism in the air and the publication of the *Female Eunuch* making a big splash. This was the time of Swinging London, especially on the Kings Road. Every other Saturday, I would walk down the Fulham Road from the South Kensington tube station to the Chelsea Football Ground to watch a match – enjoying the sun, the vibes and the beautiful people.

At Commonwealth Hall, I met some very interesting student musicians who joined up to play free-form jazz. The main players were Jonathan Tubb on tenor sax, Git Wikremasingh, who played keyboards and also trombone, and a bass player,

Nigel Simmons. We would book a room in Senate House from time to time to rehearse Tubb's arrangements. Since I'd never played free-form jazz before, it was an exciting time for me and my clarinet. One night, we were playing at a birthday party in Commonwealth Hall. The unfortunate thing was that the birthday boy's room was directly above the warden's flat. The warden was a professor of linguistics and was having some people round for a *soirée musicale*, which definitely did not include free-form jazz. After 11 pm, the warden got very upset with this raucous noise crashing directly through his ceiling, so he came up to complain. We could only suppose that he had consumed a fair bit of alcohol when he came to our room, for he banged on the door and marched in uninvited to see what was going on. At this time, Git was playing trombone and he continued to play until the warden approached him, snatched the trombone from his hands and threw it through the open window, whereupon it spiralled gracefully down five floors to hit the tarmac of Cartwright Gardens and broke into a thousand pieces. At this point, the warden said, 'Right – no more playing' and stormed out of the room. This was an unnecessary comment – we were all shocked into total silence and we packed up our gear and went home. Git was most aggrieved at the warden and made an appointment to see him the next morning. By this time, the warden had realised exactly what he'd done and was deeply apologetic. He offered to write Git a cheque to buy a new trombone and asked Git how much he'd paid for the trombone. Thinking quickly, Git explained that it had been a rather expensive trombone that cost him £250. The warden wrote out a cheque for £250 on the spot, which Git promptly banked. The next day, he bought a new electric keyboard. In fact, he had picked up the trombone for £25 on the Bayswater Road Sunday market. At this point, we entered into an electric phase, based around Git's new keyboard.

In my second year in London, I started to spread my wings and enjoyed all the cultural offerings of London theatres, films, music and museums and galleries, including one favourite – Arthur Miller's play 'The Price' – at the Haymarket Theatre, many new plays at the Royal Court Theatre and lots of great jazz. One winter's snowy night, coming out of a theatre in Leicester Square, I heard a tenor sax player improvising in a shop doorway and stood listening to his amazing music for half an hour, at which point he told me was playing in the Upper Room at Ronnie Scott's from about 1 am onwards and would I like to come as his personal guest in a warmer place? The tenor player lived in Oxford and he had so little money that he would busk outside Oxford Station till he had enough money for the train fare down to London. He would play in his concert and then busk some more to get a meal and a train fare back to Oxford. Other greats I heard at Ronnie Scott's included my particular hero, Stan Getz, playing with a Belgian backing trio. I heard Dave Brubeck and his Quintet in the Hammersmith Odeon, playing 23 choruses of 'Sweet Georgia Brown', and I would go along each Monday evening to Humphrey Littleton's Jazz Evenings for Radio 3, recorded in the Playhouse Theatre in Northumberland Avenue. My friend the guitarist, Ken Trethewey, who was a chemistry student at Leicester University, would regularly come down to London and we would busk in the Tottenham Court Road underground passage until the police moved us on. Sometimes I would go up to Leicester to play jazz with Ken in student concerts.

The Institute of Archaeology was a small, specialist college. It was founded by Sir Mortimer Wheeler in 1937 and began as an entirely postgraduate institute along the lines of the Central and Eastern European Research Institutes. But by a certain point in the late 1960s, the Institute realised that a postgrad-only model was no longer financially viable. So, from October 1968, they took in undergraduates and I was one of the second cohort of undergraduates. The most famous member of the first cohort was Ian Hodder. There was a great diversity of degree courses in the Institute, all more specialised than in most other University Archaeology programmes. In my BA in European Prehistory, there was never any teaching on the Romans or the medieval period – something I have never found to have been a handicap in my career. The degree programmes were divided by floors in the Gordon Square building, with the Conservation students – almost all women – on the sixth floor, the European Prehistorians and the Roman Imperials on the fourth floor, the Human Environmentalists on the third floor and the Middle Easterners on the second floor. The staff was an amazingly mixed group who covered a vast range of periods and places – probably the first World Archaeology programme in the UK, although never advertised as such. But none of the staff had been chosen for their talents at lecturing – and they had had only one year to hone their much-needed teaching skills before I started at the Institute.

In the first year, the star lecturer was Henry Hodges, who could turn a talk about pottery technology into a magical mystery tour. He may have been rather hazy on the dates of key technological innovations; his favourite phrase was that such and such an innovation began 'at a commendably early date'. He introduced little experiments into his lectures, the best of which was an illustration of how to perforate a stone tool with a bow-drill. Henry sat cross-legged on the large wooden dais, bowing away and showing how the bow-drill turned the wooden spindle. But, carried away by his oration on the invention of the bow-drill, he was oblivious to the drill-tip biting into the top of the dais and setting it alight. It was only when the fire alarm started to ring that Henry realised its cause.

The toughest course was undoubtedly the 'Introduction to Archaeology' lectures and especially the first term's lectures given by the Institute's Director, Professor W. F. ('Peter') Grimes (Fig. 3). Grimes was never seen in the Institute without his three-piece suit, striped shirt and carnation in his buttonhole. The Director would make a grand entrance into Room 105, blow the dust off his lecture notes and read an hour's worth, with a 15-minute coffee break before he read the next hour's lecture. It was all I could do to remain awake for each hour and the interval espresso was the best coffee of the week at the time. One week, I must have done something beastly to my fellow students for them to leave me to sleep at the end of the first hour. Grimes came up and, in an avuncular manner, tapped me on the shoulder and said,

Fig. 3. Professor W. F. Grimes

'It's OK, John, it's finished now – go for a coffee'. Off I went feeling extremely embarrassed but the director never held it against me – I suppose he understood that undergraduate lecturing was not his *forté*.

There were many other stars in the Institute staff. Geoff Dimbleby looked like the object of his favourite studies – a mature tree. He was one of the earliest supporters of what became known as the 'Green Movement'. He had a serious face that rarely broke into a smile but, when it did, it covered the room with light. It was only later that we realised that he spent much of his time caring for his seriously disabled wife. Dimbleby was Head of the Human Environment Department and knew everything about any aspect of human environment, with a fantastic breadth of coverage although a serious lecturing style. The same was true of that tragic figure of Anatolian archaeology, Mr James Mellaart. Mellaart was a British archaeologist who married a Turkish lady and together they worked in the British Institute of Archaeology in Ankara. Two scandals dogged Mellaart's career – the Dorak treasure and the mother goddesses of Çatalhöyük. In 1965, Mellaart published drawings of an Early Bronze Age treasure, which he claimed he was shown by a lady on a train. Since he remained the only person to have seen the treasure, Mellaart was accused of smuggling and was kicked out of Turkey. Worse still, the controversy over mother goddesses at Çatalhöyük led to the closure of the dig and Mellaart's second removal from Turkey. Mellaart knew everything about the Neolithic and Bronze Age of the Near East and Anatolia and had a phenomenally energetic lecturing style.

Professor John Evans was the senior professor of European Prehistory. He was tall and slender, with a distinguished face and tousled grey hair. He did his best to control his often severe stammer during his lectures, which were immensely well-informed. Others not quite so up to the mark included Mr Harry Stewart, a diffident Scot with wisps of red hair, who struggled to master the teaching of archaeological surveying, even with such high-tech devises as alidades and plane-tables. We put up with it because it was a chance to get out of the Institute and into Gordon Square (Fig. 4), where we would endlessly survey the low barrow in the middle of the square and try to ensure dogs would get tangled up with

Fig. 4. Gordon Square, outside the UCL Institute of Archaeology

our tape measures. The head of the Photography Department was Vera Conlon, a woman with a beaked nose, raven-black hair and a strong Cockney accent, who worked as an assistant with Mortimer Wheeler in the early days. Vera could take the most fantastic photographs but couldn't explain how she did it, other than, 'Well, it's straightforward, really'. There were others, like John Waechter, who took us to Regents Park in the summer term for flint-knapping demonstrations. A lot of blood was spilt on the deckchairs but, with no Health and Safety concerns, we had a great time. My favourite lecturer by a long way was John Nandris, whose Romanian parents had brought the family to London in the 1930s. He knew an enormous amount about the Balkans and everywhere else in Europe. I was to have a lot to do with John Nandris in my second year.

My first long vacation centred on a Greek trip, with an invitation from Professor John Evans to dig with him at Knossos. I happily accepted his offer to join him at Knossos and, by way of preparation, I decided to go to Greek regional museums and look at Neolithic material. I researched the main collections and sent off 25 letters, each with a European Reply Coupon, with a request to come and see their Neolithic material. It was a colossal disappointment that I received only one reply, which informed me the museum was closed and I couldn't see any material that year. It seemed a long, hard road into Greek archaeology, which prompted a decision that would shape the rest of my life.

On my way to Professor Evans' dig at Knossos, I made a trip around the Cyclades, Rhodes and the islands to Crete with my American girlfriend Steph, who had spent her sophomore year in London University. We soon realised that night-time boat trips were the best ways to move between islands, every time with unforgettable views of the Milky Way from the tourist class deck. Her Tulane University in New Orleans started a month earlier than mine in London, so she sadly had to leave no sooner had we arrived on Crete. After she flew off, I took the bus up to Knossos village from Heraklion to join the excavation. The Knossos base was the complex whose building was started by Arthur Evans and later was taken over by the British School of Archaeology in Athens – that rather bizarre Imperial concoction of learning and snobbery. It was to my great disappointment but also with a certain pride that, rather than joining in the excavation of the Neolithic levels, I had to supervise the clearing of a Roman tomb on a hillside above the village. Having proved that I could record a Roman tomb, I was taken back on board in the main Neolithic dig and, by the time I joined the team, they had reached the Early Neolithic levels in the West Court. For me, there was nothing as exciting as excavating real Neolithic finds, despite the persistently annoying (and annoyingly persistent) presence of American tourists, whose cameras probably cost more than the entire dig budget, and who kept asking, 'Is it really old?' Even the nuclear hazard signs we erected around the trench could not keep the tourists away.

The main scandal of the year involved two brothers in a family with long connections to the Knossos excavations going back to the time of Arthur Evans. Yiannis was foreman at Knossos and organised all the Greek workers. His brother Andreas was senior but not the foreman and was terribly jealous of Yiannis. This unquenchable jealousy led Andreas to do something really horrendous. He used his access to the Dig House to steal a figurine from the storeroom and plant it in Yiannis's bedroom. The loss was discovered the same day and, after a hint to the police that Yiannis might be involved, the police had to search Yiannis' house and found the figurine under Yiannis' bed. The foreman of course heatedly denied any involvement but the British School had no option but to dismiss Yiannis from his post pending an investigation and replace him temporarily with Andreas. This set off a very uncomfortable fortnight in the village, which was divided into two camps – those supporting Yiannis, who sat in the top *kafeneion* on Knossos hill, Andreas' supporters in the bottom *kafeneion* and the British diplomatically using the middle *kafeneion.* After a fortnight, Andreas couldn't bear the guilt any longer and his conscience prompted him to confess that he was the one who had stolen the figurine and planted it in his brother's room. So the figurine was restored to the Dig House, Andreas was in disgrace but not irredeemably (since he had at least confessed his crime) and Yiannis was restored to his post of foreman. It transpired that the confession was well-timed, for the reconciliation was completed in time for the treading of the grapes – a festive event that required the co-operation of everyone in the village. The British students were instructed to put on Wellington boots so they could join in despite the battalions of wasps mixed with the grapes. The village reconciliation was completed with a feast at the end of the grape-press, which enabled everyone to finish off any wine left over from the previous year. It was a dramatic end to my season at Knossos.

In my second year, I discovered a hall of residence in Bayswater reserved for Commonwealth students, applied and surprisingly was offered a place. There I met some really interesting Commonwealth students, especially those from India and Malaysia, and learned much about the anti-colonial struggles in their countries. One student who was particularly kind to me was a Malaysian law student – because Malaysian law was based on Roman law, a lot of Malaysian law students came to study in London. George soon realised that I hadn't eaten many curries, Plymouth being rather provincial in the matter of cuisine in the 1960s. So once a week George took me to a curry restaurant in Bayswater, gradually increasing the strength of the curry powder mix so that, by the end of the year, while I certainly couldn't comfortably eat a vindaloo or a madras, I could at least manage a rogan josh.

In the second year in the Institute, we had a lot more lectures devoted to the core subjects of our European Prehistory course. That was a time when I got to know John Nandris, since he delivered much of the Neolithic teaching (Plate 2). John was known to many Institute students as a character who would appear at Institute football matches in Regents Park but not play in them, fulfilling his part as Romanian observer sitting on the touchline beneath a huge shepherd's cloak that must have been over a metre high, which covered him entirely, with two tiny eye-slits to watch the goals. I gradually got to know him and appreciate his many talents. It became apparent he showed extreme manual dexterity – he could make violins and he also made a miniature loom on which he wove tiny textiles with motifs from Early Neolithic pottery. He had also spent much time in the monasteries on Mount Athos, studying Greek Orthodox texts, and in Istanbul with the Greek Orthodox Primate. In short, beneath the shepherd's cloak, he was an extraordinary man and gave some brilliant lectures. So it was a real pleasure to be invited to join his survey team, in my second long vacation, in what was then Yugoslav Macedonia.

At the end of my second year, I blew all my spare money on a trip to New Orleans to pick up the relationship with Steph, sadly interrupted by time and distance. I stayed with Steph and her father, a widower who still took the recent death of his wife very badly. Neither of the Twilbecks cooked, so I had the bizarre experience of eating out for every meal, including breakfasts in the local drugstore (grits with coffee). Lunches soon became predictable, since Mr Twilbeck always went to the same Italian restaurant he'd visited for the last 30 years. In the end, I insisted on doing some home cooking, which endeared me to Steph but not to her dad.

We had great times in and around New Orleans, escaping to the jazz clubs and the Cajun restaurants as often as possible. One afternoon, on a trip to Lake Pontchartrain, we disturbed a gigantic water snake, certainly 2 m long, if not 3, and more than a hand's-grip in diameter, which slid away into the lake, terrified of the visitors but not as terrified as we were of it. We played croquet on the top of the giant Mississippi levees, with the subtlest trick being to send the opponent's ball down the slopes of the levee. Mr Twilbeck took time off work to drive us round the Louisiana swamps, with a boat trip in Cajun country, then off on a longer trip to Florida. By a round-about route through villages like those in the film *Easy Rider*, we came to St Louis and took the paddle steamer back down to New Orleans. We visited enough *ante bellum* homes to soak up the atmosphere of Confederate America, which still permeated the southern states. But the relationship with Steph foundered.

Later that summer, I travelled extensively by bus and train around Yugoslavia. First of all, I took the train to Zagreb and met Ružica Drechsler-Bižić, a senior museum archaeologist with a taste in florid dresses and heavy make-up. A London friend had said that Ružica was susceptible to male compliments and flowers. On my second day at the Arheološki Muzej, I took a bunch of red roses, which gave me passage to the store-room full of Vinča pottery from various Croatian sites. It was not always as easy as this to gain access to museums.

I then moved on to Novi Sad to meet someone I was told was a rising star in prehistoric archaeology – Bogdan Brukner. I climbed the hill to the Vojvodjanski Muzej to meet Brukner at his museum base. I had never met him before, so when a tall, slim, middle-aged balding archaeologist offered to show me around the Vinča collections, I assumed that this was Bogdan Brukner. In the morning, 'Brukner' showed me the material from two complete house assemblages excavated at Obrež-Beletinci, passing on to the Gomolava tell Vinča material in the afternoon. All of this was pretty amazing for an undergraduate student and I was mightily disappointed when 'Brukner' said this really was the last day I could come and he was too busy to show me anything tomorrow or the next day. This was a great lesson for Balkan museums – you never know when the gates slam shut, so draw, record and study everything you can, believing the current hour is the last hour you will ever gain access to those collections. It was only much later, when I was introduced to the real Bogdan Brukner, that I realised that an impersonator had shown me Brukner's unpublished material while he was away at a meeting in Beograd. Later still, I met the impersonator in his own museum in north Bosnia at Doboj; Branko Belić had good reason to dislike Brukner and took this chance to show as much of Brukner's material as possible to a British student. I don't suppose Brukner ever found out about this deception, and he died almost 20 years ago. He was one of the so-called 'new generation' of 30–40-year-old archaeologists in Yugoslavia who were beginning to challenge the older generation – the Garašanin husband and wife team in Beograd, Alojz Benac in Sarajevo and Josip Korošec in Ljubljana – who had controlled Yugoslav prehistory throughout the 1960s and held all the key positions of institutional and committee power. The 'new generation' of Bogdan Brukner, Nicola Tasić and Borislav Jovanović was starting out on their own excavations and achieving great things with new recovery techniques. Someone who spanned this generation gap – younger than the Garašanins but slightly older than Brukner *et al.* – was Dragoslav Srejović, who by then had become a megastar because of his excavations of Lepenski Vir (Plate 4). Srejović was a portly type who always dressed smartly; on digs and in cafés, he was famous for his beautiful singing voice. My challenge was to navigate between these two generations. The social dance was complicated by the often strong likes and dislikes of the Yugoslav colleagues for my PhD supervisor, John Nandris, who had clashed dramatically with Srejović over his interpretation of Lepenski Vir. I soon learnt the principle that the friends of John Nandris were my friends, his enemies were my enemies and the enemies of John's enemies were also my friends. It would take longer to identify the *dramatis personae.*

Summer was a bad time to meet archaeologists at their home bases and so I found very few prehistorians at home in Beograd in July. I was shown what seemed to me a random kindness – the best kind perhaps? – from the only Beograd Egyptologist – Sava Tutundžić – who took me in his car to see the Vinča site of Jakovo-Kormadin in the western suburbs – the very first site visit to a Vinča settlement that I had made.

I had to wait a few days before I could arrange an audience with Professor Dragoslav Srejović. Since he didn't speak any English and my Serbo-Croat was not advanced, we had to find a translator, who turned out to be a kind lady from the Arheološka Zbirka – Dr Zagorka Letica. We managed to converse in French and I asked general questions about the Vinča culture, which the Professor answered in a very professorial way – comfortably *ex cathedra.* At one point, Srejović claimed that there were five chronological phases of the Vinča culture in the province of Srem and I asked Dr Letica what was the Professor's evidence for this statement. She looked at me in absolute horror and spat out the words, 'Mr Chapman asks what is your *evidence* for this?', with particular emphasis on the word 'evidence'. Clearly Srejović was not used to such close questioning of *ex cathedra* pronouncements. Of course, Srejović didn't have any evidence for this claim whatsoever! But the damage had been done and the questioning of a Professor for evidence was clearly not allowed. The interview didn't last much longer. Only part of this was the Nandris factor – I had clearly contributed to my own downfall. I didn't meet Professor Srejović again until the Edinburgh Mesolithic conference in 1985.

I looked for a room to rent in Beograd through the state tourist office, *Putnik,* and found one in a multi-bedroom house in the centre of town. One evening, I came back to my room and settled in to freshen up when I heard the most disgusting Serbo-Croat swear-words coming from the next room. Eventually, I met the man who was so angry – an American archaeozoologist called Charlie Schwartz, who had worked with Marija Gimbutas at Anza. This was the start of a long friendship, which ended only with Charlie's death in 2017. We would drive around the centre of town in his ancient car. One time, I made a wrong right turn near Terasija to try to go under the tunnel and two policemen stepped out from behind a pillar and flagged me down. They proceeded to call me all of the worst Serbo-Croat words they knew and were enjoying themselves enormously, thinking we couldn't understand a word of their insults, when Charlie told them '*pičku mate, jebem ti majku*'. They laughed so much that we even escaped a fine.

Soon after, I took to the road again and caught a bus to the town of Zrenjanin in the Banat, north of Belgrade. I arrived late in the afternoon and looked around for a campsite but Zrenjanin was certainly not a tourist town, so campsite there was none. I was walking along the outskirts of the town and found a canal and I thought this would be a good place to pitch my tent. So in the approaching dark, I started to pitch my tent and was just about to unpack my rucksack and find my camping stove to cook myself a simple dinner when someone came up and said in Serbo-Croat that camping here was not a good idea. It turned out this was a local who was worried that the police might catch me and arrest me for camping in the wrong place. This wonderful total stranger helped me take down my tent, pack up my things and carry them into his house. His wife cooked a delicious dinner and they gave me a bed for the night. In the morning, the couple woke up earlier than I would have and came up with the four crucial ingredients for a good Balkan breakfast: greasy fried eggs, strong *šljivovica*, Turkish coffee and freshly baked bread – a dramatic start to the day. I was deeply touched by this incredible hospitality from someone who just cared about a stranger who might very well have got himself into trouble, as indeed I did on other occasions. When I went to the museum, things didn't really improve but, despite the language barrier, the archaeologist Rastko Radišić showed me a certain amount of material from the Botoš cemetery. So a mixed trip to Zrenjanin.

After this short trip in the Banat, I took the bus south from Belgrade to Yugoslav Macedonia to join John Nandris' survey team. The four students forming the survey team were to arrive in Macedonia from all parts of Europe and Asia: Michael Roaf from Persepolis, Jacqui Paice (later Huntley) from France, Sara Lunt from Norfolk and myself from Serbia. This meant that John needed to pick a single spot for the rendezvous. The campsite information at the time suggested that the most central place was the campsite near the classical site of Stobi and we planned to meet there on a given date. We all arrived at *Stobi* only to find that the campsite was not even open for camping that season. The only visitors at Stobi comprised a large American team led by Jim Wiseman (Fig. 8), who was excavating on the Classical site. There were two problems with this team: first, they were Americans and John Nandris hated Americans and, secondly, they were excavating Classical remains and had no interest whatsoever in Macedonian prehistory. We would meet them in the cafe outside the 'campsite', but John Nandris had a trick to get rid of Americans – he would pull up his T-shirt and scratch his back hard until they were too scared of his bedbugs and left. However, we had to camp somewhere and so we camped in the woods behind the campsite in a quiet spot, which we thought would be safe.

We were unable to start the survey yet because John Nandris hadn't got the permit through and he spent much of the first three or four days shuttling between Skopje and Beograd, trying to get a permit. The safety of our camp in the woods was, unfortunately, illusory: on the third day, the local postman delivered mail to our tent. John arrived back from Belgrade that evening and, the next morning, the police came to arrest us and we were taken to Kavadarci jail and kept in prison all day and night. I must admit that the next day they served us a very good breakfast before we were taken off for trial in Negotin. The trial was an obvious set-up because the young female translator offered to us mis-translated much of what John Nandris said in our defence (he understood enough Slavic langauges to understand that his words were not being properly translated!), so there was no chance that we would escape. The really weird thing, that no one could ever explain, is how the money we were fined exactly matched the sum of money that the British Academy had given John for the expedition. So without a permit, without camping and without money, the expedition was over. We went off to the police station to pay the fine and also to have our passports stamped. Amazingly, the police thought the fine was so unjustifiably vast that they were sure the judge would make off with part of the money for a holiday in Greece, so they decided unilaterally that they wouldn't stamp anyone's passports. We left Negotin in a hurry but unwisely didn't drive straight out of Yugoslav Macedonia but went off to Anza to see the Marija Gimbutas excavations. We didn't stay there very long, which was just as well, because the police were following us and they arrived at Anza just after we left. We managed to get out of Macedonia to the north, with the expedition bankrupt but without having our passports stamped. Most of the others went their own ways but I stayed with John in the Institute Land Rover as he drove north, first to Kosovo and then to Beograd for the 1971 UISPP conference.

As a coda to this story, many years later, when I was working in Newcastle University, the professor of Archaeology from Boston University, James Wiseman, came to talk about Classical Stobi. He had no idea that there was someone in the audience who was arrested with John Nandris' team at Stobi in 1971. When I broached the arrest during post-seminar drinks, he greeted me like a long-lost brother and explained how important the Nandris event was to the Stobi Project – whenever the mood was down, he would tell stories about the year that the Brits were arrested. By the year of his visit (*c.* 1985), the time we had spent in a Macedonian prison had extended from one night to several weeks and the fines paid to thousands of pounds. It was revealing to hear an outsider's views of our project disaster.

Returning to Macedonia, the only story I heard about Anza in our short stay there concerned the Anza cow. In one of the peripheral sondas that Gimbutas had planned, amongst the many Vinča sherds was a set of articulated bones that turned out to be a complete cow skeleton. This was very exciting since no one had ever retrieved a Neolithic cow before. The students spent two days cleaning the skeleton and, on the third day, a local farmer came along and asked why they were disturbing his 'Daisy',[1] who'd died unexpectedly five years ago. A disappointment for Sándor Bökönyi![2]

In Beograd, I stayed with friends as I was broke, with no money at all to register for the conference, so I shared registration with one of my richer friends, Melanie Anderson. John Nandris came to the conference as well and he suggested that we should drive the London Institute of Archaeology Land Rover to the famous tell site of Vinča-Belo Brdo near Beograd one morning. We drove to the tell, which lies along the right bank of the River Danube with an exposed profile facing the river (Plate 3). This was the first time I had ever been to the Vinča tell but John Nandris had been several times before and he showed me some of the vantage points and the 1930s excavation trenches of the original excavator Miloje Vasić. John was also interested in taking pollen samples from the exposed profile of the Vinča tell. This meant doing something not entirely legal since we had no permission to take such samples. Nonetheless, we managed to drive the Land Rover to the foot of the section and, standing on the roof of the Land Rover, we took samples from the higher parts. The section was 8 m high. Unfortunately, just as we were in the middle of taking samples from the Land Rover roof, a convoy of buses from Belgrade arrived bringing the conference delegates to see the Vinča tell. I had never jumped off a Land Rover roof quicker and John had never driven a Land Rover away from a site quicker – we had about a minute to escape from a rather embarrassing position. Especially given our shared arrest and trial earlier that summer, this was probably not the best idea that John had ever had. However, we were not discovered by the conference delegates and we made our escape round the back road through the village of Vinča and back to Belgrade.

The UISPP was the first international meeting that I had attended. It was hard to keep track of all of the great archaeologists who were giving papers but three people stuck in my mind, all of whom talking about Anza – Milutin Garašanin, Marija Gimbutas and Vladimir Milojčić. Garašanin gave his paper in such beautiful French that I was transfixed and decided that, if ever I would work with a Belgrade archaeologist, it would be with him. Luckily, this actually happened.[3] Marija Gimbutas was an émigrée from Lithuania who arrived in America after fleeing from the Red Army invasion of Vilnius to Tübingen in the Second World War and who had become a leading specialist on fired clay figurines, which she interpreted in weird and wonderful ways. Gimbutas had a photographic memory, recalling not only the object but the museum case and shelf on which it was displayed. She was also as good a linguist as she was a superb cook, who knew local dishes and languages from all over Eastern Europe. Gimbutas gave a paper about figurines, using tricks of low lighting and exaggeration to transform the little clay figures into scary monsters on screen – a deception at once impressive and dishonest. The new Director of the Groningen

[1] Or the Serbian equivalent of a pet cow's name.

[2] Marija Gimbutas' archaeozoologist and her great friend.

[3] For more stories about Milutin Garašanin, see below, pp. 43–44.

Lab, a fresh-faced Dutchman called Wilhelm Mook, gave a paper on ^{14}C dates, using the new Anza dates as an example. Mook's arguments were demolished with great aplomb by Vladimir Milojčić, the professor of Archaeology from Heidelberg, whom I'd imagined[4] as a fat, dishevelled *Oktoberfest*-hungover German but who turned out to be dressed in an immaculate three-piece suit and looked like a top barrister. These vignettes helped me to put faces to the authors of papers I was beginning to explore – to personalise my study of Balkan prehistory.

One of the contacts I had made at the Belgrade conference was one of the three Hungarian Neolithic specialists I'd heard of – János Makkay. He was very interested to hear that my research on the origins of the Vinča group was going to become my third-year dissertation. He was very hospitable and made a big impression with his thoughts on the Neolithic in Hungary. I would return to work with him several times in later years. Ida Kutzián, the doyenne of Hungarian Neolithic studies, was also very kind and supportive, later showing me her material from Fajsz and telling me all about the Early Neolithic in Hungary. In my third year, I did indeed start writing an undergrad dissertation on the origins of the Middle Neolithic Vinča group. This was deliberately so that I could differentiate my dissertation from the doctoral thesis of John Nandris on the Early Neolithic in the Balkans – the so-called *First Temperate Neolithic*.

Much of the coursework in the third year was rather similar to the Prehistoric Europe courses in the second year but in much more detail and with a lot more seminars. At this time, I became deeply attached to the *Linearbandkeramik* and the Urnfield group and read huge amounts about both of these groups, which really helped me understand more about German approaches to prehistoric archaeology. There were two optional courses which gave me insights into parts of archaeology I hadn't really reached before. Mike Rowlands, then a second-year PhD student in the UCL Department of Anthropology, gave the first undergraduate course he had ever given – on 'Anthropology for archaeologists'. Mike introduced me to a range of approaches to possible interpretations that became fundamental to the direction I took in my later studies. The second colleague was Mark Newcomer – an American specialising in the Palaeolithic, who gave a seminar course on lithic technologies in their social context. I'd never really thought that stone tools were related to society before and this, too, opened up many new possibilities.

Near the end of the year, the agony of Finals exams began – especially tantalising because they took place at the same time as Wimbledon Fortnight. That exams fortnight was so warm that it became essential to revise outdoors on the grass in Cartwright Gardens, where the distractions were sometimes worse than the heat inside the Hall. Eventually, the exams were over and there began a three-week wait for the results. No actual marks were ever given by exam but the overall result was

[4] It is strange how archaeologists' writings conjure up for the reader an image of the author. Milojčić' papers were so poorly argued – at least to a second-year undergraduate – that I had created a quite misleading image of the man.

conveyed in a curious Institute tradition – for each course, a party was held in one of the course teachers' house or flat. The European Prehistory graduates were invited to a party at Roy Hodson's flat in Southampton Row. After making sure the students were plied with alcohol, Hodson slowly went around the room, explaining the results to each student. I was fairly disappointed about gaining an Upper Second degree but had no explanation as to why this was because we had no exam marks. In fact, I could never work out what really happened to my marks. The only European Prehistorian to win a First that year was May Ashmore, who, as well as being very bright, was incredibly well organised as a single mum. It is one of my regrets that I was not a good 'godfather' to her daughter Philippa and didn't stay in touch after my postgrad years.

The third long vacation started off with Mum and Dad's graduation present – a fortnight's boat trip around the Aegean islands with two of my friends – Ian Young and Louise Hodgson. One of my dad's Scouting friends who worked in the Royal Naval College at Dartmouth – Ken Armitstead – owned a small yacht moored in the Piraeus, near Athens. Since I was not a sailor, this was an adventurous voyage (Fig. 5), filled with sun, sand, loukoumi, retsina and chocolate cakes – a wonderful graduation present!

After the Aegean trip, I took a bus to Saloniki and then a smaller village bus to *Servia*, above the Haliakmon gorge, where I had been invited by Cressida Ridley to excavate at her Neolithic and Early Bronze Age site. The person I was really

Fig. 5. The author with Ian Young, pulling in the anchor, Aegean

going to work with was John Watson, a Cambridge student first in Natural Sciences and then in Archaeology and Anthropology, who transferred to the Institute for his PhD on animal bones. He was digging an environmental trench, where I learnt much about on-site environmental sampling. Cressida Ridley never forgave me for naming the contexts in that trench after Be Bop jazz heroes and their tunes: I don't think she knew about Dizzy Gillespie and Charlie Parker or 'Ooh Bop Sh'Bam'. The contexts needed memorable names in case the context numbers were mistranscribed – but probably not that memorable! The season with John Watson helped me to understand the potential of animal bones and begin to understand their size-related recovery and the way that animal bones fragmented – a useful experience which I kept on hold for quite a long time.[5]

One amazing trip on a Sunday off was the visit to Mount Olympus in John Watson's famous Volkswagen Beetle. We left Servia village around noon and drove up a rough track towards the Greek Army ski school – the highest building on the slopes of Mount Olympus. The road was so rough that John could hardly drive at more than 30 kmph. Suddenly, we heard a rhythmic knocking that seemed to come from the outside of the car and, when we looked out the window, we saw a mountain shepherd dog with an iron collar with iron spikes trying to eat the tyre. John heroically tried to accelerate up to 40 kmph but the sheepdog kept pace with us. It was only when he reached 50 kmph that John left the dog behind, frustrated and panting. It was a warning for the walk ahead. The ski school was halfway up the mountain and we reached there at 2 pm. We had to move off fast to cover the 12 km there and the 12 km back before nightfall. John told us to pick up two small rocks and keep them in our hands, in case of further sheepdog attack. As we climbed higher, we saw sheepdogs on the far side of the herd from us but none of them attacked. There are 32 peaks of Mount Olympus – one for each deity – so we had time to climb only one. The sun's rays shone on the high clouds, making them unforgettably golden (Fig. 6). It was hard to leave the mountain but the light was fading. We managed to descend fast and without sheepdog attack, reaching the car in the dark.

After the Servia excavation, I hitchhiked to Skopje, taking the safer option of a bus to Lake Ohrid to see the limpid blue waters of the lake and the Early Byzantine churches on their shore. I was walking around the third of these churches when I noticed the same dark-haired, bearded man that I had seen in the other churches. We talked about the churches and it turned out that he was a Macedonian architect who lived in a village near Skopje. He invited me to lunch on a whim and drove me to his home. There, a family celebration was in full swing, with food covering a huge dining table. I was made very welcome and all was going well, until I noticed that the '*baba*' (grandmother) was sending me a stream of dark looks. When I spoke to my host, he asked her what was going on and she explained that his guest must be a

[5] For the fragmentation part of my career, see Chapter 8.

Fig. 6. Three of the peaks of Mount Olympos, northern Greece

bourgeois (hence an Enemy of the People), since he was not eating any bread! I never made this mistake again in a Balkan meal.

I moved onto the towns of the Morava valley – Leskovac, Niš and Svetozarevo – where I could not see any prehistoric finds except what was on display. My next stop was the central Serbian town of Kragujevac, infamous for a Nazi massacre of Serbs in the Second World War and, more recently, famous as the biggest producer of cars (baby Fiats) in Tito's Yugoslavia. The town was close to a joint Yugoslav–American excavation at the site of Divostin and I thought I'd like to get to the town as early as possible, so as to make it to the site before dusk. I clearly had not read the Yugoslav railway timetables, for the two-carriage electric train meandered across the Serbian countryside, taking six hours to cover 120 km, stopping at every village, hamlet and farm and pausing for cows to cross the line. This created a record for the slowest train I'd ever been on in the Balkans, so I got to Kragujevac much later than I wanted. When I got off the train, I looked around for the best way to find accommodation but I needn't have bothered. I was immediately seized by two policemen, who took me off to the police station and threw me in jail for the night. After a good breakfast, the police charged me with being an unplanned foreign visitor, to which I pleaded guilty, whereupon I was fined and had my passport marked. This would come in handy later (see p. 45). The police then gave me instructions to get to the bus station, where I took the local bus to the village of Divostin, where the excavation was taking place. It was only when I got there and talked to the American co-director, Alan McPherron, that I realised that this was a traditional way of being welcomed to Kragujevac and the Divostin excavation, with the first night in jail and the next morning a bus ride to Divostin village. Alan McPherron was the first senior American archaeologist I'd met working in Yugoslavia. He and three other major projects were benefitting from a Smithsonian Institution initiative using part of the funds for post-war reparations to Yugoslavia to support archaeological excavations. The Yugoslav–American team, with Professor Srejović the Yugoslav co-director, had uncovered both Early and Late Neolithic villages. It was fascinating to meet Yugoslav students interested in the Neolithic and talk to American students working on Balkan materials. Since the team had occupied all of the village houses with spare rooms at Divostin, I spent the night in the neighbouring village of Grivac. This was the first time I had personal experience of the suffering of left-handers (I'm a left-hander myself). I felt for the little boy of about two who was not only sitting immobile in an upright baby chair but also had his left hand tied to the arm of the chair and he was being forced to eat with his right hand only. This is absolutely standard not only in Serbia but over much of the Balkans, where the superstition of the evil left hand was still prevalent. The attempts to stamp out left-handedness undoubtedly scarred many people for life.

At the Divostin excavation, I explained to the Yugoslav students that I wanted to see Lepenski Vir. They explained that it was difficult to get there but that the best way was to take a bus to the town of Zaječar in north-east Serbia and then take a village bus crossing the mountains to Boljetin near the Danube. Getting to Zaječar was easy enough and, while I was there, I thought it would be great to see another Srejović project – the Late Antique palace at Gamzigrad. Since I had a spare day, I took a village bus to Gamzigrad. On the bus, a local from the village soon started asking me questions, finding out I was a London Archaeology student who wanted to see the Gamzigrad palace. He said that the village was actually celebrating a wedding that afternoon and invited me to the wedding. Little did I expect that the wedding turned into a three-day feast from which it was almost impossible to escape. We went to the wedding feast straight off the bus and, after my host explained I was a Londoner, I soon became one of the guests of honour who sat at the foot of the table at the opposite end to the bride and groom. The main dish was roast pork, which I consumed in enormous quantities since I had been on the road for a month and had not been eating wonderfully well. It was a fantastic meal, with a party going on late into the night, of which I remember very little. When I woke up in the morning and tried to walk out of the house to find the Gamzigrad palace, I was strongly discouraged by the guests, who led me off to the party which had already restarted. The wedding feast went on for the rest of the day, the evening and night. On the third morning, I realised that I simply *had* to get out to find the Gamzigrad palace. So, most ungraciously, I left the house and started walking to the palace. It was worth the trip – an extraordinary reconstruction presenting a very fine piece of architecture. But by the time I'd seen the palace, my host had arrived and he remonstrated with me fiercely in Serbian for

10 minutes, telling me what a bad guest I was and insisting I came back for the third day of the wedding. At this point, I had about 15 minutes to catch the bus back to Zaječar and I knew that if I didn't run down the hill to the bus stop and catch the bus back to town, I would never escape from that village. So I left the man at the palace and ran down the hill, just managing to catch the already overloaded bus. It was a narrow escape but not the only one I would experience that day.

At the Zaječar bus station, I found the village bus, which was supposed to end up at Boljetin on the Danube. It was absolutely packed with the usual extended families of humans, sheep, goats, dogs and chickens. I sat on one of the few remaining seats at the very back of the bus, next to an extremely pretty teenage girl. We didn't say anything to each other but, when the bus stopped at the first village a half hour out of Zaječar, the girl stood up, looked at me passionately, took a tortoiseshell hair ornament from her head, threw it at me and stormed off the bus. I was so dumbstruck I didn't know how to react and I wondered if I should follow her. But doubts crowded in: I don't know her; I can't possibly get off the bus; I would end up in the village; I'd marry her; and there I would live for the rest of my life. Although she was extremely pretty, I couldn't make that choice so I stayed on the bus – a life-defining moment.

The bus continued to descend, first of all on a track, before veering alarmingly into a stream bed with luckily only smallish boulders. It progressed down the stream bed for at least a kilometre until it regained the semblance of another track. This extraordinary ride took me to Boljetin village, 2 km from the Danube, by about 6 pm. After two escapes in one day, I hoped that the evening would be calmer. It was a short walk from Boljetin to the site of Lepenski Vir on the banks of the Danube. The rescue excavation was completed before the waters of the Danube rose 4 m to cover all of the riverside sites. At this stage of the operations, the water had already started to rise and covered the bottom of trees along the shore and the only people at Lepenski Vir were conservation students from Belgrade, who were removing stones from as many of the houses as they could to rebuild them in a museum 50 m upslope. This was an amazing scene to watch at the very end of the Lepenski Vir project; as the conservation students took the stone blocks away, they revealed more and more of the sandy shore on which the first settlement had been built (Plate 4).

One member of the conservation team spoke good English and suggested that I came back with him to Boljetin, where at least there was a restaurant and maybe even a bed for the night. So we walked back to Boljetin, where indeed we found a good meal in the village pub but there were no beds to be had. The pub owner had a word with one of the village customers, who said: 'Yes, that would be absolutely fine – come with me'. So we went with him and started to walk back towards Lepenski Vir on a track I already felt I knew quite well. But, at a certain moment, he took off vertically up a U-shaped valley slope that got steeper and steeper. The villager was not only fleet-footed but knew the track. I really struggled to keep up, what with my heavy rucksack, and at a certain moment we reached a mountain stream with the only way across being a single pine trunk. By a combination of luck and balance, we managed to get across and we walked on up the mountain. Halfway up the hillside was his farm and our host called to ask for his wife to prepare a feast, since they had distinguished guests – one from Belgrade and one from London. She didn't look too happy but prepared everything that she could, which turned into a second dinner. After an hour, our host beckoned the Serbian student to go outside with him and they went out and the student came back five minutes later, looking extremely jolly but sworn to silence. Half an hour afterwards, it was my turn and the treat was to drink *šljivovica* straight from a plastic tube leading from an enormous barrel – a tube that unfortunately contained not only alcohol but also dead wasps, flies and bees. A hazardous enterprise but providing very good *šljivovica*. Soon after the barrel event, we were getting to the end of the meal and there was really not much else to do but sleep. I was given the bed of honour in the main room – a double bed with nice sheets and blankets – while the Serbian student was taken off somewhere else. The man went somewhere else to be with his wife but, at some ghastly hour in the morning, I felt the presence of another human in the double bed. The drunken host had clearly forgotten that he had moved his wife to another bed and so came to the main bed to snuggle up to his wife and who knows what more besides. It took a lot of patient, kind, gentle but firm resistance to stop him having his way with me but eventually he went off frustrated, hopefully to find his own wife somewhere else and not the Belgrade student. After a minimalist breakfast, we decided we'd better leave and make our way down the incredibly steep hillside. With the hangover I was nursing and the disturbed night, I was not looking forward to the pine branch bridge across the stream but, again, somehow I managed to get across and we got down to the bottom of the hill safely. We said our goodbyes, with the student returning to Lepenski Vir and I walking back to Boljetin bus stop to wait for the bus to Belgrade. After three narrow escapes in as many days, I recovered on a peaceful three-day train ride back to England, where I was to start my postgraduate studies at the Institute of Archaeology.

Looking back at my undergraduate days, I think of the Institute as a warm, friendly and supportive place for students. I had a moral tutor named Joan Sheldon who impressed Geoff Dimbleby so much as an administrative secretary that he made her a lecturer. She was kind to me, especially giving me concert tickets for gigs that she was unable to attend. But in a way she typified the Institute in not really contributing to the atmosphere of the place as a hothouse of great new ideas. Don't forget that, the year before I started out, Lewis Binford published *New Perspectives in Archaeology* and David Clarke published *Analytical Archaeology*. But this revolutionary material was not taught in the Institute – we had to discover this for ourselves. There was one amazing opportunity to host one of the two revolutionaries in London for an entire year (it would have been my third undergraduate year). In 1969, Lewis Binford was under suspicion at the University of New Mexico and was likely to be arrested. Binford had been following the funding trajectories of anthropological research in South America through the 1960s and he realised that, suddenly in the middle of the 1960s, large amounts of new money were coming into social anthropology, with the specific aim of studying local social structures. Binford couldn't find out the source of this new money but he kept delving into Government documents until he identified the source of the money as the CIA, who wanted to understand more about power relations in South America. Publication of this news made Binford so *persona non grata* that he sought refuge in Europe for a year and asked the Institute if he could come there. For some extraordinary reason, the Institute turned down the person who, at the time, was the greatest living theoretical archaeologist – a crime for which I never really forgave my *alma mater*. So the Institute carried on in its staid old ways, with Institute tea-party conversations more likely to feature gardens and rose-pruning than new ideas about subsistence strategies or systems theory. In many ways, the most stimulating theoretical thinker was Mike Rowlands, who was still not a lecturer but a PhD student in anthropology. So there was a sense of malaise about theoretical archaeology in the Institute that concerned me. I certainly didn't help my future employment prospects in British archaeology by asking a theoretical question of Roy Hodson in an Institute seminar, to which he gave the answer, 'Well, why does the chicken cross the road?'. While Roy was great on computers and brilliant on innovative methods in archaeology, he didn't really touch base on theory. In fact, it was his wife – a medical statistician – who told Roy about the famous Sokal and Sneath paper in a medical journal in 1966 which led to Roy's early insights on multivariate statistics.

So why did I stay on at the Institute to study for a PhD? I had realised that that's what I wanted to do – to continue my studies of the Vinča group. I looked around other departments of Archaeology in the UK to see who else could supervise this topic. There were really very few people who specialised in Balkan prehistory. Indeed, the only one who could have done this was John Nandris' greatest rival, who worked in UCL in the Department of Anthropology – Ruth Tringham. But in my three years at the Institute, I had never met her and John had certainly never introduced me to her. So, with theoretical qualms but Balkan contacts, I decided to stay at the Institute – because of John Nandris.

Chapter 3

Postgraduate days

I started my PhD studies at the London Institute of Archaeology in October 1972, after no break from my undergrad studies. As I had no grant, I was poorer than a church mouse and could only survive with help from my parents. I also had nowhere to live when I came back to London in September but I advertised for someone to share a room with me in a house in King Edward's Road, on the south side of Hampstead Heath. A psychology student called David Romanos was the first to reply and so we set up home. It was the only time in my life that I've shared a single room with a bloke for a whole year. The room had beds in opposite corners, a sink in another corner and a tiny table with a box cooker in the third area, near the door. The room was above a sweet shop/ice cream shop and not far from a Greek cake shop. The only saving grace was that we were near Hampstead Heath; the walks on the Heath were the only things to keep me sane in a tricky year and I certainly didn't stay in touch with David Romanos afterwards.

Although we were in different years, I had come across Ian Hodder several times in the Institute and we'd struck up a friendship. It was kind of him to invite me up to Cambridge one weekend in November 1972, when he'd already become established after his move from the Institute to Cambridge to study with David Clarke for a PhD on spatial studies. He invited me to stay in his home, where he lived with Françoise Hivernel, a French anthropologist who had worked in Africa. They were renting an Elizabethan bakery in Sutton and I spent two nights there. Ian organised a party so that I could meet the other PhD students. It was there for the first time that I met Steve and Sue Shennan, Tim and Sara Champion, Andrew Sherratt, John Bintliff and also a second-year undergraduate called Paul Halstead who seemed to be the star of the show, with everyone falling about with his imitations of Eric Higgs.

This year, it became clear to me that I needed to learn Slavic languages if I was to get anywhere with my PhD. It was my good fortune that my Institute friend, Melanie Anderson, introduced me to Celia Hawksworth, who had just started teaching at the UCL School of Slavonic and East European Studies (SSEES). Celia was generous in giving me a weekly hour's free Serbo-Croat lesson. This was the year that Asterix the Gaul was translated into Serbo-Croat, rapidly becoming our course book from which

I learnt lots of really important vocabulary (the Serbo-Croat for talents, javelins and megaliths). But Celia was really good at teaching me chat-up lines to help me with Serbian women – '*kako lepi oči imaš*' ('what beautiful eyes you have') or '*imaš divni veliki grudi*' ('you have wonderful big breasts'). Some of these lines were a real help for my next research trip in summer 1973.

On this trip, I drove alone – excepting hitchhikers – in my Morris car for three days all the way to Yugoslavia. When I had settled into the campsite on Banovo Brdo in southern Beograd, I went to the university to see if I could find anybody but most archaeologists were already in the field. The only Archaeology student I met was a final-year student called Jasmina, who was married to an American archaeologist called Greg Johnson. Mina felt obliged to take me around tourist places, but she thought that two days' hospitality was more than enough. She told me that we had to go to Banovo Brdo to meet a fellow student called Maja, who would look after me, since she (Mina) had to do some work. So I returned to Banovo Brdo to meet Maja.

This was the start of a major part of my life, since there was an obvious and immediate deep mutual attraction. Maja explained that she could show me round Beograd that day but the next day she had to go digging on Bogdan Brukner's excavations at Gomolava and why didn't I come along? I stayed there for a week, but she stayed much longer. That season, there was a Dutch team from the Bio-Archaeological Institute at Groningen, with megastars like Henrik Waterbolk and Willem Van Zeist and up-and-coming stars like Anneke Clason and Sietze Bottema. I had an amazing time talking to them about how they did archaeology in Yugoslavia. It turned out that I was there at an absolutely pivotal moment in the Gomolava excavations.

Gomolava was a 4 m tell on which Bogdan Brukner and colleagues had already excavated down through the later levels to the top of the Neolithic levels, where as yet they hadn't found any structures. Waterbolk's habit was to take his dog for a walk in the early morning before digging began. That night had been a chilly night and so there was excess humidity on the ground surface of the tell. Waterbolk walked up to the top of the tell – some 3 m above the Neolithic layer – and looked down. What he saw amazed him – rows of postholes in the moist sediment. Now whatever else Dutch archaeologists do, they could always spot a posthole – that's what they have in Holland! So Waterbolk immediately recognised line after line of postholes forming long-house structures. He rushed off the tell and found as many pieces of wood as he could and pushed a stick into each posthole so that they could recognise the postholes when the sediment dried out and they became invisible. Waterbolk then walked back to the village with his dog and woke up Bogdan Brukner, who was extremely grumpy at this disturbance, only to be told he'd got a village of Vinča houses on his tell. Even Bogdan woke up at this juncture and came to the tell. And that was the real start of the Vinča excavations at Gomolava, which arose from taking a dog for a walk.

Later on in July, I had a chance to go on excavations with John Nandris and Ghiţa Lazarovici at Gornea (Fig. 7) and Zorlenţu Mare. Gornea was an amazing Neolithic site on the banks of the Danube upstream of the Iron Gates gorge. At the end of the day's digging, Ghiţa would go out in a small boat to fish. He was an extremely good fisherman and caught every kind of Danube fish apart from sturgeon. Fried fish in the evening was the Gornea speciality. John thought that it would be really useful to buy a new Western invention, the non-stick frying pan, as a present to the team and we waited for Ghiţa to catch and fry the fish in the frying pan. After a delicious meal, the director of Reşiţa Museum, a *politikolog* called Ilie Uzum, took the pan down to the Danube to wash it in the traditional manner. He grabbed a handful of gravel and moved it slowly round the frying pan, removing all the fish from the surface perfectly, and brought it back to John minus the non-stick surface. Even without its Teflon surface, it remained a very good pan.

The next site that Ghiţa and John were excavating that summer was Zorlenţu Mare – totally different from Gornea. The site was high in the Western Carpathians at the junction of three ridges – an obvious place for transhumance. On my second excavation of a Vinča site, I was impressed by the rich house deposits of pottery and figurines. We had to camp at the edge of the site and carry all of our food up 8 km from the valley below. The first valley to the north-east was gloomy and dark, covered in dense undergrowth; the locals called it 'The Valley of the Bears' (*Valea Ursului*) because that's exactly who lived there. We were told never to go down there on our own, especially at night. I didn't really believe that there were bears in the area until,

Fig. 7. Gheorghe (Ghiţa) Lazarovici, Gornea excavations, Romania

one night, a bear visited our camp. We couldn't hear the bear padding around but, in the morning, we saw bear paw-prints all round the campfire. Luckily, the bear wasn't the hungriest of visitors, so he never tried to enter our tents. After that, I took the bears in the valley more seriously.

Ghiţa was a very handsome man, well-built with a stunning suntan, blue eyes and a shock of light brown hair (Fig. 7). With a name like Lazarovici, it was no surprise that his father was a Serb, whom I met that year and with whom I talked in unfluent Serbo-Croat (on both sides of the conversation). Although he was a heavy man, Ghiţa had extremely good balance, which meant he was not only a beautiful dancer but also a very good bike rider. One day, the director of the Reşiţa Museum challenged Ghiţa to ride his bike all the way from Reşiţa to Caransebeş – a distance of 25 km – without his hands touching the handlebars. The road went up and down over the Western Carpathian foothills but Ghiţa managed to achieve this – a great triumph for Ghiţa that we heard about several times that year (and subsequently).

After the Zorlenţu Mare excavations, I had time to visit sites and museums in Transylvania. We drove to Cluj-Napoca, the capital of Transylvania, where Ghiţa took me to the Muzeul de Istorie. There, he introduced me to the senior archaeologist, Nicolae Vlassa, who was the guardian of the Tărtăria tablets, which he had excavated back in the early 1960s. The only reason Vlassa showed me the Tărtăria tablets was because I was a friend of Ghiţa. Vlassa was an incredible guy – tall, well built with a boot-shaped face that he kept deadpan most of the time. Vlassa was multilingual apart from English and told political jokes in as many languages as he knew. He was a brilliant man to have in company and was invariably the star of any conference he attended.

Vlassa had won a Government scholarship to Vienna to study 'Romanian' finds in the National Treasury. At that stage, his German was poor and when he went into a patisserie and saw a cake he fancied, he could only ask the stately pensioner behind the counter, '*Was ist dass?*'. '*Dass, mein Herr, ist ein Buttermilch*,' she replied. Vlassa loved the cake and went back the next morning and, in confusion, asked the lady, '*Guten Tag, haben Sie Muttermilch?*'. '*Vielleicht meinen Sie Buttermilch*', replied the angry lady, at which point Vlassa ran out of the shop, never to return.

I left Cluj to drive south to Oltenia and headed for the main town of Craiova, the home base of one of the great characters of Romanian Neolithic archaeology. This was Marin Nica, who had a small head above a body that grew in girth as it went downwards. Nica came from a village near Craiova and spoke with a strong peasant dialect. He was famous for his homemade plum brandy (Romanian *ţuica*), about which more later.[1] Nica was an extremely enthusiastic speaker of French, who used to speak very fast and stood close to you looking at you directly, speaking into your face and spitting as he spoke. A half-hour of conversation with Marin Nica was like a cold shower. But Nica was very generous with showing his finds.

[1] For a story about Marin Nica's ţuica, see p. 135.

For the next stop, I made my way to the Institute of Archaeology in Bucureşti. Some of the great stars of Romanian archaeology were still working there, including Dr Eugen Comşa, who spoke French (and Russian) beautifully. Because he trained in Moscow, Comşa was regarded as a kind of Russian spy. Although he was revered for his scholarship, Comşa didn't seem to have many friends in the Romanian archaeological community but he was kind to me – a totally unknown PhD student. He accompanied me on a drive to the famous *Cernica* cemetery with the settlement nearby. Eugen Comşa had had a hard life and the authorities were particularly mean in delaying his publications. His exceptional PhD on the Boian group was delayed for over 20 years. Comşa found it hard to give straight and useful information. So if Comşa wanted to tell you about an animal bone assemblage he had excavated on a Neolithic site, he would say that 70% of the available bones were cattle, there were 300 sheep or goat bones and the colour of the pigs' hair was black. Comşa clearly wanted to make sure you had to work as hard for the information as he did himself. But there was no doubt that Eugen Comşa was a very interesting man to meet.

After my visit to Bucureşti, I drove to Hungary. Although many of my early trips to Hungary were made in the company of János Makkay, I went to other places as well. One of the kindest people who welcomed me to his museum was Otto Trogmayer, who worked in the Móra Ferenc Múzeum in Szeged. Although Otto had never met me before, he was kind enough to take me for a day trip around all of the Körös and earliest Vinča sites that he had discovered in the vicinity. Otto also showed me a lot of his material in the Museum.[2] Another famous museum near Szeged was in the small town of Hódmezővásárhely. I took a bus to the town and looked for the local museum but no one I asked had a clue where the museum was. In the end, I was directed to a private address that was the home of the local Member of Parliament, Mr János Dömötör. He was an art historian who spoke good English and brought me along to the heavily disguised museum. Dömötör instructed the archaeologist to show me whatever I wanted to see and this was an incredible piece of good fortune, since the Museum had some of the finest Late Neolithic collections in Hungary. Even better fortune for me was that Dömötör had a beautiful daughter – Rózsa – and we saw quite a lot of each other over the coming days.

Another early trip to western Hungary involved a visit to the Museum of Székesfehérvár, which was the second place where János Makkay was offered a job after he was banished from Hungarian archaeology after 1956. This museum was the place where János stored his excavation materials from the site of Bicske, where I went to excavate.[3] The museum was run by a husband-and-wife team called Mr and Mrs Fitz. While the husband was a Romanist, Mrs Fitz was an extremely kind prehistorian – actually very reminiscent of my mother in size, stature and manner. I liked her very much indeed and she helped me feel very welcome in her museum.

[2] See p. 113 for Otto's method of finding Körös sites.
[3] See p. 42 for the stories of the Bicske excavations.

After my Hungarian trip, I slowly drove back to England to start the second year of my PhD in London. Before I left, I had already fixed up to rent a room in a large house in Highbury owned by my Institute friend Melanie Anderson. When I arrived at the house, one of the other housemates explained that my room was upstairs but that she thought that somebody was in the room just now. I expressed great surprise since no one had mentioned this possibility to me so I went up to see who was there. There was the sound of not just one but two people, having an extremely enjoyable time. Not being one to spoil the occasion, I waited a bit but, at a certain point, there was an enormous crash, followed by cursing in Serbian. I instantly knew who this was – the American Charlie Schwartz, whom I had met in Beograd the summer before. Charlie had in fact been having such vigorous sex with a Polish archaeologist that they had broken my bed. Charlie was kind enough to repair my bed before I moved in a dramatic arrival in London. This was a brilliant house to stay in and I stayed there for one year before I went off to Beograd for a research year.

In parallel to my research, I had also started lecturing for the University of London Department of Extramural Studies, which at the time offered a four-year part-time degree: the first year an introduction to archaeology, the second year Near Eastern archaeology, the third year European prehistory and the fourth year British prehistory. Taking this degree was an exceptionally heavy load for anyone with a full-time job, as the coursework required a lot of reading and essay-writing and much revision for the end-of-session exams. This was the first lecturing job I'd ever taken on and so it was a steep learning curve since I had no lecturing materials of my own, not least a total lack of slides. A photographer friend told me about a Kodak ciné film that enabled you to take pictures from books and develop them without a negative stage. I used this trick to make thousands of slides in the first month of my second year and built up a slide collection that would last me well into my first university job. Using my own slide collection helped me to develop a lecturing style that I could summarise as 'point, show and talk'. With each slide, I pointed to the interesting bits and described the significance of what was on the slide before moving on to the next slide, and so on. It wasn't for decades that I'd realise that this lecturing style was developed from the times when we had family slideshows after summer holidays in Plymouth.

I started off with this style in my first Extra-Mural lectures, which took place in the Institute of Archaeology in room 410 – a lecture room too familiar to me as an Institute student. The lectures lasted two hours, with a 15-minute coffee break. One particularly kind couple were clearly coming to the class not simply to learn about European prehistory but to be with each other – an architect called Norman who worked for English Heritage and a refugee from the Soviet invasion of Czechoslovakia called Helena. They were so obviously in love with each other that it was a delight to see. I almost betrayed them on a class field trip, when Norman was accompanied by his wife. We had reached the foot of Silbury Hill, where his wife was telling me how she admired my lecturing stamina: 'After all, John, it can't be easy for you to give three hours of lectures with only short breaks in between.' At this moment, I realised exactly what she was saying and explained that, while it took a little bit of practice, eventually you got used to it. This managed to convince the wife and protect Norman and Helena.

I'd been living perhaps a month and a half in Melanie's house when I heard via a friend of a friend that Maja was in London as a tourist. I was absolutely astonished, because I felt sure she would have made contact with me. Distraught, I supposed that she didn't want to have anything to do with me anymore but Melanie comforted me, suggesting that perhaps she just wanted to get on her feet and be independent before she made contact with me. In fact, she was working as a nurse at the Royal Free Hospital, sharing a room with a Zagreb nurse called Božena. When I turned up unannounced at her door, Maja was obviously surprised but delighted that I'd found her (Plates 5–6). We started going out and that shaped much of the rest of that year. Indeed, in the summer of 1974, we decided that I would spend the next academic year in Beograd and after that we would get married.

In Easter 1974, János Makkay invited Maja and me to join his excavation team at Bicske in Transdanubia. This was a small-scale, low-budget affair, with six village workers and any volunteers that János could find. The student volunteers included Pál Raczky – the first time that I met Pali and it became the beginning of a lifetime's friendship. Maja and I were given one precious worker to help us try out the technique of froth-flotation – hitherto unknown in Hungarian archaeology.[4] We had no special tank and it was too expensive for houses to offer us running water, so the only place we could use for this operation was Bicske swimming pool. We found lots of botanical remains which indeed dated to the Neolithic – a great result for Hungarian archaeology.

By July 1974, I was all set to drive to Beograd and stay there for a year. I left Highbury Hill with the Morris Minor loaded to the gunwhales and drove off for the continent. I was supposed to meet Maja at the Sopron hillfort excavations, just outside the highly Austrianised town near the west Hungarian border but I arrived a day late, having hit very bad traffic on the German *Autobahnen*. But this was a magical reunion. We eventually reached Beograd, where Maja's family had organised a rented flat for me near their flat in Pere Todorovića. The Martinović parents – Petar and Milica – were quite strict about us not spending nights together until we were married. Indeed, Petar was used to sitting up waiting for Maja to return if she was out later than 10 pm. It soon became clear that we could not possibly wait till we returned to England in 1975 to get married, so we arranged for a winter wedding in Beograd.

When living in Beograd, I came to Maja's Pere Todorovića flat for lunch and dinner. I came to know Petar quite well. Milica would prepare a light lunch for us

[4] The idea behind froth flotation was that seeds, shells, animal bones and even copper beads were so small that they were not routinely recovered with pick-and-shovel excavation techniques. Washing a bucket of soil through a tank full of water would separate out the micro-finds from the soil, allowing specialists to find out more about the site and its subsistence.

both and I would listen to Petar's stories of life in the pre-First World War Balkans. One story he told me epitomises the Montenegran character. One town was under Ottoman siege and there was a narrow mountain pass by which the relieving army could reach the town. But the pass was wide enough for only one soldier at a time and the army never crossed it because the army marched in pairs and no one would agree to be second to pass.

The most intriguing story concerned a talented Montenegran chef at the royal court with a penchant for alcohol. One evening, unexpected guests arrived at the court and the King sent Martinović with a message to the kitchen to prepare a special extra meal and send up four bottles of champagne. This was unfortunate, since the chef had drunk all but one bottle. Martinović was so angry that he hit the chef with an empty bottle, accidentally killing him. In turn, the King was so angry with Martinović that he called for his arrest. Luckily, Martinović was on good terms with the Queen, who hid him in her bedroom until he could escape the next morning. Martinović was sent into exile, which lasted 20 years. These were fascinating, heroic tales from another world, which made me appreciate the descendant of the courtly Martinovićs.

As soon as term began, I registered in the University of Beograd as a foreign student – not an easy task because there was no official exchange scheme between the Universities of London and Beograd. I was assigned as supervisor the senior professor of Prehistory, Branko Gavela, who had no discernible interest in the Vinča group. Although I met him once, at my initial registration meeting, I never went to any supervision with Gavela. It was quite clear that the person who would be most valuable to me as the finest scholar of his generation was Milutin Garašanin,[5] whose position in the University was under doubt because the regime mistrusted the grandson of a former prime minister in the era of the Kingdom of Yugoslavia. Indeed, sometime in the 1960s, Garašanin (Fig. 8) had finished teaching a class on Roman archaeology at the University and, when he came out of the lecture theatre around 12 o'clock, he was arrested by uniformed officers who took him away and he was forced to dig ditches in the Vojvodina for two weeks and then returned to the University. I never dared to talk to him about this experience but it must have made him extremely insecure.

At the time of his death in November 1956, Professor Miloje Vasić held the chairs of both Prehistory and Classical Archaeology in Beograd. After Vasić' death, Branko Gavela, effectively a philosopher, was appointed as Professor of Prehistory, and Garašanin, an eminent prehistorian, was appointed as Professor of Classical Archaeology. In this position, Garašanin could not take me as a supervised student, so the only time I could see him safely was outside the University. We agreed that I would go along to his flat in Trg Marksa i Engelsa, in the centre of town, every Tuesday afternoon at 5 pm after his siesta. The professor would open the door and usher me into his library room – a wonderful long, narrow space with a small window and a

[5] The same Professor Garašanin whom I'd heard give a lecture about Anza in wonderful French in 1971.

Fig. 8. Milutin Garašanin (left) with James Wiseman (Boston University) at the Classical site of Skupi

door but with the rest of the room covered in library shelves full of books. The high point of my week was our meeting, when we would talk in French about the Neolithic. I owe an enormous debt to Milutin Garašanin for helping me understand the Vinča group. He could talk authoritatively about every single Vinča site that had ever been excavated. Once we got into a meeting rhythm, we would often begin the talk with a glass of *crnogorski lozovača*. I felt I was approaching as close as I could get to the master of the Vinča group in Yugoslavia. As far as I'm aware, nobody else in the university knew about these meetings and so they put Garašanin in no political danger.

However, my own inattention to detail put me in political danger, since, in late October or early November, my three-month tourist visa had run out and I became an illegal immigrant. Even though I missed the deadline by two days, this was potentially very serious and could easily have led to my deportation. It was my great good fortune that I could draw on the assistance of Maja's father, who was an academic of the Yugoslav Academy of Arts and Sciences. Petar contacted the Academy lawyer who looked into my case the next day (only far later would I realise the unprecedented speed at which the lawyer moved). He asked to see my passport and asked about the stamp on the passport made by the Kragujevac police. I explained that I had been travelling through Serbia without proper registration. The Academy lawyer found a loophole, since I could not be punished for the same offence twice. So I immediately got another three-month visa and then another and then another and managed to spend my full year in Beograd. But I was very close to being expelled and losing not only my scholarship year in Yugoslavia but also, perhaps, my marriage.

That autumn, I was working in the Beograd museums, whether the National Museum or the Muzej Grada Beograda (Town Museum of Belgrade), or reading in the two great libraries – the Archaeological Institute or the Academy Library, both on Knez Miloša. From time to time, Maja and I, or just Chapman solo, would make trips outside Beograd. The National Museum in Vršac, in the Eastern Banat near the Romanian border, was a local museum with immensely rich Vinča collections thanks almost single-handedly to the research of Béla Milleker, born when Vršac was still in the Austro-Hungarian Empire and later to become 'Felix' after the First World War. Milleker collected or purchased thousands of finds from key Vinča sites in and around the town. Vršac was only 85 km from Beograd, meaning return bus trips inside a day. I had made two trips before Maja wished to accompany me on the third, which we made by car. While I was studying the museum collections, Maja was walking round the main Vršac market, where she met an old gypsy driving a horse and carriage. She soon realised that this gypsy traded in antiques and arranged a meeting in his house after museum hours. We arrived at the gypsy's house, which was a treasure-house mixture of beautiful and kitsch *objets d'art*. It also became clear that the gypsy would sell his own grandmother to any visitor to turn a profit. The finest object in the house was a 19th-century bronze lamp suspended from the ceiling of the main room by a brass chain. Maja negotiated long and hard over the lamp, eventually reaching a deal whereby she would get the lamp in exchange for a new French washing machine – an innovation that had barely spread beyond Beograd. So all we had to do was to find a French washing machine and transport it from Beograd to the gypsy's house in Vršac. This was when I was beginning to find out things about Maja that I had not realised before. She not only ordered a washing machine but organised friends in Beograd to provide an open-backed truck to carry the item to Vršac. By the end of the day, Maja brought the lamp back to Beograd in triumph. It was the start of many years of antique collecting.

Another solo trip that I made that autumn was down the Morava valley. I had reached Paraćin, where I camped in a small campsite next to the motel and also next to a gypsy encampment. I stayed there three nights and went into the museum in the next town of Svetozarevo to study the Vinča collections there. On the Sunday morning, I packed my tent and went to the motel reception to collect my passport, only to find that it had disappeared. This was serious and I drove straight back to the main British Consulate in Beograd on Monday morning. However, being an innocent in these matters, I hadn't registered the loss with the Paraćin police so the consulate insisted that I had to drive back and get the local police documents. That took the rest of Monday afternoon and I drove back to the consulate that evening. I was at the consulate first thing Tuesday morning but so was someone else. There was a man inside the consulate already, who was shouting and screaming in Serbo-Croat at the top of his voice. This man was a dwarf and he was protesting violently against abuses to him. It was only when the Yugoslav police arrived and they controlled the protesting man that it was possible to open the British Consulate. After much delay, I presented the police documents and supporting evidence and the consulate promised to process these as soon as possible – which meant that I had to return in two days for a new passport. As a coda to this story, I received my old passport back after six years, with a photo not closely related to my own and with stamps across the Near East as far as the Khyber Pass, where the passport had been seized. So it was not the Paraćin gypsies but the Oriental travellers who had stolen my passport in the first place.

With my new passport in hand, I drove down the Morava valley to Niš – a town which I always felt to be strange and cold to visitors. The principal monument on the main street was the famous *Čele kula* (Skull Tower), which was a monument built mainly from the skulls of the victims of Ottoman killings in the town, which left a gloomy atmosphere over Niš that never dissipated. On my previous visit, I had not been able to see any prehistoric finds in the museum, mainly because there was no exhibition space in the town museum. But this time I came armed with a letter from Milutin Garašanin to one of his former students – Radmila Ajdić – currently the museum archaeologist in Niš. Radmila showed me the Neolithic material in the store in the main museum but she also took me out to the museum outstation in a preserved Nazi concentration camp on the edge of Niš. A Skull Tower and a Nazi concentration camp more or less summed up for me the essence of Niš. Nonetheless, I drove my Morris straight into the concentration camp (Plate 7) and sat down in one of the barracks to look at the material from the Bubanj Hum and Pločnik tells.

Back in Beograd, I was able to work in the National Museum with Blaženka (Seka to her friends) Stalio, Dušan Krstić, who was about to start the *Selevac* project with Ruth Tringham and Milutin Garašanin's wife Draga (*Lalka* – Serbo-Croat for 'doll' – to her friends). Between them, they guaranteed me access not only to the main National Museum store in the basement but also the gold treasure room, with Thracian and Roman coins and other golden treasures, which was locked and securely placed at the back of the basement store. So these were extraordinary days for a British PhD student.

My favourite archaeologist of the Brukner–Tasić–Jovanović generation was Borislav (Bora) Jovanović, who had already started work in the Archaeological Institute where he would spend his entire career. He was just in the middle of a groundbreaking project to excavate the first securely dated copper mine known in the Vinča group. The site was Rudna Glava in north-east Serbia and Bora was writing short articles about Rudna Glava for as many journals as he could and he wanted me, as a native speaker, to edit his already good English texts. So, that autumn, I was earning pin money by polishing Rudna Glava texts. This work led to a visit to Rudna Glava.

Bora Jovanović had organised a field trip to north-east Serbia to look at metallurgical remains, not only Vinča sites but also Bronze Age and Roman sites. He had invited several foreign metallurgical luminaries, principally Theodore Wertime and Jim Muhly from America and Ronald Tylecote from the UK. The trip was scheduled for a weekend, with Tylecote due to arrive at Beograd airport on the Friday afternoon. I was still in my flat in Banovo Brdo that Friday afternoon when Maja ran over and said there was an emergency – the Institute of Archaeology's only field car had broken down and could I please collect Professor Tylecote from the airport: his flight was due to arrive at 3 pm and I should bring him to the Institute. I agreed and Maja ran back to confirm the arrangement with Bora. So, after an hour, I fired up my ancient Morris Minor – only 20 years old at the time – and drove to Beograd airport and sat waiting for the Heathrow flight to arrive.

A man in his 50s with a pronounced limp, walking with a stick and holding a British passport and a copy of the London Times, walked across the terminal, announcing to everyone concerned that this was a British professor abroad. I introduced myself, we walked to the car and I drove him to the Institute in the city centre. Tylecote was extremely grateful to me for meeting him and invited me to dinner that night, suggesting I choose a restaurant near the Institute. There were many excellent restaurants but I decided that the most atmospheric was one in the only preserved Turkish street in the centre of town – the so-called Skadarlija. We had an extremely fine and very jolly meal there, during which Ronnie told me the story of his life. After falling off a mountain cut short his mountaineering career, Ronnie became Britain's leading archaeo-metallurgist through the 1960s and 1970s.

Next morning, the group were driven off to north-east Serbia, with Bora Jovanović the prehistoric guide and Vladimir Condić, the director of the National Museum, the guide to the Roman sites. On the first morning, we drove to Rudna Glava, which we approached via the Saška Reka (the Valley of the Saxons). When we reached the top of the Saška Reka, we had to walk 3 km up the slope to Rudna Glava, where the first sign of mining that we saw consisted of an enormous V-shaped trench cut into the limestone ridge. This was the remains of a Roman mining operation but, as we looked carefully, we could see the traces of semi-circular shafts in the side of the Roman cut. These small shafts were the remains of the Vinča mining. At the top of each shaft was a platform, sometimes containing Vinča pottery. The shafts were so small that full-grown adults couldn't go down, so this must have meant child labour at an early stage of mining. The discovery of the site was revolutionary for the study of Balkan metallurgy and mining, confirming the independent discovery of copper metallurgy in the Balkan Neolithic.

Jovanović realised that the Bor-Majdanpek area in north-east Serbia was one of the great metallurgical centres in the medieval period, so if one was to find prehistoric finds anywhere, this would be the place. In the late 1960s, he started to look for such sites. In the Museum of Mining at Bor, he systematically went through every box in the storeroom and came upon a box with a Vinča deer-terminal lamp and one sherd of Vinča dark burnished ware, with a scruffy note in the box, stating 'Rudna Glava, found in Roman mine'. This note was what led Bora to the discovery of the Rudna Glava mine.

The visit to the earliest known copper mine in the world was an amazing experience for me. We spent the night in Majdanpek and had the meatiest dinner I had ever experienced – a Serbian speciality called '*mešano meso*' (mixed grill), including steak, pork chops, meatballs, kevapčići, liver and lamb chops. What was even more intriguing was the discussions about the significance of Rudna Glava, with Bora leading the charge by maintaining this meant independent copper metallurgy in the Balkans and the great diffusionist Theodore Wertime trying to defend his corner under heavy pressure.

Back in Beograd in mid-October, I noticed an article in the daily newspaper *Politika* announcing a sudden change of policy by the Romanian state as regards foreign visitors. The article stated that, on 1 November, the Romanian state would institute a new US $10 tax on foreigners coming into the country. This would mean, that every day they spend in Romania, foreigners would have to change $10 into Romanian lei, undoubtedly at a poor rate of exchange. I had quite a lot of work to complete in Transylvania and this left me very little time to make my final visit to Cluj-Napoca. So I sent a telegram that day to Ghiţa Lazarovici with the wording: '*10 dollars crise: Chapman arrive demain*'. I took the night train to Cluj-Napoca from Beograd and got there around 8 am next morning. After a good breakfast at the station, I turned up at the Museum. My friends and colleagues were astonished to see me there and I asked them: 'Did you not get my telegram?' They said, 'Yes, we did' but there was something about a $10 crisis and the arrival of champagne. The telegrapher had clearly misspelt my name and my friends were very disappointed that it was only me that had arrived the next day. They soon recovered and I had the chance over the next week to finish all of my studies of Vinča pottery that I needed to in Cluj-Napoca before the deadline of 1 November. At this point, I bade farewell to my friends and colleagues and returned to Beograd on the day train.

The other Museum in which I worked in Beograd was the Muzej Grada Beograda (Town Museum), whose lack of separate public exhibition space meant that everything in their collections was in store. The leading prehistorian was a short, stocky *bon viveur* called Jovan (Giovanni) Todorović, who, after his first heart attack, was on strict doctor's orders not to drink, especially *rakia* or *šljivovica*. This was an impossible demand on Giovanni, who kept drinking and had on average one heart attack per year until his 11th fit killed him in the late 1970s. But he was such good company that no one wanted to persuade him to follow doctor's orders.

There were two particular features of the museum that were both rather endearing. The first one was that, once you were accepted as one of the museum family, there was a regular half-hour coffee break in which people would meet every two hours to drink very strong Turkish coffee, have a gossipy chat and then return to work. So 25% of the work time in the museum was devoted to socialisation, which was fine as far as I was concerned because I was working extremely intensively with a large amount of pottery to study and could well do with frequent coffee breaks. Once the museum staff realised I was quite happy left on my own to work in the store, they allowed me to go anywhere I wanted. The second endearing feature of the museum was the museum rat, who, by the time of my visit, had become a member of the museum family, living in the store and not really bothering anybody. It was certainly a shock the first time you saw the rat but, after that, you simply treated him as another member of the museum staff.

I had explained before that Maja and I had decided to get married while we were still in Yugoslavia. The date of the civil wedding was set for 22 December 1974, because there was no other free time before that in the Town Hall calendar. Earlier, we went to the town hall, so that the Registrar could explain what was going to happen. He said that the Town Hall was adept at mixed language weddings, which could be quite long since the Serbo-Croat text had to be translated into English. Indeed, a civil wedding in Yugoslavia was very much a contract in which your responsibilities and your duties were laid out in remarkable detail. We would have to sign up to all of the clauses before our guests and witnesses. We were also told that there would be music during the long ceremony and this turned out to be an amazing gypsy violinist who, while producing a very fine tone with his vintage violin, had a narrow range of tunes suitable for a civil marriage. When he'd finished tune A, he moved onto tune B and then returned to tune A. Thus a marriage in Opština Čukarica consisted of a long ceremony with a tedious musical accompaniment.

It was quite a challenge to draw up a guest list for the wedding. I invited as many of my relatives and friends as I could contact at short notice but in fact only my parents came over with Aunt Ruth. Ruth was the senior aunt on my father's side, lived in Sydenham in South London in the old family home, had extremely poor eyesight and was the only member of the family who was a true believer with a High Church Anglican background.[6] But the family trio managed to come on a three-day train trip and arrive just before the wedding. We certainly invited Milutin Garašanin and his wife Lalka. We desperately wanted to invite Mina and Greg since it was Mina who had introduced me to Maja in the first place but Mina and Greg were in America at the time and couldn't come over. We invited all of Maja's extended family and quite a lot of people from the block, as well as the students who knew both of us.

The day of the wedding arrived and it was snowing lightly – not enough to stop us walking down to the Town Hall. So the wedding party left from the Pere Todorovića flat and we walked half a kilometre or so to the Town Hall. Just as we were entering the Town Hall, Maja cried out with horror that she had forgotten her *lična karta* (personal ID card), which was essential for the wedding ceremony. So I had to go back up the hill through the snow to get the *lična karta*.

[6] See pp. 64–65 for a story about the improbably naughty side of Aunt Ruth.

This diversion gave everyone time to relax inside the Town Hall and for people to meet each other. It also allowed the violinist to tune up and start his ABABABA sequence. While the guests sat, we stood through what did indeed transpire to be a long service – over an hour and a half because of the translations. Eventually, we signed on the dotted line, with signatures from our witnesses, thus completing the formalities in the Town Hall. So, as man and wife, we walked with families and guests back up the hill through the snow to a reception in the Martinović flat. The main dish of the feast was indeed the very fine suckling pigs, while the newly decorated wedding cake bowled everyone over. Everyone squeezed into the flat and there was lots of very jolly music and dancing till the wee hours.

My parents had never been to Yugoslavia before and never seen Dubrovnik, so I persuaded Maja to let them come with us on the honeymoon, not to be gooseberries but simply to enjoy the Adriatic coast in their own time and space while leaving us to do the same. All four of us went for a week's honeymoon in Dubrovnik and we booked into a newish hotel outside the old town, with a swimming pool in front of the hotel. However, on our very first night, the *bura* – the Yugoslav equivalent of the *mistral* – blew so hard that it took the roof off the hotel. Our rooms were not on the top floor of the hotel, so we weren't flooded out. But when we woke up the next morning, we found the hotel roof sitting in the swimming pool. All the guests were extremely worried and even the hotel staff suggested that we find another place to stay. Since this was December, it was no problem at all to book two rooms in a 16th-century house in the old town. Our new place was a beautiful old building – much more atmospheric than our hotel – and we were safe from the *bura*, which had blown many times and never knocked the city walls down. The *bura* kept blowing, though less fiercely, for another two or three days. During one walk round the harbour, it was extremely lucky that my father was holding my mum's hand, as a huge gust lifted her off her feet and would otherwise have dumped her in the water.

After the wedding, I gave up my flat at the other end of the Banovo Brdo street and moved into the Martinović flat. Of course, over the next few months, I got to know Petar and Milica much better – especially Petar, with whom I shared not only lunch but also a wealth of his stories most days. I owe Petar a vastly improved knowledge of genetics and evolution; I think he was pleased that there was finally someone in his family who was interested in biology.

The next year was divided between expeditions to museums in the provinces and working on material in the National Museum in Beograd. We reversed what was a typical programme for people living in Beograd, which was to work in Beograd during the week and go out to their summerhouse – the so-called *vikendica* – at the weekend. Instead, we worked outside Beograd in provincial museums for the week and then came back to Beograd for the weekend. These visits to local museums were facilitated by the contacts that Maja had with her fellow students or ex-students who had got museum jobs. Almost everywhere, this helped me greatly to look at Vinča material in the museum stores.

The one exception was the Priština Museum in Kosovo, where Dr Jovan Glišić was still the principal archaeologist and whom I had met in the company of John Nandris in 1971. In the 1950s and 60s, Glišić had excavated a series of really important Vinča sites and he had under his control other important material too. When I went to Priština Museum on the first day and asked if I could talk with Dr Glišić, the museum staff said, 'Not today, come back tomorrow', so I looked in great detail at the Vinča pottery on display. I came back the next day to be told the same. On the third day, I was told that Dr Glišić was not available but that I could meet him in the evening in his flat – I was given his address and told be there at 7 pm. I went along to the Glišić flat, knocked on the door and was met not by Dr Glišić but by his wife, who said she had a message from her husband for me: 'There is no way that you can study any Vinča material in my museum – not even if you were *Drug Tito* (Comrade Tito) himself. Goodbye.' And that was why Priština Museum was the only museum in which it was totally impossible for me to study Vinča collections. Years later, I discovered that only two people had ever been given access to the Vinča collections in Priština. One case was quite understandable, since Stojan Dimitrijević – later a famous professor of Archaeology in Zagreb University – was a classmate of Glišić. But the other person who was able to access the Priština Museum Vinča collection was a University of Bucureşti professor called Vladimir Dumitrescu – the senior prehistorian in Romania. I have asked many people why Vladimir Dumitrescu was so privileged but no one has ever been able to shed light on this Priština Museum mystery.

Many of the trips we made to provincial museums that year took me to parts of former Yugoslavia we had never visited before. For instance, we made a trip to Odžaci, a village with houses in the Austro-Hungarian style in Srem – the western part of the Vojvodina lowlands. An amateur archaeologist called Sergei Karmanski had arrived from Russia seeking asylum in the 1950s and had soon learnt Serbo-Croat well enough to become the village schoolteacher. Karmanski's special interest was the Neolithic. He would ask his schoolchildren if their parents ever found prehistoric pottery in their fields and then visit these sites to produce accurate maps of Neolithic sites in the Odžaci area. He started small-scale excavations at some of the key sites, the most important of which was Donja Branjevina. His excavations produced some extraordinarily rich Early Neolithic material, of which the local professional archaeologists were understandably jealous. Since Karmanski very rarely met with the local big boss, Bogdan Brukner, the boss decided that it was time that he took over excavations on the site. As a professional, he had no difficulties in getting a permit to excavate at the site and so, without talking to Karmanski although he had clearly read his preliminary reports, Brukner and a team from Novi Sad came over one summer and laid out two small trenches in what he took to be the middle of the site. Once he started to go down through the ploughsoil, Brukner hit homogenous deposits that went on for another metre without any finds at all. After enquiries with the landowner, Brukner was crestfallen to find that he had been digging in a pigpen – obviously a very long-lasting pigpen – and had excavated a stratified deposit of pig-shit. At this point, Brukner abandoned Donja Branjevina, never returning to Odžaci and certainly never speaking again to Karmanski.

Not very far from the tell of Gomolava, but on the other bank of the River Sava. was the town of *Šabac* – another town dominated by its Austro-Hungarian architectural past. In Šabac was that rare beast – a museum enthusiast – a wonderful archaeologist called Milivoj Vasiljević. In collaboration with Vojislav Trbuhović from the Beograd Institute of Archaeology, Vasiljević had extended the Karmanski principle of local informants bringing pottery to him to include every pub in the Sava lowlands and higher, up to the Ćer Planina. The team went back time and time again to the bars and pubs of the area and, every time they bought a drink for someone, they got more information about a new prehistoric site. It was the sheer intensity of the drinking research that made this an interesting project, for, by the end of their pub-work and follow-up fieldwork, the team had discovered almost 200 new Vinča sites – a far greater density of Vinča sites than anyone else had found by any other method. Vasiljević was extremely generous with this material and allowed me to mark the location of all the Neolithic sites on copies of 1:50,000 soil maps, which I had procured from another kind and generous colleague – Professor Gligorije Antonović[7] of the Academy Pedological Institute. Šabac was a rich hunting ground for me and invaluable in my study of Vinča settlement patterns. I also drank some of the best Serbian beers in those pubs I visited with Vasiljević.

An interesting point about the overall Vinča distribution was its extension well to the west into Bosnia and Herzegovina. So it was important to visit all three of the key museums in Bosnia to look at Vinča material – in Sarajevo, Doboj and Tuzla. Maja had a distant relative in Sarajevo – a lady of great grace and charm who was married to one of the foremost Sarajevo doctors. On our very first weekend in Sarajevo, we were invited to Sunday afternoon tea in a beautiful and spacious second-floor apartment on one of the main streets. The doctor being absent, the wife entertained us in her *salon* and explained her upbringing in the 1950s. She showed us a vast copper dish that was about a metre in diameter (a *tepsija*) and told us that this was one of the key elements of the preparation of tea in Sarajevo and a young lady was expected to know how to bake enough cakes to fill the entire dish. Later, we were able to buy a matching set of a *džugun* and *tepsija* in the Muslim coppersmiths' quarter of Baš Čarsija and carry them back to England. Even though there were only three of us for tea, our hostess still cooked a very large cake that covered all of the *tepsija*. It was a beautiful welcome to Sarajevo.

Sarajevo had two famous archaeologists who specialised in the Neolithic period – Alojz Benac and Borivoj Čović. Benac was the senior prehistorian in the Academy Institute of Archaeology. To say that Benac was a serious archaeologist would be to underplay the term 'serious'. He was simply a bishop compared to most archaeologists

---

[7] The father of Dragana Antonović, who became an important geo-archaeologist.

who were parish priests. He looked the Episcopal part, as if most of the time he spent communing with the deity and gaining insights about the Neolithic from God. He was an extraordinarily dignified and sober academic and scholar, who was kind to colleagues without ever showing any personal emotions. But he did agree to me looking at the Neolithic material from his sites. The prehistorian who had excavated more Bosnian Vinča sites than anyone else was Borivoj Čović, who, although not as serious as Benac, was certainly a careful archaeologist who excavated well for the time. He was kind enough to let me see all of his finds from his 1950s excavations at the important tell of Gornja Tuzla, which formed a central part of my Vinča studies in Bosnia.

When we arrived in Doboj, I finally got to identify the archaeologist who had impersonated Bogdan Brukner back in 1971 – the museum archaeologist Branko Belić. He had taken a leaf out of Milivoj Vasiljević's book and used pub research to discover several important Bosnian Vinča sites.

One of the most striking towns in Bosnia was the salt town of Tuzla (the Turkish word for 'salt' is '*tuz*'). When the Ottomans arrived in Bosnia, they were already very well aware of the location of this rich salt source. The Turkish town of Tuzla was built directly above salt pans, which were themselves the lower part of a very extensive marshland. The main method of salt extraction was to tunnel into the salt pan below the marsh, which led to the collapse of numerous buildings. It was fascinating to see 16th–17th-century Turkish buildings right next to much more recent, 19th-century stone Austro-Hungarian style buildings, which had replaced the buildings that had subsided into the salt deposit. It was hardly surprising that the main known Vinča site (Donja Tuzla) was found in the centre of town, immediately above the salt pans. The site contained large quantities of what were known as 'salt-pots' of a particular shape (aka the 'Tuzla type'), which were known from a number of Vinča sites in the Vojvodina and which suggested salt exchange from the uplands into the plains.

The last really intriguing place that we visited was the town of what was then called 'Titovo Užice'[8] in south-west Serbia, not far from the Drina valley. The name signified a very important group of resistance fighters in the Second World War, who established an independent republic for a few months before the Nazis overran the town. In the small town museum worked an archaeologist called Mihailo Zotović, who had carried out some excavations and also some pub research. One of the most interesting Vinča sites was a single house site called Kuline-Rog, with an impressive ceramic assemblage that had been stored in the house before burning. Near Kuline was the home village of a famous potter who was still producing pots although well into his 60s. I was particularly interested in his pots because he had developed an interesting parallel practice to those of Neolithic potters – he would make a mark on the base of his wheel-made pottery to identify his vessel. These so-called 'potter's

[8] The name 'Titovo' has been removed from the town's name, which remains 'Užice'.

marks' were very similar to the Vinča incised signs that I'd studied in several Beograd sites. Like most craftpersons, the potter was happy to explain his technique used in producing what seemed to me quite like Iron Age wheel-made pottery with very heavy limestone tempering. The potter explained that he took a solid block of limestone and broke it into smaller pieces, then ground them down into a powder to make temper. The temper probably weighed about as much as the clay for making the vessels. As well as making storage jars, the potter would make large, wide shallow dishes for the separation of curds from whey in dairy production – a pottery shape well known from Late Vinča pottery assemblages.

At the end of this trip to Bosnia and Western Serbia, it became clear that my year in Beograd was coming to an end and we needed to drive back to London in our baby Morris. The problem immediately became what to take and what to leave – the choice between personal items, the ethnographic collection that we'd amassed over the year and the books and periodicals that we had also collected over the year. The Yugoslav post office made a great profit from us, with several large boxes being sent off to England.

Maja had a Yugoslav friend in London called Mira Djisalov – an engineer teaching in a secondary school in Chiswick. Mira very kindly offered us a room in her house in Speldhurst Road in Chiswick, which she vacated for the summer during her return visit to Pančevo. Not entirely vacated, however, because two relatives of Mira, who were in London to learn English, had rooms in the house too. Once we moved into the house, we were living in the main bedroom but expanded to take over most of the house. We had never lived in a house before so the possibilities of expanding into a much larger space had never presented itself – but we soon managed it. This proved a very comfortable place for us during the beautifully warm summer. This expansion was to prove complicated when Mira returned from Pančevo in September.

I still had a lot of writing-up to do, which was my main task while in Chiswick, and still had a little money left over from my University postgrad grant. But Maja wanted to work and she tried several museums through my Institute contacts and eventually one of them turned up trumps in the Museum of London Archaeology Service (the so-called 'MOLAS'). At the time, MOLAS was run by Brian Hobley, previously a millionaire garage owner with amateur interests in Roman archaeology. A Welsh friend called Charlie put in a good word for Maja, who got a job as a finds assistant in the Bonehill Street finds store. This was a rundown warehouse that MOLAS rented as a store in the city. The caretaker was a Hungarian called István, who sat in front of a huge cauldron filled most of the time with *gulyas* but in which István occasionally used to wash his socks. The Bonehill Street store was more or less habitable in the summer of 1975 but it became so cold in the winter of 1975–1976 that it prompted the very first strike in British museum archaeology. The archaeologists in Bonehill Street walked out when the temperature failed to rise above 5°C for two successive days. Even though Brian Hobley had run a garage, he had no experience of dealing with striking archaeologists and eventually bought several electric heaters, which saved the situation. After Maja's day in the city, we had lovely evenings in the garden at Speldhurst Road and in the many delightful Chiswick parks. Meanwhile, I was re-establishing contacts with the University Extramural Studies Department and I was going to start giving lectures in European prehistory again in October.

Eventually, Mira did return to Chiswick and soon found the tensions of being crowded out of her own house too much to bear. After a couple of rows, it became obvious that we had to move out and so we advertised for a house-sharing couple and found a pleasant New Zealand couple – Ron and Pam – who needed house partners. We looked round places all over London but eventually found a vacant house in Edgware, in a leafy, bourgeois suburb. Despite its pretensions, we had signed a contract to take the house over for one year. I was the main occupant of the house in Stoneyfields Lane simply because I was still writing up my thesis. Ron seemed to be unemployed most of the time but had the occasional casual work. Pam was a company secretary in the West End and Maja was still taking the Northern Line into the city to work for MOLAS (Museum of London Archaeological Service).

In those days, there was an annual Young Archaeologists Conference to which I thought I should contribute a paper after three years of researching the Vinča group. In 1977, the conference was at the University of Reading and this turned out to be my first conference paper. My theme of 'Trade and exchange in Balkan prehistory' included some good material and the talk went well. But when the first question from Andrew Selkirk, the editor of *Current Archaeology*, asked me to distinguish between 'trade' and 'exchange', I froze. This really made the point to me that I'd better tidy up my theoretical act for future events. Reading was a useful experience for me but I still found it pretty terrifying to speak at a conference, even of 150 postgraduates. I was obviously still suffering from the experience I'd had in my first year at Devonport High School[9] and my Cambridge Peterhouse interview.[10]

It was around November that tests showed that Maja was pregnant. Although totally unexpected, this was amazing news for us – something that was really important and to which we gave our total commitment. There was a time in late November–early December when life became difficult and Maja got very tired at her work, prompting a discussion with her boss Mike Rhodes about whether she should keep the baby. We owe Mike our everlasting gratitude that he dissuaded Maja from doing anything drastic. The pregnancy went reasonably well, although I experienced morning sickness far worse than the expectant mother and internal bleeding meant that Maja almost lost the baby in January. This meant a month of complete rest in Edgware Hospital, which saved the situation and prompted Maja to leave MOLAS earlier than planned. Everything was fine after that, so I continued

[9] See p. 7 for my first speaking experience at DHS.
[10] See p. 15 for my Peterhouse interview experience.

to work on the writing-up of the thesis but at a faster pace. But our financial state was so poor that I had to look for a job. The ideal place would have been a university job, which would have enabled me to carry on with Balkan prehistory, but there was no such job available at the time. In April, the post of Assistant Curator in Carlisle Museum was advertised. I applied and was given an interview. I took the train to Carlisle, stayed overnight, went to the interview the next morning and was offered the job the day after. My postgraduate life was about to end abruptly and we moved to Carlisle in time for me to start my first paid job on May Day 1976.

Chapter 4

Museum intermezzo

Our move to Carlisle took place in the final days of April 1976. We organised our move in two vehicles. I drove Maja in the Morris Minor, while we put the rather small collection of our belongings in Ron's smallest furniture van. In those days, the surface of most motorways was rather bumpy and it was quite surprising that the long road trip didn't actually induce Eleanor's birth by the time we got to Carlisle.

The City Council had organised a council house for us and, when we got there with Ron and unpacked our belongings, it seemed rather bare. We had no table, only one sofa-bed and very few chairs; it was at that point that we understood the full meaning of the term 'unfurnished'. But it was a pleasant house, about 2 km from Carlisle centre in the direction of Wigtown. We had friendly and welcoming neighbours – Norman and Irene, who were very proud of their cottage garden in the front of the house, which produced tomatoes and beans so small as to be almost invisible, even in the morning light.

Fig. 9. The author with Maja in Balkan ethnographic costume, Carlisle Great Fair

So we settled down to life in Carlisle – a city of about 75,000 people (Fig. 9). Apart from being on Hadrian's Wall, Carlisle's main claim to fame was the Carlisle Experiment, the State Management Scheme for breweries, which had been running since 1921 and which sponsored a large number of pubs with cheap, subsidised beer. It seemed a pity that the Experiment was privatised by the Edward Heath government in 1971, leading to the closure of 20 pubs. But that still left over 50 pubs to sample! Many of them (allegedly) featured Cumbrian folk music – not at all the kind of music that Maja and I appreciated. Sadly, there were no jazz pubs that we could find and few outlets for classical music. In fact, I can't even recall Carlisle having a bespoke concert hall, so large-scale music events took place in the cathedral. Carlisle's music scene did not inspire us greatly.

Carlisle Museum was in the centre of town just off Castle Street. It opened in 1893 in a Jacobean townhouse but its present interior was created in the 1930s by R. G. Collingwood, the great Roman archaeologist and Oxford Professor of History. The Museum was more or less as Collingwood had designed it in the 1930s, with a particularly grand exhibit of a horizontal panel 6 m long, with a Roman inscription of about 40 words of which just three letters had survived from the original inscription (an old epigrapher's trick) (Fig. 10). However, Collingwood justified its importance as the only inscription which related the foundation of Hadrian's Wall. Thus, Carlisle Museum in the old building known as Tullie House was, in effect, a museum of a museum – an extraordinary period piece. Apart from the superfluity of Roman exhibits, there was quite a lot of prehistory on display, with stone axes of Group 6 Langdale type packed into exhibition cases.

The museum staff consisted of the recently appointed curator David Clarke (a biologist), the newly appointed costume expert, Judith Clarke (the curator's wife), a social historian called Dennis Perriam, a photographer called Guy Berisford, the museum secretary called Mrs Scaife and two museum caretakers – Joe and Barry. Joe's most impressive skill was cutting the museum lawn with a scythe. Tullie House was neighbours with the city library, where colleagues in the local history section were also interested in archaeology. But the one person whose personality most strongly permeated the museum was the former curator Robert (Bob) Hogg, a geologist by training, who had served as curator for over 30 years. Bob Hogg's interest in geology focused on the rich mineralogy of the North Pennines. He was not above exchanging inventoried museum objects from the prehistoric collection with Penrith Museum for special mineral samples. It took me a year to realise that as many as 30 polished

Fig. 10. Inscription recording the foundation of Hadrian's Wall (in Tullie House, Carlisle Museum)

stone axes from the prehistory collections were missing and they all turned up in Penrith Museum, whose curator was an archaeologist. The other famous aspect of the Carlisle Museum holdings was their collection of Pre-Raphaelite paintings. The artists' deep attachment to Lake District landscapes led to the museum holding a collection of over 80 paintings, including some of the very finest paintings that the group ever made. In the 1930s, a habit developed for Carlisle councillors to borrow Pre-Raphaelite paintings from the museum collection to adorn their front rooms. I'm not sure how many of these paintings were displayed in the house at the time of a councillor's death but the house's possessions would often pass to the next of kin, with the museum title to the painting lapsing. But the principal legacies of Bob Hogg's curatorship were the unchanging displays and the resultant low level of finances required for the museum from the City Council,[1] under long-term, fiscally tight Conservative control and with seemingly little interest in culture.

The first weeks of my job were taken up with learning standard museum procedures: what was on display, what was in store, how I could find whatever I was looking for, how I could use inventory books and how I should answer archaeological queries made at the museum. In the first month, I had my first archaeological query. A man came to the door asking if I could suggest the location of any Roman fort near Carlisle. Since I had the strong suspicion that he was a metal detectorist, I suggested that there was an excellent Roman fort on Cross Fell – the highest hill in the Pennines – and that he would be sure to find interesting artefacts there. He never came back.

As far I could tell, there were minimal security procedures for the museum and hardly anything which had such intrinsic value that it would be a target for thieves. But I'd reckoned without the museum birds' egg collection, which was stored in a passage off the natural history exhibition. Within two months of my arrival, there was an attempted theft of birds' eggs from the store by someone who was well-known to the German police for stealing birds' eggs from nests in Germany. I took from this incident that there was an international trade in birds' eggs and that no museum was safe from theft.

When I finished my museum work, I would go back to our council house and share my day with Maja, who was finding Carlisle very difficult. In these early months, Maja hadn't met anyone from outside the county, let alone the country, so life on a council estate was dispiriting for her. She looked forward to my return after 5 pm but agreed that it was a top priority to complete the PhD thesis before the birth of our child. So every evening after dinner, I would work away at this task. Within a month of arriving in Carlisle, I had completed the writing up of the PhD for submission to the University of London by the end of May 1976.

The other event at the end of May 1976 was my first salary cheque from my first full-time job. I remember seeing, with total horror, that the sum total of my earnings,

[1] This all changed in the New Millennium, when the new Carlisle City Museum opened (2000–1).

after all deductions, had reached a mighty £149.40. This was well below the PhD student grant that I had received from the University of London. Now with a wife to support and a baby on the way, it seemed a paltry sum and I must admit did not persuade me to make any long-term plans for staying in Cumbria.

By June, Maja was eight months pregnant and had lost a lot of mobility. I was extremely relieved that I'd finished writing up the PhD and was able to spend more time with her. On the evening of Friday 21 July, her waters broke and I drove her to the maternity ward of Carlisle General Hospital. At that point, Maja started a 14-hour labour, not made easier by the fact that, on this Saturday, there was only one doctor on duty in the maternity ward who had to devote her attention to another, more complicated case. So Maja had two nurses to help in the delivery. At least I was able to sit with her and comfort her as much as I could but she underwent a lot of pain and needed oxygen from near the start. The first 'disaster' came when the first canister of oxygen ran out and the nurses didn't know how to disconnect it. I helped with that but, when the second canister was supposed to come on stream, we realised that it was empty. Eventually, a third canister was brought and Maja breathed again after five minutes of pain. But she still had another six hours to go. Finally, the doctor delivered the other baby and was free for perhaps the 13th hour of Maja's delivery. She realised immediately that the baby's head was stuck in the birth canal and needed to operate with a small cut followed by a forceps delivery. To my great chagrin, I was ushered out of the ward, despite having spent 12 hours supporting Maja. Eventually, the news came that the mother was safe and she had given birth to a baby girl. If the baby was a girl, we had previously decided to call her 'Eleanor' since the name was easily transliterated into the Serbo-Croat 'Jelena' and also because it was an ancient, probably Neolithic, name.[2] The inspiration for Eleanor's second name – Fleur – was the character in Galsworthy's novels *The Forsyte Sagas*. So Eleanor Fleur was born and Maja was so exhausted that she stayed an extra three days in hospital. On the Wednesday morning, I drove them back to our council house and so Eleanor's life in Carlisle began. Eleanor was an ethnic Cumbrian – if ever Cumbria declares UDI, she would get a passport but we wouldn't.

Now that Eleanor was at home with us, my parents offered to come up from Plymouth to help with the baby. It wasn't really possible for Maja's parents Milica and Petar to come over from Yugoslavia – they would have to wait until the summer to see Eleanor. For my parents' visit, we had to buy some furniture – a dining table, two chairs and an extra divan bed for them. We managed to do this despite my monthly salary. The table was actually a washstand with a marble top – pretty but extremely narrow, perhaps 70 cm wide – so dinners were a little complicated. But my parents put up with this and it was certainly very helpful to have them around, even though, after 25 years, my mum had forgotten most of her mothering skills. They stayed a

[2] From Homer's work, Helen of Troy was certainly a Dark Age, if not a Bronze Age name, so the name 'Eleni' was very likely to be an Indo-European name and therefore probably Neolithic.

week and a half and that helped us to get on our feet. In those days, there was no such thing as paternity leave and it was too soon in my employment to ask for annual leave, so each weekday I was working in the museum and it was a great comfort that Mum and Dad were in the house with Maja and Eleanor.

Not surprisingly, in Eleanor's first year, we had to limit our travels around Cumbria but we still took her out in the sun as much as we could. We had a feeding interval of three to four hours, so we could go up to an hour and a half's drive in any direction. This meant that we were confined to the northern lakes, especially Bassenthwaite, but also nearby was the Solway coast with its views across to Scotland, the Eden Valley and the Penrith area. Here were wonderful Neolithic monuments, such as Long Meg and her Daughters and the henges near Penrith. One of our favourite places was Wetheriggs Pottery, which started off as a working pottery producing drainage tiles for local estates in the mid-19th century but, after closing down in 1962, had opened up as an art pottery. Their specialty was imitation post-medieval slipware, with white patterns on rich Chelsea blue surfaces. Our most treasured possession in these early days was the blue and white slipware model cot decorated with Eleanor's name – still in the family. East of Eden was the Tyne–Solway corridor, with a spectacular medieval church at Brampton and the stunning ruin of Lanercost Priory.

Summer 1976 was a season of serious drought and we did everything we could to keep cool and hydrated, with Eleanor protected from direct sunlight as much as possible. There was so little water in the Lake District lakes that there were several instances of soil coming out of the taps instead of water – another threat to Eleanor's health. But the fine, warm weather was good for Eleanor's health and prepared her for her first visit to Yugoslavia.

Maja had found contacts among a babysitting circle, so she was able to escape once or twice a week to the centre of Carlisle. It was there that she discovered a passion for antiques that would last her and my wallet for the rest of her life. Maja discovered the excitement of looking at antiques – although maybe not acquiring them yet – and heard about the twice-weekly antiques auction in the Carlisle Market Hall. Maja was to spend hours of her free time sitting in auctions, observing and, later at home, reading about antiques. She developed a good general knowledge of antiques, which later helped to turn a decent profit for her when she started to trade.

Maja would also visit the only Continental health food shop in Carlisle in Castle Street, run by two refugees from Czechoslovakia, Mr Becko and his wife. Mr Becko's Continental food was essential to us. While Mr Becko was friendly to his customers, he treated his wife rather differently. While we liked the shop, we hated Mr Becko.

I had learned from Dennis Perriam that there was what one might call an unbalanced relationship between the museum and the two leading university archaeologists who did fieldwork in Cumbria. Both universities wanted to claim Cumbria – at the time without a university of its own – as a province of their own university and both of the archaeologists were Romanists. Tim Potter worked in Lancaster University and was excavating a Roman fort at Bowness-on-Solway on the Forth – thought to be the

Westernmost fort on Hadrian's Wall. I paid him a site visit one hot day and was given the impression that Tim considered the museum simply to be a place where he could store his materials after the completion of post-ex but that otherwise any interactions would be minimal. The drought summer of 1976 produced ideal conditions for aerial photography, of which Barrie Jones of Manchester University took full advantage. Professor Jones had initiated a programme of block flying of the Solway Lowlands and south-west Scotland, with dramatic results. He discovered hundreds of enclosed sites south of Hadrian's Wall and very few enclosed sites north of the wall – potentially evidence for major economic differences caused by the building of the wall. But Professor Jones never contacted the museum. Although both these projects fell clearly within the museum collection area of North Cumbria, there was no sense that the museum could benefit from this research and no notion of a museum exhibition to popularise their findings with the general public. Perhaps it didn't help that I was a recent appointment and, even worse, a prehistorian. But this taught me a very valuable lesson about how archaeologists could interact with their museum counterparts, wherever they were in the world.

Near the end of the summer, my two examiners had finished reading my PhD. In those days, it was University of London practice for one's supervisor to be an internal examiner – a potentially flawed practice that I think was soon abandoned. The external examiner was Colin Renfrew, who, at 35, had recently become a young professor at the University of Southampton. Although this was a University of London thesis, Colin Renfrew refused to travel to London for the day, so the mountains had to travel to Muhammad. It was clear from the beginning of the viva that only minor changes were to be made, since the first version of the thesis was extremely data heavy. In fact, I spent so much time collecting data and analysing site pottery assemblages that I didn't have time to complete any broader secondary analysis of the material. The examiners accepted that this was a limitation of the thesis but felt it was important that the thesis should be accepted so that this material would be available in public for anyone who wanted to work on it. Professor Renfrew raised only two minor quibbles – both relating to his own research. He felt that I was not making enough of his work on the radiocarbon calibration curve and not paying enough attention to his analysis of the Tărtăria tablets and their implications for Balkan chronology. These were minor re-writes which I finished in a week and so the thesis was accepted by London University in 1976, slightly less than four years since I began and a cause for great celebration. One of the few lasting achievements of my 250,000-word thesis was that it stimulated the University of London to impose an upper word limit of 100,000 words on archaeology PhD theses.

I was able to make one trip in late summer that year thanks to Carlisle Council's generous decision to give me a week's paid leave. This let me participate in the UISPP (*Union des Sciences Pré- et Proto-historiques*) conference held in Nice, where I represented Carlisle City Museum and read a paper on my Vinča research. One of the other delegates, working in Durham University, to which he had recently moved from the British Museum, was Anthony Harding. He had recently married Lesley and we exchanged newlywed stories. Anthony could not understand how any married person could read general books, since his previous habit was to read himself to sleep. As we walked the streets of Nice in the warm late evening air, passing casinos and bars full of attractive young ladies, we felt very remote from our wives in the north of England. I was totally reinvigorated by the conference, which was the first chance for me to discuss Balkan prehistory with anyone in many months. I realised that this was the milieu in which I wanted to work – the only question was 'how?'.

Soon after Nice, I had accumulated enough working months to be able to take annual leave, so we flew to Beograd to take Eleanor to meet her grandparents for the first time. This was an exciting time for them and we had two weeks of blissful Balkan food and great good cheer. I also started to rebuild links with the Beograd prehistorians with whom I had previously worked. The experience was utterly typical of Balkan friendships: we took up exactly where we had left off our relationship over a year ago, as if nothing had happened in between (even though it had, in the case of Eleanor) and as if we were still the closest of friends. This shrinking of friendship time was one vital way to keep in touch with people one couldn't meet very often.

One visit to Carlisle which really perked me up was a professional visit to the Museum. The Greens – Stephen and Miranda – came to Tullie House for almost a week. Stephen was an expert on the Neolithic, writing a PhD about flint arrowheads in the British Neolithic, while Miranda was an Iron Age specialist researching Celtic art in Britain. They were the first prehistorians to visit me in the museum and it made a huge difference to be able to talk about new ideas and trends in archaeology. Perhaps the Greens may have been a bit overwhelmed by my enthusiasm for their company – I hardly let them out of my sight for five days. Their visit gave me a huge boost at a time when things in the museum were pretty humdrum.

The main aspect of my work in that first autumn in Carlisle centred on the documentation of our prehistoric collections. One new approach to museum documentation currently circulating in museum circles in Britain was the so-called 'IRGMA' documentation system, developed by the Museums Association. The goal was to work out a unified, comparable documentation format for inventoried museum finds so that they could be eventually computerised. The green, two-sided IRGMA card wasn't quite a punchcard design but it was designed for later computer input. I suggested to the curator that I went through the entire Carlisle Museum prehistoric collection and put all of the items onto IRGMA cards and he was very much in favour of this. So I started this after the summer of 1976 and it was an extremely good way of getting to know the collection. I had to go through every single box in the museum store and all of the displays in order to link up accession numbers to objects. I then had to go through all of the inventory books and make that same link, slowly building up a very large pile of IRGMA cards. For the third documentation pillar, I needed strong support from colleagues in the local history section of Carlisle Library. This involved me going through the entire microfiched record of the two local newspapers – the

Carlisle Journal, starting in 1801 and the *Carlisle Patriot*, which started rather later, in 1815 – up to the 1940s, when archaeological finds were more professionally recorded. I needed library training to become an efficient microfiche reader but I could then go through a huge number of newspapers and make links to many objects in the collection, as well as recording objects that had never entered the collections of our museum or had never been published.

Another aspect of museum life which brought me in contact with mostly amateur archaeologists – a very interesting and very knowledgeable group – was the Cumberland and Westmoreland Archaeological and Antiquarian Society – usually called the 'Cumbersome and Wearisome'. The C & W had a monthly lecture series through the winter and spring months, with most talks held in Carlisle Museum. I would go along to these, whatever the subject. By far the most impressive lecturer was the famous architectural historian Niklaus Pevsner, who had already published his volumes on the buildings of Cumberland, Westmoreland and Lancashire North of the Sands. He came up to give a general lecture on the architecture of Cumbria and I was asked to meet Pevsner and set up his audio-visuals (in those days, a slide projector and slides). After making him feel as welcome as possible, I asked if he'd like to give me his slides so that I could set up the slide projector. Pevsner looked through his bag twice and even checked his coat and it became obvious that the great man had forgotten his slides. 'Don't worry,' said Pevsner, 'just turn the projector on and I will speak and I will stamp on the floor with my stick when I want you to change slides.' Once the audience was seated and the speaker introduced, Pevsner started off with a few general comments and said that he'd like to take us all back to one of the earliest surviving buildings, at which point he banged the floor. I switched on the projector and he proceeded to talk for two or three minutes about a 14th-century tithe barn located near Windermere. He continued his lecture with learned commentaries on 50 more non-existent slides, often mentioning constructional details and decorative elements, all the while talking with total self-confidence. Pevsner was a star and managed to bring off one of the most enjoyable un-illustrated lectures on architectural history I've ever heard.

At Christmas in 1976, the guest of honour was Aunt Ruth, who was so appreciated by Maja's family for coming all the way to Beograd for our wedding. She decided she wanted to come up to Carlisle to see Eleanor, with my parents coming up slightly later, since we didn't have enough beds to host the whole family. Aunt Ruth was very worried that we hadn't managed to find a Christmas tree for Eleanor's first Christmas and she wondered where we could find one. I explained that I believed the Forestry Commission had ready-cut trees and Ruth said, 'Let's drive to the nearest Forestry Commission plantation and see if we can buy one.' So we drove just over the Scottish border and found a small plantation in which a number of Christmas trees were lying in a ditch by the edge of the track but where no Commission workers were present. Aunt Ruth told me to collect a small tree from the ditch and I put it in the back of the Morris Minor Traveller and we drove back to Carlisle with our prize. I could hardly believe what my aunt had just done because she was the most God-fearing and devout member of my entire family and the idea that Aunt Ruth would go out and steal a Christmas tree was little short of incredible. But that's exactly what happened – and Aunt Ruth appeared to enjoy herself considerably. Maybe she regretted missing out on a life of crime in Sydenham? She just exclaimed what a very wonderful tree it was and we bought some simple tree decorations, which certainly enlivened Eleanor's first Christmas.

One piece of fieldwork was connected to Professor Barrie Jones's block-flying of the Solway Lowlands.[3] Minor roadworks appeared to be about to disturb one of the hitherto undated enclosed sites found from the air, so it was useful to conduct what would now be called a 'watching brief' near one of the lowland villages. When I arrived at the site, I spotted a fieldwalker looking very carefully into the JCB trench. It transpired that he was a soil scientist called Barry Matthews, from the Soil Survey of England and Wales, and he was interested in studying an exposure of the buried soil sequence underneath the banks of what turned out to be an Iron Age enclosure. I took notes and made photos and sketches of the profiles and Barry Matthews worked out the soil sequence – perhaps the first one ever to have been recorded for a Cumbrian Iron Age enclosure.

I met Barry Matthews a few times that summer but then he went off the radar completely. It wasn't until late in 1977 that I caught up with him to find out what had happened. He was doing some fieldwork along the Cumbrian coast near the Windscale nuclear reactor and he'd realised at an early stage that the plant was leaking radioactive liquid into the Irish Sea – a fact not officially recognised by the authorities but well recorded by local environmentalists and Greenpeace. One day, Barry decided to have lunch on the beach just south of Windscale, where he drove in his Soil Survey van. He took his pack of sandwiches and sat down on the beach, which was deserted apart from a family with two young children, who were just about to go swimming. Since Barry was certain the beach was contaminated, he approached the family and explained that it wasn't wise for children to bathe in this water. The family thanked Barry and indeed didn't go swimming and that appeared to be the end of that. But the couple complained to the local council about this 'official intervention' by a civil servant in an official vehicle and, as Barry was the only soil scientist working in West Cumbria, he was easily tracked down and fired for potentially saving lives. This seemed to me such a misuse of public goodwill and trust that I could never trust Windscale again.[4] But that was why I didn't see any more of Barry Matthews in the Solway Lowlands. Incidentally, the best-funded travelling exhibition, with the smartest design and the largest schools education/propaganda programme, ever presented in Carlisle Museum in my time there was the BNF (British Nuclear Fuels) exhibition in 1977.

[3] See p. 62.
[4] See pp. 67–68 for Jim Cherry's story of the start of operations at Windscale.

The English Heritage archaeologist, Dorothy Charlesworth, kept a very close watch on building developments proposed for the centre of Carlisle. One major project was the 'Lanes Project', involving the demolition of post-medieval houses and a shopping re-development in the Roman and medieval core of the city over a 2.8 ha area. Since this project was far too big for Dorothy Charlesworth and all the local Carlisle resources, she negotiated with English Heritage for the assistance of the Central Archaeological Unit. This was Head Archaeologist Geoff Wainwright's baby, which operated in Wessex with two criteria for the choice of sites: the site had to be on the chalk (so as to facilitate the recognition of cut features with dark fill) and within 1 km of a pub. Carlisle worked very well for the second criterion but not so well for the first, so Geoff Wainwright delegated the job of Project Director to David Neal, a Romanist who was a specialist in Roman mosaics. David Neal was quintessentially a military man, who ran everything according to a precise schedule and considered himself the commander of his workers. It was quite a shock for a laid-back Assistant Curator to watch David Neal in action. One of his diggers was Tony Wilkinson, who was not at all military and whom I found a much more congenial companion. I got to know Tony quite well during the Lanes Project, before he went off to Chicago to work in the Field School on Near Eastern landscape archaeology. It would not be until he joined Durham in the 2000s that I met him again.

A major event in the summer of 1977 was the Prehistoric Society's British Field Trip. Every year, the Prehistoric Society – the leading national society for prehistorians in the UK – holds a British field excursion lasting a week. That year, the Society had decided to base their trip on Cumbria, partly because there was a new County Archaeologist, recently appointed in Kendal, called Tom Clare, who knew colleagues on the Society's Council, but also in honour of one of the oldest and most vigorous long-term Prehistoric Society members, Clare Fell. A member of the county set, Clare was the *doyenne* of Cumbrian archaeology and, although in her 70s, she behaved as if she was in her 40s. I joined up this special field trip on the second day, when the tour looked at the Penrith and Eden Valley sites. That day, the group was supposed to visit Carlisle Museum for a guided tour. I had organised for a buffet dinner to be laid out in the museum and persuaded the normally mean city council to fund it. However, wires were crossed and the Society returned to their accommodation in the Newton Rigg agricultural training college West of Penrith for 6 pm dinner. It became clear that the Prehistoric Society group were not going to arrive in Carlisle Museum for 6.30 pm, when the Lord Mayor was due to give a welcoming address. All I could do was telephone the museum to explain the mistake and we turned up an hour late in Carlisle Museum. To say that the Lord Mayor, in full regalia, was miffed was a gross understatement. He became apoplectic when he realised that most of the guests would not be able to eat a great deal of the very fine spread that he had funded. This was the last occasion when I managed to persuade Carlisle City Council to sponsor any kind of archaeological event.

The most curious aspect of the buffet dinner concerned teaspoons. To complete the savoury buffet, the Council had laid on a beautiful series of plates of cakes and jellies, with appropriate cutlery (one teaspoon had been provided for each member of the group and the Carlisle party – a total of 32 teaspoons). At the end of the reception, the Society went on a tour of the prehistoric exhibitions, together with a set of Group VI axes specially brought out from the store. After the Prehistoric Society's Vice-President thanked the Lord Mayor very much for his kind hospitality, the group returned to their coach and I stayed behind to help clear up. At the end of the washing-up, the mysterious fact emerged there were only five teaspoons remaining in the museum. What did this mean? Were there 27 thieves in the Prehistoric Society, each of whom made off with one teaspoon? Or could it be a single kleptomaniac who put 27 teaspoons in their knapsack and escaped to Penrith? This was an unsolved mystery both for the Prehistoric Society and for Carlisle City Council and, for years, remained a very sore point between the City Council and Carlisle Museum.

One of the most enterprising members of the Prehistoric Society to come on that trip was Jim Cherry, who lived in Leeds and travelled every weekend to the Cumbrian coast to complete an amazing research project – to locate every single Mesolithic and Neolithic site within a 2 km range of the coastline. If you looked at a map of Mesolithic and Neolithic finds in Cumbria, there was the *Jim Cherry culture* along the coast and an apparently random scatter of dots in the Cumbrian fells, which indicated where Jim had been on holiday.

Jim was an amazing character and, once he had found a promising site, nothing could move him before he had completed proper documentation. One Sunday late morning, Jim was out on St Bees' Head – a limestone promontory extremely rich in Mesolithic flints of the smallest variety (known as 'microliths'). Once Jim started work, he became totally absorbed in the discovery of the microliths, having to keep his head close to the thin vegetation to see the tiny tools. Unbeknown to Jim, a group of 25 people surrounded him – he was collecting flints in the centre circle of the St Bees' football pitch and the players and referees did not know what to do. Jim was faced with a stark choice: abandon the site (never!), ask people to go away (unlikely to succeed, because outnumbered by 25 to 1) or play mad dog and scare them off. Jim chose the third option and gazed straight into the footballers' eyes, barking as fiercely as a Mesolithic archaeologist could bark for a minute. At this point, the referee called off the match because a madman had invaded the pitch and left Jim to continue his collection of microliths – one of his finest collections from the Cumbrian coast.

Jim was a great raconteur, who liked telling stories about the early days of the Windscale nuclear plant, since he was one of the engineers who helped design and build the plant. Perhaps his best story concerned the day when Windscale started production of nuclear energy. A lot of Windscale workers, including Jim, lived in Windscale village, which was separated from the plant by a low hill. On the day of the opening, Jim decided that he would have a lie-in and cycle to the plant a little later than usual. He cycled up the low hill and saw a wisp of radioactive smoke coming from the main dome of the plant. Jim was absolutely terrified and quickly biked back downhill, went inside his house and stayed there for the rest of the day. When he went to the pub in the evening, he could not believe the rumours that were going around that you could tell the plant had started because it was producing smoke. Jim tried to explain that Windscale was not like a normal industrial plant, with smoke indicating production, and that no one should go anywhere near it, but no one believed him. So Windscale started with a radioactive leak on its very first day – an accident that, according to Jim, has never been recorded in the annals of the Windscale plant and, I can confirm, does not appear in John May's *Greenpeace Book of the Nuclear Age* (1989).

One of the many things I learnt about provincial museums in England – and I'm sure it's the same everywhere else in the world – is that each one has a hidden gem in their collections which is often not exploited. So it was with Carlisle Museum and I found out about our treasure quite by chance. One day, I had an early lunch and came back to the museum to let the other staff go for a snack. I was sitting in the curator's office, reading a book, when the phone rang and a representative from the famous London violin company, J. & A. Beare, was on the line. He explained that, later that year, on 20 December, it was the 400th anniversary of the death of Andrea Amati of Cremona, the famous string-instrument maker who had created the form of the modern violin. He explained that Beares would very much like to borrow the Carlisle Amati violin, which was one of only nine surviving Amatis in the world, for inclusion in a special anniversary exhibition in Cremona. The gentleman confirmed that his firm would pay for the safe transport of the violin, for the insurance and for the security of the violin in the exhibition. The question was whether Carlisle City Council, as owner of the violin, would like to consider making this loan for the exhibition. I played for time and said that I was sure that Carlisle would be extremely interested but that I'd need first of all to consult my curator and then he would need to consult the Lord Mayor but that we would get back to him in three days. The gentleman was satisfied with this reply and rang off.

At this point, I experienced a total panic, since I had heard not one word about the existence of an Amati violin in Carlisle Museum. When my colleagues returned from lunch, my fears quadrupled because none of the other four had heard of the Amati violin at all – in fact, none of the others knew who Amati was. So the first task was to find the Amati violin. The staff looked in all of the stores and found absolutely nothing. There were few places left to look but I started to make a systematic search of all of the cupboards in the curator's office. In one cupboard right at the back lay a simple violin case containing the greatest treasure of Carlisle Museum. I am very interested in classical music, so one of the most amazing moments of my life was when, with all of the museum staff assembled, I opened the violin case and I held an Amati violin in my hands with the greatest of care and respect. I didn't, of course, play it, although there was a bow in the case. I told David Clarke that he had better contact the City Treasurer and get him to double the museum insurance premium and then ask for a secure, environmentally sensitive exhibition case to display this treasure to the people of Carlisle as soon as possible. David took my advice and contacted the Treasurer and we rearranged the museum insurance based upon a valuation for this amazing instrument. The Works Department constructed a very beautiful, environmentally controlled, aluminium display case in which the Amati was placed. Two days later, we called Beares to confirm that Carlisle City Council had agreed to the loan of our Amati violin for the Cremona exhibition. This was an amazing episode and it shows what fun people can have in provincial museums if they encounter the unexpected.

Nonetheless, I was beginning to get restless after a tough year for the family's finances and the realisation that the completion of the IRGMA cataloguing of the entire prehistoric collection left me without any other major projects. In the autumn of 1977, I started to look for a new post. Since there were still no academic jobs available. I focused on museum curatorial posts. I noticed that there was a vacancy for the post of museum director in Harlow Museum, in Essex. I thought that Harlow was an excellent location, halfway between London and Cambridge, enabling me to commute to London to carry on Extra-Mural teaching and have access to academic libraries in London and Cambridge. Also being a museum director would provide a more secure financial base and the potential to learn new things. I applied for the Harlow job, was invited to interview, performed well and was offered the job. I accepted the offer of a job that would start in the New Year in 1978.

Moving to Harlow was the second big move for our family and the first involving Eleanor. After the long drive, we moved into a council house that had only been built a few months ago, provided rent-free by Harlow Council and right on the edge of the new town. This was still very much the Wild West of Harlow; every part of the new town must have been like this at some stage. The estate consisted of a tarmac approach road, with mud roads leading to groups of houses. We had a house in a cluster of perhaps 15 semi-detached houses, each with gardens front and back. The council promised that we would have a real road there in a month, followed by a medical centre and later a pub. But, after three months, no construction had begun.

This was the first time that Maja or I had lived in a new town in Britain. Harlow had many appealing landscape features which we liked a lot. The town planner for the project was Frederick (by then Lord Frederick) Gibberd, whose starting point was a very rural area with villages connected by winding lanes. The lanes were converted into bicycle tracks and superimposed on the bicycle tracks was a new road network for cars, with roundabouts linking each new housing estate to a main road. The town centre – the so-called 'High', on the highest hill in Harlow and the windiest place in town – was the only built-up area that you might consider an urban space. Everywhere else, there were new housing estates linked by new roads. Gibberd's other favourite planning principle was to have small areas of green starting from the High and expanding outwards in wedge shapes. These 'green wedges' defined much of the inner part of Harlow and the museum was located in such a green wedge.

As with most New Towns, Harlow was built and designed after the end of the Second World War to provide new housing for people whose houses had been flattened during bombing. Harlow attracted large numbers of homeless people from the East End of London, principally West Ham supporters who filled the whole town – an unappealing facet of the new town for a long-term Chelsea fan! The new town had a built-in Labour majority and the Labour council was extremely keen on developing the museum and would invest heavily in a good project. This was a total difference in attitude to museums and museum spending from the one I'd encountered, sometimes despairingly, in Carlisle.

I'm afraid that our loyalty to Harlow New Town was not strong enough to stop us moving out after four or five months. It was partly the mud but also the lack of local facilities. We decided that it would be preferable to live in an established village, so we treacherously moved out of the new town, over the county line into Hertfordshire, to a village called Sawbridgeworth. This was the first house that we had purchased together. The house had been built in the 1940s and shared a common feature with other houses in Church Crescent – a far higher ratio of windows to wall than any other house we had seen. Some time after we bought it, we asked the neighbours about this feature and they explained that the man who built all of these houses was in fact using stolen bricks from a nearby builder's yard and, whenever he ran out of stolen bricks, he had to put in a window. We thought that this was quite exciting to live in stolen property and the neighbours agreed, saying that no one had ever tried to reclaim the bricks. It was an attractive and airy flint-cobbled cottage, with nice gardens back and front. The village had a station with a direct line to Cambridge and to Liverpool Street in London. Walking down the hill where we lived, we were in countryside in two minutes, with a field with two retired donkeys – Eleanor's favourites – at the bottom of the hill and, a little further, a pub next to the River Stort with a very fine pub garden whose principal attraction was a chatty West Ham-supporting mynah bird who delighted customers with his knowledge of Cockney slang and swear words. In short, it was a very pleasant village and we were really happy to live there.

In Harlow-speak, my job running Harlow Museum was termed 'Museum Officer'. The Museum Officer was a medium-ranking council official, with the museum in the Leisure Services Department, run by my line manager, Alan Jackson. A well-built, ruddy-cheeked Yorkshireman who looked like a farmer, Mr Jackson was not only extremely efficient but also very receptive to new ideas. Parallel to the museum in the Council hierarchy but much bigger was the Parks Section, whose manager was Robin Bletsoe. There was little doubt which department had more weight in the Leisure Services empire. From day one, I would regularly attend Leisure Services management meetings – the first time I'd ever been involved in Council decision-making and its own world of bureaucratic niceties.

The museum was founded in 1976 and the first Museum Officer was Katharine Davison. Katharine developed the museum in her own image and made it her own. The museum had a single base when I moved there. The building was originally a medieval manor house surrounded by a moat and with wooded grounds. Much later, the house was Georgianised and three sides of the moat were filled in to leave the fourth as an ornamental pond. Several other walled parts of the grounds near the house were created and survive to this day, the most attractive being a garden, whose wonderful fragrances attracted a huge variety of butterflies. The museum was designed primarily for children and families, with a general exhibition and no specialist displays at all. The main parts were the natural history and social history galleries, the latter featuring items such as Singer sewing machines and carbolic soaps used by Old Harlow folks when they were children before WWII. There was a small archaeological display of mostly Roman antiquities – perhaps not surprising since I was the first archaeologist to be appointed in the museum.

Two members of the staff were a married couple, the husband, Albert Story, a conservator who looked after the collection, and his wife Jackie Story who was the museum secretary. Another member was Ian Jones, a social historian with a strong interest in military history, who was popularly known as 'Führer' Jones. The museum cleaner was Annie, a Glaswegian from the Gorbals, who came from a very large family and, being the youngest, had to take responsibility for absolutely everything. Annie was really the unofficial museum officer, who was quite capable of organising everything and everyone. I was very grateful to her for often doing that as I learned the ropes. Annie was also the ideal buffer between Katharine and any changes which I felt were necessary. It was essential to keep Katharine onside for any changes to 'her' museum. There were two museum receptionists – the older one was Harry Bryant, a typical East Ender and West Ham United fan, the younger person, Anne Wallett. What was great about the entire staff was their devotion to the museum and their skill with family visitors.

My job introduced me to many new elements of museum and local authority life. I had to prepare committee reports and cases for the next year's museum budget for the Leisure Services Committee. I was responsible for a non-staff annual budget which totalled £75,000 and had to look after six members of staff. I was also responsible for the exhibition programme, which Maja helped to develop in the second year we were at Harlow. I was liaising with the Essex County Museums Group and periodically visited towns I hadn't seen before, such as Colchester and Chelmsford. I was involved in the archaeological collections but not too closely, since most of the archaeology came from the earlier New Town – Roman Harlow. But the Roman collections provided a link to the Friends of Harlow Museum, who met once a week in the evening and which the curatorial staff took in turn to manage. That was an important and also a new experience for me. But the main strategic point about my appointment was that I'd been hired to take the museum further. After three or four years, the museum was consolidated as a presence in the town. But how would the museum develop?

The direction of change was thrust upon me utterly by chance. One day, a man came into the museum and introduced himself as John Collins. He said that, until recently, he owned a bicycle-repair shop in Old Harlow, which in fact went back five generations and was therefore probably the oldest bicycle repair shop in the country. John explained that everyone in Old Harlow knew that he lived above the shop and, even if the shop was closed, they would throw stones at his window until he came down and agreed to repair the bike. At his age, and John was around 60, he was getting fed up with this and wanted to sell the family business. The crucial thing about John Collins was that he had amassed an enormous collection of 75 veteran cycles, stretching from the 1810s to the last decade. The Collins collection included multiple examples of all stages in the bicycle story – from the Denis Johnson Hobby-Horse through boneshakers, penny-farthings and the earliest bikes with gears right through to the present (Fig. 11). John had built up this fantastic collection over 30 years of travel in East Anglia. He had repaired and restored all the machines himself, so they were all in excellent condition and needing virtually no extra conservation. The offer that John Collins put to me was

Fig. 11. John Collins with one of the boneshakers in the Harlow Museum collection

that, if Harlow Council would hire him as a museum bicycle curator for the five years until he retired, he would sell the collection to Harlow Museum for £25,000 to develop one of the finest bicycle museums in the country.

This was a pretty astonishing afternoon for me since – and I didn't admitted this to John Collins for a very long time – I didn't actually know how to ride a bicycle, following a childhood learning disaster. I had no idea what Alan Jackson would say to this idea and I had no notion of where a bicycle exhibition could be located – certainly not in the existing Harlow Museum. Moreover, I didn't know if there was any chance of getting a grant for the purchase price or even whether Harlow would want to purchase the collection in the first place. But there were several factors in favour of the idea: Harlow had one of the best cycle track networks in the country; John Collins was a well-known local; and most of the cycles in his collection came from the region. So, with some aces up my sleeve, I went up to see Alan Jackson and I was delighted that he agreed that Harlow would find the money while encouraging me to try to find a matching grant. When Alan talked to the Parks manager, Robin confirmed that a Parks outstation in the western part of Harlow called Mark Hall, which was a 16th-century coaching stables, was surplus to requirements. So, with its transport associations and historic potential, Mark Hall was the obvious place to become a bicycle museum.

At this point, things began to move fast. Alan Jackson persuaded the Council to approve the purchase, subject to me finding a matching grant and, vitally, to approve the appointment of John Collins to the museum staff. My next job was to explain this to John Collins and tell him that he would soon be hired by Harlow Council but that this depended upon finding a matching purchase grant for his collection. He did not have any ideas at all about funding but, after researching UK bicycle collections, I realised that the Science Museum in London had such a purchase fund and it would put up 50% of the purchase price of an exceptional scientific collection. Not knowing anything about cycle collections, I had to do a lot of reading to identify the other museums with fine collections. It became clear to me after one month's research that the Collins Collection could indeed be a very exciting and very significant collection at the national level. Over the next fortnight, I visited the key bicycle collections in Britain. The Science Museum had the largest collection of over 100 machines, while Nottingham and Coventry Museums each had a collection of about the same size as John Collins. Snowshill Manor in Oxfordshire once had an eccentric aristocratic owner, whose profits from the West Indian sugar trade were spent on three particular interests – Japanese samurai armour, County wooden farm cart models and boneshakers. My visits to these top collections confirmed in me the belief that John Collins had a very significant collection and we were thus able to complete an application form to the Science Museum for a purchase grant.

About three weeks later, the principal curator of the Science Museum bicycle collection came to interview the Harlow staff. I introduced him to John Collins and spent one of the most fascinating afternoons I have ever spent listening to two specialists exploring the contours of their field. The Science Museum expert started by asking a couple of basic questions to test John Collins, following up with what John explained to me afterwards were a couple of trick questions, which John dealt with in style. Having gained each other's confidence, the specialists continued a three-hour discussion on the technicalities of John's bikes. I had to separate the two specialists at about 6 o'clock, since John could easily talk for an hour about each of his machines. But, by this time, it was perfectly obvious that we would get the Science Museum grant, which was confirmed the following week. So Harlow had a curator of cycles, a building that could be turned into a bicycle museum and a fine collection to put in it. This was a fantastic start and my discussions with Alan Jackson showed that the next challenge was to find a sympathetic architect for the Mark Hall conversion. Through local connections, we approached an architect called Ray Hooper, who had an office in London but lived in Hertfordshire, and Ray agreed to be the project architect. So, for much of the next year and a half from June 1978 through to the end of my job in Harlow, my main job was researching bicycle collections and liaising with John Collins and Ray Hooper to design the Mark Hall conversion and the bicycle display. This was an amazing experience, which I thought would stand me in really good stead for the future and for later projects. The fact that it didn't is neither here nor there but these 18 months at Harlow were extremely exciting.

Another exciting project was a rescue archaeological excavation which started up in April 1978. I needed to assemble a team of diggers who would be working against a very tight schedule to excavate a Romano-British settlement in Harlow industrial estate, near the Harlow Temple where Mortimer Wheeler had excavated in 1928. This was the first rescue dig I had ever directed and I relied heavily on the site supervisor, Simon Ellis, who had just finished his PhD thesis on Roman Carthage, for details about Roman excavations. Simon looked after the site when I was away doing other things. We had a late burst of snow that year, so we had to convince the excavators that they had to continue through a light snowfall. Simon and I managed to do this by digging alongside the excavators ourselves. This two-month excavation produced huge quantities of material, meaning lots of new work for Albert the conservator and lots of post-excavation work for the Friends of Harlow Museum. I learned much from this rescue excavation, identifying mistakes in excavation strategy and recording systems that I would try to avoid in future excavations (*e.g.* in the Balkans).

Another project that took off at the time was the Friends of Harlow Museum. The FHM was a very mixed group of people – some who lived in Harlow but didn't know much about museums but liked to help out and other skilled professionals who supported the museum with their skills, such as a professional photographer called George Taylor. To their credit, the FHM had already completed a sizeable post-excavation project under the leadership of Ian Miller by preparing for publication the material from an excavation in the garden of a house in the Felmongers estate. This dig had turned up an enormous Roman pit full of a wide range of material culture, including one of the finest assemblages of glassware known in Roman Britain and published by Jenny Price – later to become a colleague of mine in Durham University. I was confident that the FHM would be able to manage at least some of the post-ex sorting and marking for the Industrial Excavations, which started in summer 1978 and carried on over the next year and a half.

While I had some idea about provincial differences across Britain, I really had no idea about the depth to which localism penetrated places and cultures until I came to Harlow. I had visited Epping Forest and its twin villages, Waltham Abbey and Waltham Cross. I have already mentioned the photographer George Taylor, who lived in Waltham Abbey, and whose daughter was going steady with a 'local' man. At one meeting of the Friends of Harlow Museum, George came in looking crestfallen. Since he was normally an open, cheerful chap, I asked him what was the matter. 'It's terrible!' said George, 'my daughter is getting married.' I replied that this seemed like a happy event and what was wrong with that. Rolling his eyes upwards and speaking slowly and with great emphasis, as if to an idiot, George said, 'But the husband-to-be is from Waltham Cross!' It was impossible to persuade George that perhaps one person from Waltham Cross might be a decent bloke.

In an exciting year, one great event marked the summer – Eleanor's second birthday. We had wonderful weather and organised a garden party, borrowing trestle tables from the museum for the cold buffet. The centrepiece of the buffet was a vast bowl of strawberries that we had picked ourselves from a nearby farm. At this point, Charlie Schwartz re-entered the story as Eleanor's godfather. At the time, Charlie was in the final year of his PhD in the London Institute of Archaeology, which I'd helped to set up for him with the Human Environment Department. Charlie came to Eleanor's birthday party and distinguished himself by polishing off probably half of the strawberries, leaving enough for Eleanor but hardly for the rest of us. We were utterly amazed at the greed of this great Californian buddy, who was forgiven because he was Eleanor's godfather. Eleanor remembers the strawberry party to this very day.

Another wonderful event for Eleanor was an exhibition that Maja designed using the museum costume collection of Victorian dresses, caps and accessories. Maja also took the opportunity to develop her graphic skills and she designed a very beautiful green and white poster for the exhibition, which was called 'The swing of our childhood'. The poster (Fig. 12) showed Eleanor, in Victorian bobcap and frilly dress, on a swing. This was the first exhibition that Maja had ever designed in a British institution and the whole family was very proud of the exhibition, which went on for three months in the summer of 1979.

The other opportunity offered by living in the south-east was that I could resume my lecturing in the London Department of Extramural Studies. In October 1978, I started up a the third-year Prehistoric Europe class for the Extra-Mural Diploma, which was essential for getting additional lecturing experience, which soon was to turn out to be extremely valuable.

Fig. 12. Poster for the exhibition 'The swing of our childhood', Harlow Museum, 1979

I have mentioned that there had been very few new university posts in European prehistory since I took my PhD in 1976. The first post was for a lectureship in Balkan prehistory at Sheffield and, although there was a strong presumption that Andrew Sherratt would get the job, Graeme Barker talked the hind leg off the Sheffield donkey and won the competition. The second post was for an Assistant Keeper in the Ashmolean Museum at Oxford and here Andrew Sherratt showed his class and took the post. The third such post was a lectureship in European Prehistory at the University of Newcastle upon Tyne.

The professor of Archaeology at Newcastle was Martin Harrison, a Byzantinist, who had devised a scheme of pre-interview selection by which he contacted all of the professors/heads of departments of Archaeology and asked if they had any recommendations for his new post. I was lucky enough to get *two* letters of recommendation. The first one was the obvious letter of strong support from my old professor of Archaeology, John D. Evans, who by then was the Director of the Institute. The other letter came from an unexpected source. While I was a postgrad, I had met Richard Harrison, who was working in the Department of Prehistoric and Romano-British Antiquities at the British Museum. Since he was the 'new boy', his boss Ian Longworth had tasked him with giving a series of lunchtime lectures about Romanian prehistory to coincide with the 'Dacian Exhibition' in the BM. Richard specialised in Iberian prehistory and had no visual materials for these talks. He heard about my research and came to ask if I could lend him any colour slides of Romanian prehistory. By good fortune, I had purchased a set of 12 slides of the most striking exhibits from the Museum of Romanian National History in Bucharest the year before. My loan of 12 slides helped him in two ways – first, by giving him great *kudos* in the eyes of his boss and, secondly, ensuring that his excellent lectures were well illustrated. Shortly after these lectures, Richard took up a lecturing post in Bristol, so when the professor in Bristol – Peter Warren – asked Richard if he could recommend anyone for the Newcastle post, Richard suggested me. He passed on my details to Peter Warren and so Martin Harrison received two letters of recommendation for me. This must have helped me to get an interview.

Maja insisted on coming up to Newcastle with me for the interview. When we arrived on campus in the morning before the interview, we were met by Martin Harrison, who asked Maja why she had come up to Newcastle and Martin was deeply impressed when Maja said she'd come up to look at houses. In preparation for the interview, I had gathered some information about Martin Harrison from two London friends – Ralph and Barbara Hoddinott – who were Thracian specialists but who knew that Harrison had excavated the currently unpublished church of St Polyeuktos in Istanbul. So, as we were walking around the campus, I slipped a casual question into our conversation: 'By the way, how's Polyeuktos?' Martin stopped for a moment and looked at me – the moment in which I think that I clinched the job – and said, 'Polyeuktos is very well, thank you.' With two letters of recommendation and two crucial interventions before the interview, I was well set up for the formal interview (in those days, formal presentations were rare). At the interview, I don't remember any particularly difficult questions, so I was able to impress them as far as I could. I thought that I must be in a reasonably strong position and so I was, for that evening I was offered the job and of course accepted it.

A long time later, I found out how close I was to losing the job because of the stiff competition. I thought the star of the short-list was Heinrich Härke, who had completed a German undergraduate degree and Masters before moving to Cambridge to complete his PhD on Anglo-Saxon archaeology. He had started digging when he was still at school and had published his prehistoric, Romano-German and medieval excavations by the time he applied for a university place. Heinrich's application consisted of 12 densely packed pages, which included an impressive publication list, which I could certainly not rival. There was only one detail that was not specified in the application – the sport in which Heinrich had won a half-blue in Cambridge. The interview committee picked up on this and the Vice Chancellor said, in a German accent: 'It's probably pistol-shooting', which everyone found very amusing. At the end of the interview, in which Heinrich had performed wonderfully well, the Vice Chancellor said: 'Oh, just one question, Dr Härke. You won a half-blue at Cambridge – in which sport was that?' and Heinrich almost clicked his heels when he replied 'pistol-shooting'. Everyone on the panel had to keep a very straight face until Heinrich had left the room and apparently that did it for Heinrich. When I found this out later, I felt really sorry about the way I had unwittingly benefitted from a blatant case of racism.

Fortunately, Heinrich's qualities soon won him a lectureship – this time in Queen's University Belfast. The only positive side to Heinrich's pistol-shooting that I know about arose at the time that Heinrich was there. One of his colleagues there was 'Big Jim' Mallory – a Marija Gimbutas student from UCLA who was a specialist on Indo-European languages and archaeology, whom I'd met at Balkan conferences. Big Jim told me how he was driving Heinrich to the Navan Fort near Belfast to prepare for a student field trip. This was the time of the Troubles, with roadblocks on every major road in and out of Belfast. Jim slowed down and stopped at one such roadblock. One policeman came to Jim and asked for his passport, so Jim produced his American passport. The second policeman asked Heinrich for his passport and Heinrich produced his German passport. At this moment, the policeman looked at Heinrich in sheer delight and said (in broad Irish brogue) 'Well, Dr Härke, it *is* a pleasure to meet you face-to-face for the first time. Please, drive on!' With both passports returned, Jim drove off to the Navan and asked Heinrich: 'What the hell was all that about?' Heinrich explained that, when he was a student at Cambridge, he used to enjoy pistol-shooting and he later became interested in the ballistics of pistol-shooting. 'So,' said Heinrich, 'I've written three technical articles for the Ulster Police Journal and these articles have clearly made me famous.' So Heinrich's pistol-shooting stopped him for getting one job but saved him a lot of trouble in another university.

Chapter 5

Newcastle upon Tyne

My job in Newcastle University began in January 1980. When I joined the staff, it was a university with all seven faculties but dominated by two – Medicine and Agriculture. One of the previous Vice-Chancellors, Henry Miller, often expressed his distaste for small arts departments in what was the science wing of Durham University from 1937 until it gained independence from Durham in 1963. Post-divorce, Newcastle developed its own arts and social science departments to become a more broadly based university. I joined a Millerian Small Arts Department, with our offices in a long corridor above the Museum of Antiquities (aka the Museum of Ambiguities). Newcastle was very much a centre-of-town campus. The dominance of the Agricultural Faculty was reflected in a strange way in the Students' Union each term-time Thursday evening, when the Union bar became Agrics' Night and the Agric students got drunk and smashed up not just lots of glasses but also lots of furniture. The average weekly cost of this ritual to the university was said to be £5,000, which a Dean of Agriculture justified, in the 1980s, on the grounds that this was a fine tradition stretching back 50 years, in which he himself had participated!

In those days, university staff contracts specified one-third of our time should be spent teaching, with one-third research and one-third admin. I devote separate chapters to the two principal research projects I helped to direct while at Newcastle: Chapter 6 on the Neothermal Dalmatia Project and Chapter 8 on the Upper Tisza Project. I hope you will forgive me for overlooking my admin tasks at Newcastle. The teaching was actually very straightforward for me. In my main second-year course, I covered the whole of post-7000 BC prehistoric Europe down to the Roman Conquest. This was exactly what I'd been teaching in the London University Extra-Mural Department so, when I moved to Newcastle, I had my slides ready and all I had to do was to update their content. I also taught a small group of third-years my special subject in the Balkan Mesolithic, Neolithic and Copper Age. The other teaching consisted of any contributions to the team-taught courses that I was asked to make. In my first few years, Martin Harrison was extremely kind to his new lecturer with my inclusion in relatively few team-taught courses. In retrospect, the Newcastle teaching load was remarkably light.

New members of staff often have to undergo a trial by fire early on in their new post, which involves meeting senior members of faculty and university and other newly appointed members of staff. This particular test of nerve in the Faculty of Arts occurred in February. My professor soon introduced me to Professor Max Hammerton, in Psychology, whom I later learnt was usually referred to as 'Mad Max' because of his curious social behaviour. It was perhaps not so surprising, since Max had been locked up in Auschwitz and survived it with the aid of a pocket Bible, with which he used to memorise verses. So if you asked Max for the contents of 2 Kings 3, 9, he would recite the verse to you from memory. Of course, I knew nothing of this when Martin introduced me to Professor Hammerton, telling him that I was deeply interested in Japanese samurai swords – one of Max' pet subjects. This was a useful conversational icebreaker and Max asked me who were my favourite sword-masters. I deflected this question by recollecting my visit to Snowshill Manor, which I had visited in my tour of veteran cycle collections in Britain,[1] and where there was a magnificent collection of samurai swords and suits of armour. I felt rather pleased that Max had never actually visited this collection; knowing about Snowshill ensured that I passed the Faculty of Arts test with flying colours.

There were some real characters in the department at the time. Martin Harrison had completed two years' study in Italy when Mortimer Wheeler contacted him to ask if he would become Assistant Controller of Antiquities for Cyrenaica, Libya. Although only in his mid-20s, Martin agreed to Wheeler's request – who would dare turn him down? – and went off to Cyrenaica. After a subsequent year's teaching in Bryn Mawr College, Pennsylvania, Martin returned to the UK to take up a lectureship in Newcastle. Soon after, he began the excavations of the Palace Church of St Juliana in Istanbul. His greatest achievement there was the re-fitting of many of the 20,000+ architectural sculpture fragments to demonstrate that the church had been modelled on the Temple of Solomon in Jerusalem. Martin was instrumental in establishing a separate Department of Archaeology in Newcastle, for which he became the first professor. He kept himself fit after a stroke by walking across the Town Moor from his home in Gosforth and back in the evening. He lived in a large Gosforth house with his wife Elizabeth and their three children. As far as I knew, Martin Harrison was afraid of only one other archaeologist – the professor of Archaeology in Durham, Rosemary Cramp. Martin used to get very worried when he had to go down to meetings in Durham for there was no way to avoid Rosemary. One evening, Martin invited Maja and me to dinner with Rosemary Cramp in Gosforth. After a splendid, bibulous dinner, Rosemary offered to give us a lift home, since at the time we lived in Spital Tongues, just the other side of the Town Moor. Rosemary drove down towards the centre of town and turned onto the inner-city motorway. To reach Spiteful Tongues, she had to turn up a slip road to a roundabout. But when she reached the top of the slip road, Rosemary went round the roundabout in the wrong direction, narrowly

[1] See p. 73 for the Snowshill Manor boneshaker collection.

missing a lorry. We were speechless with fear and sat rigid, hoping that we would get home safely. Which we did.

Martin Harrison remained in Newcastle for five years after I moved there before being offered the post of Professor of Archaeology of the Roman Empire in Oxford – his *alma mater*. So he left for Oxford, with no more walks across the Town Moor and a surfeit of rich food at New College Oxford, where he had been made a Fellow. I am sure that both of these factors had an effect on Martin, who had a fatal stroke after two years in Oxford and didn't survive – a sad loss to Oxford and Byzantine archaeology.

One of the two older colleagues in the department was George Jobey, who'd had one eye shot out in the Second World War, which won him a George Medal for his bravery. One-eyed George was the most terrifying driver of the departmental Land Rover, careering down narrow Northumberland lanes and asking his passengers if they could see any sheep coming. He was a great field archaeologist and single-handedly invented the *George Jobey culture* – a tribal grouping of Bronze Age–Iron Age enclosed and fortified sites in the Cheviots. George was an original Geordie and told me lots of stories about Tyneside in the old days. He could picture the road from North Shields into the centre of Newcastle, with stotties fresh from the oven cooling on the outside windowsills and how nobody would have their doors locked at night. George gave me two really good pieces of advice about undergraduates: 'Don't kiss 'em' and 'Don't hit 'em'. Looking back, this advice from the 1980s seems just as appropriate now.

The other senior colleague was John Gillam, one of the UK's finest Roman coarse pottery specialists. John had served in India in the Second World War and learned Urdu. He still spoke it fluently and so he was always trying to persuade the department to celebrate an occasion in an Indian restaurant, where he became the Master of Ceremonies, ordering everything in patois. John hated departmental meetings, which he could tolerate for up to one and a half hours on a good day. At a given moment of excruciation, he would always excuse himself with having to attend an urgent meeting of the British Legion in town. John Gillam was also very creative with the invention of an entirely fictitious Field Club with its own journal – the *Journal of the Fennybentley Field Club*. One of his favourite letters of all time came from a German Professor of Roman archaeology in Cologne, who wrote complaining that, even though Köln had an extremely good Roman library, they didn't have copies of this Journal and would it please be possible for him to send offprints of his Fennybentley articles. I think John had this letter framed and hung in his loo.

John enjoyed a liquid lunch, so it was a bit risky to meet him early afternoon after lunch. One day, he was due to interview students for undergraduate places in the department and one particular candidate had an interview at 2.30 pm. Being a nervous type, she knocked on his door at 2.20 pm, just to make sure everything was all right. The door was ajar and, when she knocked on it, the door flew open and smoke came billowing out of John's room. The sensible applicant ran immediately to the Secretary's office to call the Fire Brigade and they managed to put out the fire in John's waste bin. What had happened was that, after the normal beer chased with whiskey chased with beer, John had returned and sat down in his armchair with a cigar. He fell fast asleep and the cigar fell out of his hand into the bin. Since the departmental offices were directly above the Museum of Ambiguities, this could have had severe effects on the future course of studies of Hadrian's Wall. Luckily, the student saved the day and was definitely offered a place. Whether she accepted it cannot be revealed.

When Martin Harrison went to Oxford, the university chose Peter Fowler to be our new professor. Peter was a prehistorian but he had also worked as a landscape archaeologist for most of his career (Plate 8). He had been in the Extra-Mural Department at Bristol University at the time of the building of the M5 motorway and so had run a great deal of rescue excavation. He was also a founder member of the protest group 'Rescue' and, on the basis of these achievements, was appointed as Secretary of the Royal Commission for Historical Monuments (England), operating out of York. So he had accomplished a lot of very good landscape archaeology in the North. As a new professor, Peter had lots of goodwill going for him but that evaporated quite rapidly after the demise of one of the best departmental secretaries – Wendy Dennis – I ever came across in my whole career. Wendy knew everything about the department and got on well with everybody, providing a safety-valve for complaints about the professor. But Peter had his eye on providing a job for his partner Cilla Boniface. Within a year of Peter's arrival, Wendy left the department and Cilla took over as secretary.

Peter Fowler's view of the department was that there was a chain of command and he was the professor at the top of the chain. This view was simply the result of Peter's previous jobs, which were always hierarchical with Peter at the top, elevated from the second-in-command by some distance. But, in the Newcastle department, there was a strong egalitarian feeling that the professor was a *primus inter pares* – a first among equals – rather than a Big Boss, so from time to time other members of the department would meet quietly at lunchtime. We would go up and down the corridor, watching for Cilla and Peter, and when they weren't around, we would slip into somebody's office and lay plans for what we had to do to derail autocratic and bureaucratic traps. In those years, from a staff perspective Newcastle was not a happy department and everyone worked on their own projects, avoiding uncomfortable situations, leaving the museum and the Archaeological Practice to do their own thing.

I've mentioned already that there were two older members of the department – George Jobey and John Gillam – and both of them retired within a few years of my arrival (no causal connection). Because there were four other colleagues who were Romanists or could teach Classical archaeology in the department, John Gillam wasn't replaced. This loss of a staff member meant that the department was down to only six academic staff.

When George Jobey retired, Martin Harrison's principle to allow me to teach only European prehistory and never to touch British prehistory worked very well, because the department could claim they really did need a specialist British prehistorian to replace George. Chris Smith – a landscape archaeologist with particular interests in the Mesolithic – was appointed from the Welsh Royal Commission and joined us in 1984. Chris was a countryman at heart and bought a cottage in Wylam, partly so as to live out of Newcastle but also as a place for his bees. Chris was a keen fieldwalker and, after several years, set up a big Tynedale fieldwalking project with members of the local amateur archaeological societies along the Tyne Valley and with the Society of Antiquaries of Newcastle. Over the years, Chris accumulated a detailed record of the lithic tools in ploughed fields up and down Tynedale, which will be a major contribution to early prehistory in this area when published.

Although Newcastle University had several social science departments, its Department of Anthropology wasn't a strong one, with only three anthropologists there. When one retired, it became clear that this was not a viable department, so the anthropologists were moved into the Sociology Department where they were heavily outnumbered by the sociologists. The weak position of the anthropologists became increasingly visible in the story of the George Brown Collection. George Brown was a Methodist minister in Oceania and collected between 1860 and 1907. On his death, the ethnographic collection was sold to the Bowes Museum, who later sold it to the Hancock Museum of the University of Newcastle. In the mid-1980s, the University had several serious funding issues and the Vice Chancellor was looking around to dispose of 'assets'. He spotted the George Brown collection and correctly surmised that the sale of part of that collection would bring in a considerable sum. In putting up objects from the Brown Collection for sale, the V-C clearly overlooked the provisions of George Brown's will. The anthropology lecturers soon mobilised a student campaign against the sale; the principal organiser of the protests amongst the Archaeology students was Rupert Brakespear, whose complaint against university policy was summarised as 'it's dog eat dog'. The combined opposition of the museums, the staff and the students made it very difficult for the Vice Chancellor to sell the whole collection but he did sell part of it. At this point, the university museums informed the Museums Association of the sale and the Association wrote a strong protest to the V-C, putting all of the university museums on the black list for museum grants for three years. This was a severe punishment for the museums; moreover, the Vice Chancellor was never really trusted again by the staff. However, the majority of the George Brown Collection was saved and much of it is now on display in the Museum of the North.

After losing a Romanist with the retirement of John Gillam, the university made the most unexpected and far-seeing appointment in my time at Newcastle. This concerned the arrival in Newcastle of Pavel Dolukhanov (Plate 8) with his wife Mariana and their teenage son Pyotr. In the mid-1980s, Pavel was a senior scientist working as Head of the Archaeology Laboratory in the Sankt-Petersburg Institute of Archaeology, run by Vadim Masson. Pavel had a stellar career, with doctorates in Archaeology, geography and linguistics, and was one of the most talented prehistorians in the Soviet Union. But Mariana was Jewish at a time when Jewish academics and their families were under constant threat from the regime.

Mariana persuaded Pavel that, in 1989, with the Fall of the Wall, it really was time to go, so they applied to leave on an economic hardship visa, flew to Vienna and later travelled on to Rome.

Pavel managed to find a part-time post in the British School at Rome, where we had colleagues friendly to Newcastle at the time. They suggested that, if we could come up with a job offer, we might find Pavel receptive to coming to Newcastle. At the time, there were two junior fellowships vacant in the Faculty of Arts and Peter Fowler and I persuaded the Dean, Jerry Patterson, that there was an opportunity to hire a stunning Russian academic if the university would agree to combine the two fellowships into the post of a junior lectureship for a year. The Dean agreed and the Vice Chancellor concurred, so the university offered Pavel a job and he came with his family to Newcastle in 1990. The Vice Chancellor came up with funds to cover a second year for Pavel and, before his second year was over, the university employed him as a permanent member of staff.

Pavel was an extraordinarily well-read archaeologist who knew a fantastic amount about the Russian environment and landscape but, when it came to basic admin, Pavel was a lost cause. It's unfair to blame him for not having any experience in the administration of a British university department but what we hadn't realised was that, as the Lab Director, Pavel did no admin at all. In British universities, little admin support was offered to the academics, who have to know how to do everything. So when it became clear that even photocopying an article was a challenge for Pavel, we realised that this small department with seven staff now had three non-functioning members who did no admin, rather than the two we had previously had. This became quite a heavy load, especially for Kevin Greene but also for me because I was Pavel's mentor. Pavel also struggled with the new technology of overhead projection, placing his transparencies upside down or back to front or both.

Pavel's contacts stretched far and wide. One of the first delegations to arrive at the 1986 World Archaeological Congress in Southampton was from Leningrad, led by Vadim Masson, the chief of the Institute of Archaeology – Pavel's old boss, whom Peter Ucko, as Professor of Archaeology at Southampton, had previously met. When Masson and his delegation arrived, Ucko happened to be out of his office and Masson asked the Departmental Secretary where the room for their delegation was. The unfortunate secretary didn't know what to do, so she put the Russians in the main departmental laboratory, which Masson commandeered for the next two weeks. When Ucko returned, the secretary told him what had happened and he went along and got on extremely well with Masson. On the basis of this newfound friendship, the two wheeler-dealers organised an Anglo-Russian Exchange Agreement, which was eventually ratified through the British Academy, lasting four years (1987–91). I should confirm that all rumours that the purpose of the scheme was to procure Christmas shopping trips for Masson's wife Dr Korobkova are completely false. One of the benefits of this new deal for Southampton was that it underpinned Peter Ucko's drive to recruit Eastern European and Russian specialists for Southampton.

As part of this drive, he invited me to join their department. Unfortunately, when Maja and I went to Southampton to check out the cost of housing, we found that selling a house in Newcastle would only allow us to purchase a one-bedroom flat in Southampton, so I turned down Peter Ucko's offer. Instead, he invited Julian Thomas to join Southampton from Lampeter, which he did with alacrity.

The first trip of the Anglo-Russian scheme concerned a visit to the famous Kapovaya gorge in the Urals, where the first discovery of Palaeolithic rock art in Russia had been made in the 1960s. Russia Palaeolithic archaeologists were always very jealous of the rock and figural art known from Central and Western Europe and desperately wanted their own rock art. The Kapovaya find was discovered and published in the 1960s and Peter Ucko, who had written extensively on Palaeolithic art, wrote a review dismissing Kapovaya as a fake – a view that rankled with all the Russian Palaeolithic specialists. So a visit to Kapovaya was an interesting choice of first events in the Anglo-Russian programme. The plan was for Ucko and his Southampton colleague Tim Champion to fly to Leningrad to meet Masson and a Palaeolithic specialist, fly on to Moscow, then to Ufa and eventually take a small plane to an airstrip near the gorge. Here, a small camping site had been organised with four tents – a Russian sleeping tent, a British sleeping tent, a food tent and a loo tent. Ucko and Champion were assigned to their tent and asked to come and meet Masson in 20 minutes in the food tent. When they arrived, there was a table with two documents and Masson said to Ucko, 'If you want to see the Kapovaya cave, you need to sign these documents first.' Paraphrasing, the document stated: 'I, Peter John Ucko, retract my claim that the Kapovaya cave rock art was a forgery and I believe it was indeed truly painted in the Palaeolithic period.' Above all, Ucko was a pragmatist and he wanted to see the site for himself, so he signed both documents, took his copy and they all went off to look at the rock art. Ucko came away moderately convinced and wrote a paper stating that he had changed his mind. However, as a coda to the story, when I was in Hungary in the 1990s, I met the leading Hungarian Palaeolithic specialist Miklos Gábori, who told me that he had paid a visit to the Kapovaya cave in the 1940s and there was *no* rock art in the cave. So Ucko was right the first time.

The second great event in the Anglo-Russian Exchange Scheme was the Maikop international conference, in which a large group of British later prehistorians, myself included, went to the North Caucasus to visit the great Early Bronze Age Maikop barrows, study the finds and debate their significance. This seemed a great opportunity and the British side flew first to Moscow and then on to Maikop. At this point, we were informed that Masson had switched the site of the conference from Maikop to Novorossisk on the Black Sea coast, meaning that it would be impossible to visit the Maikop barrows from Novorossisk because it was more than the day trip there and back. After digesting this disappointment, we held an epic six-day conference with English–Russian translations in sequence rather than in parallel. This tedious procedure was enlivened by visits to Lermontov's cottage and the Abrau-Durso champagne factory established by the French in the 1890s and which continued with French expertise right through the Soviet period. Although we weren't allowed to buy any champagne at the factory, the members of the Novorossisk Museum staff spent a hefty chunk of their small salaries to buy us each a bottle. The director of the museum further angered Masson by organising a coach trip to the Caucasian port-hole dolmens – a local form of megalithic monument. After the conference, most of us took the train back to Leningrad – an amazing 36-hour train trip across the vastness of the Russian steppe, in a buffet car that served hot and cold food and drink all the way. Masson and Ucko flew back to Leningrad in four hours to co-organise the second part of the trip – the study of the Maikop materials in the Hermitage Museum. We had two days in the Hermitage to see the Maikop finds. On the first day, the person with the key to the Maikop room could not be found and, on the second day, he was unexpectedly called away to Moscow. So Masson had broken his promise to show us the Maikop finds and the site barrows – a classic piece of Masson trickery. However, as a consolation prize, we were allowed into the Pazaryk Room to see the wonderfully preserved remains of the wooden burial chambers and their miraculous finds. If only we had seen the Maikop finds.

One opportunity came out of Pavel's appointment – the creation of a new Research Centre – a species very much in vogue at the time. I had already enjoyed a collaboration with Durham and Bradford in the termly research seminar organised by John Bintliff called 'NUARS' – the Northern Universities Archaeological Research Seminar. This provided an opportunity for sharing new research from the Universities of Newcastle (with me in charge), Durham (with Anthony Harding in charge) and Bradford (with John Bintliff in charge) and helped us to dispel the isolation that we sometimes felt in northern universities. There was one seminar in each venue per year. We were grateful to John Bintliff for such a great idea and happy that he moved to Durham soon after. Since Anthony Harding and John Bintliff both had interests in the Balkans and Eastern Europe, we thought that Pavel's arrival was a great chance for an inter-university collaboration. The result of this critical mass of four active researchers was the Centre for the Archaeology of Central and Eastern Europe (aka 'CACEE'), which was a great success for 12 years (1994–2005) before staff mobility undermined its *raison d'être*. CACEE invited several outstanding scholars to Durham or Newcastle, including Leo Klejn from Leningrad, Ludmila Koryakova from Yekaterinburg, Božidar Slapšak from Ljubljana and Ivana Radovanović from Beograd. CACEE also organised a number of conferences. The first Newcastle conference on 'Cultural Interactions' was co-organised with Peter Ucko, the British co-director of the Anglo-Russian Exchange programme with Vadim Masson.

The Newcastle conference on cultural interactions got off to an appalling start. Peter Ucko had brought with him a group from Southampton, including Tim Champion and Clive Gamble and the Russian translator Cathy Judelson. Peter Ucko insisted that all of the lectures would be translated from Russian into English or vice versa in sequence rather than in parallel. Ucko gave the keynote address and, instead of speaking for 15 minutes with five minutes of questions, he spoke for 35 minutes (*i.e.* 70 minutes including translation), at which point I signalled the chair of the session, Pavel Dolukhanov, to stop him. Not only did Peter Ucko stop but, in a fit of fury, marched out of the conference, collected his bags from the Hall of Residence and immediately took a train back to Southampton. By this time, he had already failed to pay for his accommodation and the conference fee. Fortunately, the sum owed to the conference exactly matched the fee the conference would have paid to Cathy the translator, so we told Cathy to collect her payment from Ucko, which she did. We were quits.

In 1995 we learned that, in 2001, the Higher Education Council was going to implement its third research review of the output of every department in all subjects across all British universities – the so-called Research Academic Exercise (or RAE). At the time, Newcastle was quite a small department by British standards, with only seven academic staff. It became strategically obvious that we had to expand the department by several new members of staff to survive in such a competitive atmosphere. I talked to many friends and colleagues across the sector and developed a plan for attracting three or four colleagues from other universities to Newcastle to give our department a viable size for the medium term. The principal by-product of the plan was that it would mean a lot of extra work for the departmental staff. When I put the plan to the other six staff and received support from only one of them, I realised that my plan to become Head of an expanded, thriving department was doomed.

While we were in Newcastle. Maja actively sought new challenges on the basis that there were no academic or museum jobs at the time. She came into contact with an interesting group of former sea captains, whether from the Royal Navy or the merchant marine, who worked in the Newcastle branch of Trinity House, in Broad Chare on the Newcastle Quayside. Their house was a wonderful 16th century historic building and the captains decided that they wanted to convert a warehouse forming part of the house into the Trinity Maritime Museum – a museum telling the maritime story of Newcastle. Since the sea captains had little notion about museums or exhibitions, it was fortuitous for them that they came into contact with Maja with the museum exhibitions skills she had developed in Harlow and also lucky that they met me at a time when I was actively researching Newcastle history. I had been studying Newcastle history for about a year in my spare time and continued to work on this for the next year. My exhibition concept turned time on its head. The display started off at the present time and worked backwards through the centuries until the Roman period. This backward-moving display was designed by Maja, who installed it in the Trinity Maritime Museum, opening in 1984. However, the sea captains were confused by the idea of time working backwards and they claimed that many visitors felt the same way. So the museum display only lasted two years before it was taken down; and although there was the occasional temporary display after that, the Trinity

Maritime Museum really foundered with the demise of the main exhibition. For Maja, this was a great opportunity to show her display talents, while, for me, it was a great way to find out about Newcastle history.

With the end of the Trinity Maritime Museum, the door to more permanent jobs was closing for Maja and she decided she would try her hand at teaching. So she started an Education Teaching Diploma at the Coach Lane campus of Northumbria Polytechnic. The fact that she didn't know the British primary education system and didn't like it when she grew to understand it made this a career *cul-de-sac*. This led to Maja turning her hand to interior design of houses and house renovation, thereby introducing a tension in our lives that lasted for over 10 years. The plan was to renovate the house we were living in, design beautiful interiors and sell it for enough profit so that we could buy a smaller house to live in and a second house for further renovation. But the fatal flaw in the plan was that we never made enough profit from the sale of the redesigned houses and so, every time we wanted to sell to make a profit, we had to move house. We moved house in Newcastle six times in the 11 years, which made our family life hell.

At one point, Maja had another cunning plan – to create a children's restaurant, in which we would take children off their parents' hands for an hour or two while they went to do something that didn't appeal to children, with healthy food, musical instruments and games to play. While this was a great idea, we didn't think it would work in Newcastle, so Maja went to York to check for retail locations. She found a place in Grape Lane, just off Stonegate – the main shopping street – which was not too expensive and, after receiving planning consent, we bought the house, converted it and opened up as the first children's restaurant in York. The Grape Lane house was an amazing 14th-century building connected by a passageway at first floor level to an Italian restaurant, which had its own ghost story. Sometime in the 1880s, there was a murder in the restaurant and the killer dragged the body across the passageway into the other house. It was a week before the body was discovered and the murderer was caught, prosecuted and hanged. When we lived in Grape Lane, the York ghost tours were in full flood and so, every night, one or two ghost tours would stop outside our restaurant to repeat the story, with the climax of a ghost popping up from the courtyard of the Italian restaurant to terrify the punters. This provided an opportunity to sell non-alcoholic drinks to the ghost tourists and we made quite a lot of money out of this. This was just as well because the children's restaurant was not doing well: we needed four children-hours per day to break even and we never reached this in the first summer. This was partly due to the fall-off in American tourism after President Reagan's bombing of Colonel Gaddafi's regime in Libya and partly due to the legendary meanness of Yorkshire visitors.[2] Moreover, my attempts to leaflet visitors to York would have undoubtedly

[2] A York Chamber of Commerce survey of tourism in the city (1986) showed that visitors from Leeds spent an average of 26 p per day in York.

prompted the question: 'Would you want to leave your child with this man?' After a year of financial struggle, Maja's health deteriorated and she had a minor heart condition, which, combined with threats from the local York freemasons who owned the adjacent property,[3] made us decide to sell the children's restaurant at a decent profit to someone who turned it into a wine bar. This sale made us enough money to come back to Newcastle to buy a house in Jesmond. Our time in York was exciting, allowing us to get to know the city. The best time was early evening, between 7 and 9 pm, when the tourists were eating dinner or in the pubs and York reverted to our city, with few other people on the streets.

The combination of the toxic allegations of repeated sexual harassment by a member of staff against female students and secretaries and the rejection of my planned expansion of the department for the RAE made me want to leave the department and I decided to apply for one of the posts that were opening up because of the RAE. I applied for the post of Reader in Prehistoric Archaeology at the University of Glasgow, where an ex-Durham medievalist and Rosemary Cramp *protégé*, Chris Morris, was Head of Department. I was offered the post but several factors intervened to make me turn it down. The personal factor was that the train trip to Plymouth, where my parents still lived, was two hours longer than from Newcastle and would have made weekend trips more complicated. The academic factor was the absence of an Anthropology Department in the University and that was becoming increasingly important to my way of studying archaeology. The contractual factor was that Glasgow refused to honour an entire research leave year that I was due next year. The financial factor was that they refused to pay me any removals expenses or legal expenses for buying a house in Glasgow. These four reasons combined to make me decide against Glasgow. Some time later, Glasgow decided to appoint Bernie Knapp, who had completed outstanding research on the Cypriot Bronze Age.

Friends of mine in Durham whom I regularly met in the Durham research seminars had realised that I was keen to move from Newcastle and they told me of their interest in recruiting me. I invited Anthony Harding and Colin Haselgrove to dinner one evening, cooked them a seafood pasta and was confidentially assured that the job was mine as long as I sat successfully through an interview. This seemed to be a wonderful opportunity to join a large, ambitious department, so I went down for the interview in June 1996. I answered basic questions with confidence, until Alan Bilsborough, a professor of anthropology, asked me what I thought about the claims for early hominins in the Georgian caves. My answer incorporated a spectacular amount of detail, impressed everyone around the table and sealed the job for me. I never let on to my new colleagues that I had marked exam scripts for a Pavel Dolukhanov course on exactly this question, so I really was quite well briefed on matters Georgian.

[3] These threats included allusions to the school our daughter Eleanor attended and were made in retaliation for Maja's research into the potentially illegal contravention of the Cathedral Faculty for burial by the fruiterers next door.

Incidentally, Durham were quite happy to offer me removal expenses, even for a 26.5 km move, and were also happy to honour my research leave year. So I became Reader in Archaeology, with a starting date of October 1996 but an actual starting date a year later, after the year's research leave.

Before I left Newcastle, there was a Farewell drinks reception for me and also for the department's librarian Pat Southern in the Museum of Ambiguities. Whereas Pat made an extremely witty speech that charmed everyone, I gave a potted account of each of the heads of department under whom I had worked, making some caustic comments about Peter Fowler and casting doubts on the person who was to become the new head of department – a museum biologist called Peter Davis with no archaeological network to draw on for the upcoming RAE. My speech went down like a lead balloon and effectively broke most remaining links with the Newcastle Department of Archaeology.

Chapter 6

The Neothermal Dalmatia Project

Up to now, I have followed a chronological narrative of my life but, in this chapter, as in Chapters 8 and 13, I turn to an account of my three principal fieldwork projects, beginning with the Neothermal Dalmatia Project (or 'NDP'). Chapter 7 provides a background to the Third Balkan War.

It was clear from my experience of Ruth Tringham's Selevac Project in 1977 that I was not going to be able to conduct an intensive, systematic field survey in Serbia, in the area of the Starčevo and Vinča groups, which would have been the ideal fieldwork follow-up to my PhD. As in other parts of the Balkans, fieldworking was illegal in Serbia at the time. However, this was not the case in Croatia, as my friends in Zagreb confirmed. It occurred to me that one of the areas of the Balkans that was relatively neglected in terms of prehistoric settlement data, subsistence information, ^{14}C dates and, most of all, social interpretations, was Dalmatia on the Adriatic coast. Our current understanding of prehistoric settlement rested on three *idées fixes* – Neolithic sites were found on the best land, Bronze Age people were mobile pastoralists who had no permanent settlements and Iron Age people lived in hillforts. These three hypotheses could ideally be tested by intensive, systematic fieldwalking, which would cover parts of the landscape archaeologists had not normally investigated.

With the research problems defined, the next question was the choice of a suitable study region. I thought that the simplest way to investigate this was to make a trip down the Adriatic coast from Trieste in the north as far as the Albanian border in the south, visiting as many known Mesolithic and Neolithic sites as I could on the way. I hoped to identify a study region and a colleague to work with, so we could set up a five-year project. This involved following what the locals called the '*magistrala*' – the Adriatic Coastal Highway, built in 1961–5 with a combination of foreign loans and a huge volunteer effort in manual labour from coastal communities.

I started off in the summer of 1980 in my Renault 4 Napoleon, full of camping gear, since this reconnaissance was done on a shoestring budget. The site documentation I had to locate the Mesolithic and Neolithic sites was primitive; few sites were tightly located on the maps in the site reports. But, as I would discover, the key point was to know the name of the village nearest the cave.

I started off in the Quarnero islands – where the villages still had bilingual street names in Italian and Serbo-Croat and whose inhabitants spoke with a curious local Italo-Croatian dialect. There were important hunter-gatherer sites on Cres and Lošinj. I managed to hire a fisherman to take me by boat to Jami na Sredi on the coast of Cres. But reaching the Velika pećina near the top of the main limestone ridge running down the centre of Lošinj was a challenge of a different order. I talked to people in cafés about the cave and they put me in touch with a mountain guide who, for a small sum, would take me for a night walk through the pine forests to reach the cave before sunrise. We met at a café at midnight and set out through the pine forests with the guide's dog, who proved to be an extremely capable ferret-hunter. The guide was extremely competent and took me right up to the cave in a five-hour walk, so we arrived there before sunrise, had an hour's rest until there was light enough to take photographs (Plate 9) and see the views from the extraordinary cave and then walked back down again, arriving after a 12-hour trip.

This trip was a great way to see a cave site but many caves were closer to 'their' villages than Velika pećina. Wherever I wanted to visit a cave site, I went to the local village and explained that I was an archaeologist from London who had come to see their cave and could the villagers please show me where it was. In every case, the villagers were extremely proud of their cave and very happy to show it to a foreigner who had travelled so far. What came over was a real sense of personal identity about the caves, which I'd never really experienced before, since there were few cave sites in the Vinča distribution. The open sites were much harder to find, since they were in ploughed fields and lacked obvious defining characteristics and therefore no local 'identity'. For open sites, I needed occasionally available archaeological help.

On the island of Rab, there was an open coastal site on the northern peninsula next to the Bay of Lopar. It was one of the few sites whose location was closely defined on a map. When I reached the neck of the peninsula, I found that it was protected by a 3 m-high fence, with a locked gate across the only access track. I followed the perimeter fence, getting as close to the open site as I could. When I looked through the wire mesh, I could see a row of luxury villas and out of one of them came a portly gentleman clasping a scantily clad lady. I suddenly realised that these were probably the holiday villas of Socialist politicians which had to be carefully screened from the masses.

The hardest site to reach was the Gudnja cave, high up on a limestone ridge above the village and at the far end of the Pelješac Peninsula. I was particularly keen to visit Gudnja because it lay near the town of Ston, which had a reputation for the finest oysters on the Adriatic coast. I set out from Ston to drive to the village of Česvinica but, unusually, could find no adults who were prepared to take me to the cave – I supposed because it was a very steep climb. Eventually, two children offered to take me as far as they could, so we started the climb. Soon it became clear why nobody wanted to accompany me on this walk – there had been a forest fire over the entire hillside and the surface was extremely slippery, with many sharp pine trunks, roots and branches still projecting from the ground surface. It was a difficult walk and I could hear that the kids were becoming restive for a kilometre before they told me that was far enough for them. They told me to keep going up in a certain direction and that I couldn't miss it. Astonishingly, this turned out to be the case and so I reached the Gudnja cave, with its fantastic views over the sea. On the way down, I managed to slip on some pine charcoal and impaled my left hand on a pine spike, which perforated my hand. I was stuck on the pine spike and it took a lot of pain and blood to pull my hand away. I descended the mountain very slowly and cautiously, looking a pretty sorry sight with my T-shirt covered in charcoal and blood. When I got to the village, I realised that I somehow had to drive back to Ston, which, I assumed, had a medical centre. The 5 km drive with one hand took 10 minutes and was extremely painful. Maja looked in horror at me and realised that we had to get to the medical centre immediately. She found a taxi driver to take us to the sparkling new medical centre, conveniently located 3 km outside the town. The doctor cleaned up the wound, administered a mammoth penicillin injection in my bottom and told me to come back for one more injection for each of the next two days. Worst of all, she insisted that I keep a very strict boiled potato or rice diet for the next week – which put paid to the Ston oysters.[1] When we came out of the medical centre, there were no taxis and the next bus wasn't for two hours, so we hitched a lift from the next person to drive back to the town from the hospital. The loss of the oysters was a heavy price to pay for reaching the Gudnja cave.

The next cave on my target list was the Močiljska pećina, some 10 km inland from Dubrovnik. I found the city archaeologist – Spomenka Petrak – in the Archaeological Museum and she agreed to show me the cave. We arranged to meet at the museum one morning and, as I was walking to the museum through the main square, I was astonished to find the Kalicz family there, drinking coffee. I knew Nándor Kalicz from his Hungarian Neolithic research, although I hadn't met his wife Rózsa. I asked them what they were doing there and Nándor explained that, being loyal citizens of Hungary and high-status archaeologists, they obtained a tourist visa to visit Dalmatia every two years and this year they were visiting Dubrovnik. I kept to myself my thoughts of the contrast between János Makkay's fate as an 'enemy of the people'[2] and the Kalicz's loyalty to the Party and asked the Kaliczes if they would like to come and see a Neolithic cave. They naturally accepted my offer and we walked to the museum to meet Gospodja Petrak. We drove up some serpentine roads to the village of Močilja, which was very close to the cave. When we reached the cave, we found the security grill firmly locked with a big padlock, as Spomenka had expected. Spomenka and I walked into the village to find the cave guard, who gave Spomenka the key and we walked back to the cave. The only problem was that the key didn't work: it wouldn't open the padlock whichever way we tried to make it work. Nándor stood by patiently and diplomatically, waiting for the hosts to solve the problem,

[1] In fact, to this day, I have still never tried Ston oysters.

[2] For János Makkay's background, see p. 40.

But, after 15 minutes, when he realised the hosts were not finding a solution, he asked very modestly if he could please have a look. He took one look at the padlock and said, 'Ah, it's Hungarian – no problem!', stepped back and gave it a massive kick. The padlock obediently sprung open at once and Nándor said, 'No problem, Hungarian padlock', and so we entered the cave. This was quite characteristic of Nándor – he could solve problems and rarely caused any. He demonstrated the principle that, if you want to visit a cave, take a Hungarian with you.

The next stop south of Dubrovnik was the town of Kotor. I had poor documentation for the Kotor sites and was not very hopeful of finding an archaeologist to show me the local sites. I was walking around the town centre when I had the shock of my life: I met a Yugoslav who had previously worked for me in Harlow Museum on the Roman rescue excavation in Easter 1979.[3] He told me the story of his last year. He had made enough money by working in Harlow to buy his own JCB (small digger), so that he could return to Kotor to set up his own building company. One day, he was renovating a 19th-century building in the centre of town when the infamous Kotor earthquake struck. This was such a savage earthquake (Richter scale of 6.9) that it destroyed not only most of Kotor but also the entire harbour installation at the port of Bar, in which the Yugoslav government had invested millions of dollars to become the terminus of the newly-constructed Belgrade–Bar railway and the outlet for exports to Italy. This earthquake struck the building where my friend was working on the first floor and he described it like this: 'One moment, I was standing to the right of the door. The next moment, the door was on the other side and, the moment after that, the door had moved to the other side of the room.' He was utterly terrified and thought he was going to die. Somehow, he survived but his hair changed colour from a sleek, black Dalmatian head of hair to pure white in 15 minutes. We had a drink to celebrate his survival.

The 1980 reconnaissance clearly demonstrated one feature of the coastline – that about 90% of the modern coast was extremely steep, with very little coastal plain and the coastal plain in those sectors was so narrow that, in all probability, sediment washed down from the adjacent hills or mountains would have covered any prehistoric site with hillwash. This meant that the sites wouldn't have been detectable from field survey. This was the case on most Adriatic islands, where there was a 'soft centre' flanked by limestone ridges but with hillwash several metres deep, covering any lowland sites. There was only one large coastal plain – the Plain of Zadar (aka Ravni Kotari), which was fortunately near a university base. The University of Zadar was then an outstation of the University of Split, having migrated from the University of Zagreb in the 1970s, but had its own History Faculty which included a senior archaeologist, Professor Šime Batović (Plate 10). He was Professor of Archaeology in the university and also had a team of collaborators in the Archaeological Museum in Zadar. Batović was extremely keen on collaboration and took me to see the open

[3] For the Harlow Roman rescue excavations, see p. 74.

sites of Nin, near the salt pans of that village, as well as to his own excavation sites at Smilčić and Islam Grčki. Batović was the most senior prehistorian then working in Dalmatia and his position of power in the university and museum, combined with the lowland expanse of the Plain of Zadar, made this the only sensible place to base a fieldwalking project. The plain covered perhaps 60 × 35 km, all of which was basically lowland but with limestone ridges interspersed with lowland valleys. It was decided that we should start a project. I suggested a name for the project – the Neothermal Dalmatia Project (or 'NDP') – to which Batović agreed.

Since the start of my Newcastle post in January 1980, I had a relatively light teaching load, which allowed me to begin the task of converting my PhD thesis into a book. Before my Adriatic reconnaissance and later, in parallel to the new project, I was working on the analysis of the PhD material that I'd collected. This also meant the agonies of cutting three-quarters of the word count, from 225,000 words to 75,000 words, for a two-volume BAR publication.[4] I managed to complete this by March 1981 and my Vinča BAR has remained the only synthesis of the Vinča group ever since.[5]

The other unpublished project that I had worked on in Yugoslavia the 1970s was the Selevac site-visiting season, which Ruth Tringham thought should be included in her Selevac monograph despite the lack of intensive, systematic fieldwalking. Ruth insisted that this was a priority, since she wished to publish the monograph speedily. So, despite the obvious advantages of paying a consolidating visit to Zadar and strengthening links with Professor Batović, I decided to complete my Selevac settlement chapter, with much work on soil and environmental reconstructions. I managed to complete the chapter by October 1981 but the majority of authors had not done the same. In fact, I had to wait nine years for the publication of the Selevac monograph. This was the last time that I prioritised other colleagues' publication demands over my own projects.

The Selevac research meant that the start of the NDP was delayed until summer 1982, by which time I had raised modest funding for the first season. At that time, there were no five-year project funding strategies, so I had to apply every year for funding to the British Academy, the Society of Antiquaries of London and Newcastle University, with success based on the previous summer's results but also heavily dependent upon competition from other projects. I managed to recruit a team of Newcastle students for the first season, matched by Batović' team of Zadar students. We were ready to start in the first week of September and there was only one problem – so far, we had no fieldwork permit.

Batović had been unable to start the complicated process of gaining a permit until I arrived in Dalmatia. At this point, he explained to me that the permit process started

[4] 'BAR' stands for British Archaeological Reports – an innovative publishing house set up by Geoffrey Hands and David Walker in 1974, which focused on the publication of recent PhD theses.

[5] In 2019, I was invited to give the keynote speech to the 'LBK-Vinča Conference' in Tübingen, where I gave a review of the fate of the Vinča synthesis I had published in 1981 (Chapman 2020).

with a signature of approval from the Zadar City Council, followed by the signature of the Republican Ministry of Culture in Zagreb and then a third signature from the national Ministry of Culture in Beograd. We then had to return to Zagreb for a counter signature from the Republican Ministry of Culture and a final countersignature of the other signatures by the Zadar City Council. This five-stage process took quite a lot of money for flights but we managed to achieve everything through family contacts. The father of Maja's friend Branka Šulc was a top governmental lawyer in Zagreb, who leant on a friend in the Ministry of Culture, while Maja's father in Belgrade smoothed the way for the National Ministry of Culture's signature through his contacts with the President of the Serbian Academy of Sciences. Much to Batović's amazement, we managed to complete the permit process in a week and started the field season only one week late.

Perhaps the most important member of the project team was the yellow Ford Transit van called 'Pretty Polly', whom we'd driven out to Dalmatia in August. Without Pretty Polly, the logistics of the project would have been in serious jeopardy (Figs 13 and 14). The local archaeologists who made the biggest contributions to

Fig. 13. Pretty Polly, the Ford Transit minibus at Nadin hillfort, Croatia, 1986

Fig. 14. The author climbing Nadin hill, Croatia, 1986

the project worked for the Zadar Archaeological Museum. Ivo Fadić was a Roman glass specialist who would come on some of the fieldwalking days, as would Smiljan Gluščević, the museum conservator. But the three most prominent museum staff who helped all the time was a group whom one might loosely call the 'Batović Trio' – Branka Nedved, Marija Kolega and Ljilja Klarin. This trio had worked on all of Batović's recent projects and formed a compact, loyal and highly talented team of field archaeologists. They took part in the project almost every day and, without Branka, Marija and Ljilja, we certainly wouldn't have completed the project in the way that we did. Jasenka Lulić was the ethnographer who joined the project unofficially. She worked in the Ethnographic Museum and was keen to work with an international project, contributing her expertise in two directions – Iška pottery and modern villagers' land use in the Plain of Zadar.

Our accommodation in Zadar was rather varied. When we first arrived, we managed to rent rooms in individual flats in the centre of Zadar for the team of 10 but, during that season, we found accommodation with the same landladies which lasted for the rest of the project. Our favourite landlady was a lady whom we called 'Moma' – a large, jolly, Croatian village lady in her 50s who owned a townhouse in the old town with five rooms to let. This was ideal for our student accommodation and so, from year two onwards, the students would sleep in Moma's town house.

The other regular landlady, who provided a place for the Chapmans from the third season onwards, was Fanika, who had a third floor flat in one of the old Italianate palaces on one of the main shopping streets in Zadar, now called Ulica Šimuna Kožičića Benje, so we lived extremely centrally when we stayed with her. Fanika had recently been widowed. Her husband was Chief Architect in Zadar and, some years before, he had been approached to join the Masonic Lodge. His promotion to Chief Architect was very much welcomed by the Lodge, who had obviously supported his candidature but this support came at a price. He was expected to approve plans for any Masonic entrepreneurial scheme in the old town, many of which were utterly out of character with the essentially 17th-century old town. Much tension arose from this clash of interests and, at a certain point, the architect decided to leave the Masons. But before he did this, a leading Mason came round to his flat and advised him strongly against quitting – otherwise something would certainly happen to him. But the tension was too great and he left the Masons. A month later, his lifeless body was found in a boat drifting off the main harbour of Zadar. While nobody was ever found guilty of this crime, Fanika was in absolutely no doubt that the Masons had killed her husband.

One of the project flats was distressingly close to the Zadar Cathedral bell-tower, with its half-hourly eruptions, especially dramatic early on our free days. One of our family isssues was childcare for our daughter Eleanor, who was six when the project started. We found two places – the Archaeological Museum, where a kind-hearted receptionist called Ana spent many hours entertaining Eleanor, and the nuns in the convent next to the museum. These childcare arrangements continued even when we lived at Fanika's flat and helped Eleanor to improve her Serbo-Croat, become self-reliant and cope with day-to-day tasks in the old town.

After the first two years of purely field survey, the NDP fieldwork was a combination of field survey and trial excavations. The field survey was based on two long transects to investigate landscape and settlement relations and one large block survey to target diachronic settlement patterns. In the first season, we managed to complete one long transect from the coast near Ražanac across the Plain of Zadar to the former lake Bokanjačko Blato. This transect passed through three lowland valleys and two limestone ridges and was designed to provide a sample of settlement evidence from each kind of topographical unit in the entire Plain of Zadar.

The method of working in the field was quite new to the Zadar archaeologists and indeed to the majority of Newcastle students as well. We started off in a line using regular distancing, at 25 m spacing between walkers for lowland areas and 50 m for rocky areas. We walked on a fixed compass bearing across the landscape, trying to keep accurate spacings and recording single finds and clusters of objects which may have been 'sites'. If a 'site scatter' was found, walkers would mark their place along the transect and come to help make a gridded, timed collection before returning to 'their' line. This method meant that everyone was their own fieldworker – that each person decided in detail where to go, what to collect and how to record. This was a quite different form of archaeological fieldwork from anything that Batović had ever organised in the past. His normal way of working was as the field director, with a number of other people working for him, including a site supervisor, who filled in the site notebook, a site photographer and an off-site pottery specialist from the museum who looked after the finds. Through this hierarchical system, Batović controlled absolutely everything in all stages of the fieldwork process, through pre-excavation, excavation and post-excavation. I had not appreciated how different the NDP process was from the Batović method but it became obvious that Batović was not happy with the new system because it undermined his control of the Zadar team. Perhaps unbeknown to him, the Zadar Museum colleagues were delighted to be working on their own, taking responsibility for fieldwork decisions and sites and finds recording. This underlying tension ran throughout the project and did not help the integration of the final results.

By and large, the field recording system worked reasonably well. In fact, the biggest hindrance was the quality and scale of the maps. The 1:25,000 maps from the Zadar City Council made field accuracy very difficult to achieve – recall that this was long before the days of GIS or GPS – and so we could record sites within the limitations of the mapping cover. There was only one area of the survey in which the vegetation cover was so thick that we could not have walked through the forest – a 1 km^2 block of dense karstic pine forest near the Buta Jama just inland from the Adriatic. The other main problem was snakes. Dalmatia has 15 species of snakes, of which three are poisonous – the common adder, the Karst meadow viper and the nose-horned viper – or '*poskok*' – a jumping snake that bites you soon after it jumps. The variety of snakes that we could meet meant that we had to carry anti-snake serum with us in the field. While the British team was in principle happy to use this, every single Zadar student preferred to be bitten by a snake and go to hospital rather than be injected with the horse-based serum, which they thought would kill them. Indeed, if you were bitten by a *poskok*, you had 45 minutes to get to hospital for treatment and the areas we were surveying were right on the outer limits of this time threshold. Fortunately, although we sometimes saw *poskoci* on a terrace from higher up the hill, we had only three incidents with snakes. In year two, the transect passed through a forest which the Zadar students refused to cross because they said the forest was famous for its tree snakes – snakes which lived in the trees and hung down, waiting to attack Archaeology students. I had to explain the problem to the Newcastle students, who were *macho* enough to go through this forest, which they did without seeing a single snake. There were very few snakes which came close to a team member. One day, Rupert Brakspear saw a snake near him and the snake was so terrified of Rupert that it went straight for him. Rupert jumped in the air and the snake passed underneath him to find the only adjacent hiding-place – a bush from which the snake never emerged. The other person who suffered from a snake was Maja. One afternoon in the first season, Maja was taking a pee behind a dry-stone wall when a snake passed beneath her body. This was the last day Maja came out in the field; after that, she stayed behind in the museum and looked after post-fieldwork finds processing.

Although systematic fieldwalking was within the law in Croatia, this project was the first to use the technique over an entire lowland landscape. So it was perhaps not surprising that military spotter planes flying high above the Plain of Zadar were keeping tabs on our progress each day of fieldwalking. But what happened at the end of our first season was utterly bizarre. Our transect finished at the north shore of the former Bokanačko Blato, not far from a military 'polygon' that was not marked on our maps but about which everyone knew. We rested for an hour after finishing the transect and then walked to the main road to return to Zadar. On that evening's news, there were scenes out of Hell as military officers burnt the entire hillside where we had rested at the end of the transect with flame-throwers – presumably to make sure that we had not left any surveillance equipment.

Already by the first fieldwalking season, it became clear that Professor Batović and I had divergent interpretations of the project's many field remains. I had walked over enough limestone landscapes to realise that it was possible to identify dry-stone cairns which could date to any period potentially but whose associated surface ceramic material could help to date them to the Bronze Age. Another feature which we found in the second season was the dry-stone wall, which Professor Batović interpreted as the remains of modern constructions built by the Yugoslav National Army (aka the 'JNA') in the 1950s–1960s during training exercises. It proved hard to persuade him to change his mind until we were recording the Pridraga cairnfield, above Karinsko More. Here, we came upon a dry-stone wall which lay stratigraphically beneath a cairn full to bursting with Bronze Age pottery. At this point, Professor Batović's JNA interpretation became untenable.

An even more serious dispute occurred in the third season, when we found the *Čauševica* enclosed site – a complicated set of three or four interlocking dry-stone-walled enclosures with multiple associated cairns. After our surveyors had plotted this site and we sent Professor Batović the plan, he refused to accept it, stating that the site bore no resemblance to the plan at all. Early in the fourth season, we went out to check this and found in fact that the plan was accurate. But the damage had been done and it was difficult to see how we could reconcile different interpretations of field remains when the two co-directors could not even agree on the factual basis of a survey plan. The interpretational divide between Professor Batović and myself became a yawning gulf, which we never managed to bridge.

Nonetheless, much of the archaeology turned out to be very exciting and we managed to test all of the three main hypotheses that I mentioned which defined the accepted prehistoric settlement patterns. An essential part of the programme consisted of the surveying of landscape features like enclosures, dry-stone walls and hillforts. For this, we had to thank a husband-and-wife team from the Newcastle Surveying Department, Robin and Barbara Fursdon, who drove over to Dalmatia in their camper van and did a fantastic job in producing all of the plans over the entire five years. Later, the planning of the dry-stone features led to what was innovative certainly for Dalmatia and possibly for much of prehistoric Europe – the attempt to work out estimates of construction times for dry-stone monuments. This research led me into very interesting discussions with members of a bespoke group – the British Dry Stone Walling Association (aka 'DSWA') – who provided expert guidance for my logistical estimates.

The other really innovative research for the Balkans concerned the soils research and land-use reconstructions done by Robert Shiel from the Newcastle Agriculture Faculty. Robert (Plate 13) made soil maps of all of our survey areas and worked with the Zadar ethnographer, Jasenka Lulić, in talking to many local farmers to work out the current land use of the five land-use units he'd identified in the Plain of Zadar. He then fed a model of climatic change into the static modern model, which enabled him to suggest which were the better soils for each kind of activity – arable, pastoralism, fruit trees, etc – for each phase in the Holocene climatic sequence. This enabled us to compare the settlement distributions we produced with the land-use retro-dictions that Robert had produced.

Halfway through the project, Robert had a life-changing accident while on a British Council soils trip to Zimbabwe. He was on the back seat of an open-topped car that was speeding along a country road when a tyre burst and he was hurled into the air. As he fell, he tried to save the colleague's daughter who was sitting next to him, only to land on, and break, his own spine. Robert was fortunate that the main Harare hospital had recently been equipped with modern spinal injuries facilities, which probably saved his life. He flew back to the UK with his wife, Alison, and spent months in Stoke Mandeville Hospital and then the Spinal Injuries Unit of Hexham Hospital – eventually asking the doctors if he could go back to work as a university lecturer. In each hospital where he was recovering, Robert left earlier than expected and showed wonderful spirit in facing life in a wheelchair. For a fieldworker like Robert, a sad prospect indeed.

In the third year of our fieldwork, my PhD supervisor John Nandris came out to Zadar for a few days to work on his upland ethno-archaeology project. This was a curious role reversal, since up to now I had been a student on projects directed by John. He drove out in the Institute of Archaeology Land Rover from Romania with the idea of talking to shepherds in the Velebit Mountains – the first coastal range inland from the sea and whose foothills were washed by the Adriatic. John could stay with us only three days and unfortunately he chose one of the rainiest days of the whole season for a small team of four of us to go up into the mountains to make a measured plan of what John called a '*stina*' (Romanian – summer shepherd's enclosure; Croatian – '*stan*'). In the morning, we started to make a plan of the *stan* but, in the last hour before lunch, it rained continuously. After we had sheltered in the nearby shepherds' hut and saved ourselves with hot soup, we found it extremely difficult to go back out into the wet, cold atmosphere, so, unfortunately for John, the plan of the *stan* was never completed. But what John did on his other Velebit days was to drive around and talk to as many local shepherds as he could. One of the finer points of upland ethno-archaeology was the way that shepherds counted their sheep. Although the shepherds talked to John in Serbo-Croatian most of the time, when it came to counting sheep, they reverted to an obscure, archaic form of Romanian, which John interpreted as suggesting a link with the Vlachs of Romania and Macedonia, who also counted in a 'Latin' language. So at least John made one interesting discovery in his three days on the project.

The *Iška keramika* found in the medieval and later periods in Dalmatia comprised a very important part of our fieldwork material – a poorly fired red coarse ware with dense calcite temper. The Newcastle team was initially unaware of the significance of this red ware which was so plentiful in the fields of the first season. The Zadar archaeologists and ethnographers told us that *Iška keramika* came from the island of Veli Iž – an island in the third line of Adriatic islands. Moreover, there were still two or three very old potters who made *Iška keramika* for exchange on the islands. Ethnographic accounts showed that the wares were exchanged widely up and down the Adriatic and also inland some hundred kilometres or more in the 19th century and possibly earlier. *Iška keramika* became the focus of two lines of project research – one by Rupert Brakspear and the other by Richard Carlton. Rupert collected as much clay and calcite from Veli Iž as could be safely fitted into Pretty Polly. Back in Newcastle, Rupert made experimental pots using the clay and the calcite temper and fired them in kilns in the Faculty of Agriculture labs. It was an enormous shock to all of us that, when Rupert took the batch out of the kiln after firing it to 800°C, there was nothing left but crushed sherds. We had not realised that you could not fire calcite-gritted pots to above 650°C without causing the vessels to explode. This truncated Rupert's experimental programme but gave the project an important technological baseline for firing temperature analysis. Richard Carlton came on the project for all five years and, halfway through, decided he would like to write a PhD thesis on *Iška keramika* – a thesis which he completed some years after the end of the project. Richard came up with an approximate dating method for *Iška keramika* based on the density of the calcite gritting. Richard dated the earliest occurrence of this pottery to the Iron Age. Thereafter, the calcite temper became more frequent but finer all the way through into the 19th century, giving a coarse-grained[6] possibility for discriminating Iron Age pottery from medieval and modern pottery.

One feature of the field seasons, especially in the second year, was that Robert Shiel would drop the fieldwalkers off and drive Pretty Polly away to do some soils fieldwork with his soil student. One morning, Robert had driven Pretty Polly along the limestone track on the first limestone ridge in from the coast, near Buta Jama, dropped us off above the gorge and drove back along the road towards Turanj. He descended from the limestone ridge into a hamlet and at this point was flagged down by an old lady with a six- or seven-year-old granddaughter. The old lady went around with great surprise to the wrong side of the vehicle and Robert wound down the window. The lady pointed at her granddaughter and said '*škola, škola*'. Even with Robert's basic knowledge of Serbo-Croat, it was clear that the lady wanted him to drive the granddaughter to school in the first village. In the 1980s, this would have seemed a risky procedure that involved a degree of trust hardly ever found in Britain and Rob Shiel was so delighted by this that he always used to tell the story with great fondness. Here was a total stranger – a foreigner in a strange vehicle who did not speak her language – and the grandmother had entrusted her granddaughter for a 5 or 6 km trip to her school with total confidence that the foreigner would deliver the girl safely to school. Which Robert did!

As the project progressed, we began to realise how many wonderful places there were on the coast. Ljubač Bay, West of Zadar, became a firm favourite, not least of the combination of vast, sandy beach and a *boules* pitch in the village. We used to have a round or two of what the locals call *boćanje*, using roughly shaped limestone balls ('*balote*'), before swimming in the bay. Every year, on one of our Sunday free days, we would organise a mussel party on the beach at Karinsko More. This 'sea' had a narrow neck connecting to the Adriatic but also received fresh water from the streams flowing in. This provided a perfect environment for the growth of mussels, who appreciate a mix of freshwater and salty water. The team would drive out to the beach and those who could dive went down to about 4 m, where there was an underwater reef coated with mussels. One year, we met a journalist who announced himself only as 'Anonymous' but who had a full mussel-diving kit, including a large, fine-netted bag, which he attached to his shoulder and into which he placed the

[6] Apologies for this.

mussels. It was a difficult job to knock the mussels and break their hold on the reef. With clear instructions from Anonymous, several of the students who were good at diving managed to collect vast piles of mussels. I am not such a strong swimmer so I stayed on the shore, made the fire and helped to cook the mussels in a garlic butter and white wine sauce in a huge, iron cauldron. One year, we sent an invitation to see our Zadar season to my Hungarian friends, János Makkay, his wife Magda and her daughter Lila. János turned out to be a great mussel cook and made the very best of the mussel stews that we'd ever had.

On another visit to Split, my museum friend Branko Kirigin, or Kiro as he is known, had offered to take me to see some spectacular sites inland from Split near Trilj. We drove up some tortuous roads and Kiro showed me some very interesting cartwheel-ruts, probably Roman in date, cut into the limestone. We were about to drive off to see some Roman villas when I riskily tried to overtake a car on the narrow road, only to realise that a yoghurt lorry was coming the opposite way. I couldn't avoid the yoghurt lorry entirely and we 'kissed' with a glancing blow, which damaged Pretty Polly more than it damaged the yoghurt lorry. According to Yugoslav law, you had to report any road accident to the police and so Kiro found a phone box and called the local police. But, in the hottest part of the day, the police did not come very quickly. Every 10 minutes longer that we waited, the temperature of the yoghurt and the yoghurt lorry driver increased. Eventually, after two hours, the police turned up and took statements from the three of us and noted the position of the vehicles. I accepted that I was at fault so the policeman told me that they would send a letter to me via Kiro, explaining the date and time of my trial. At that point, the yoghurt lorry driver complained bitterly about the destruction of his load and drove off as fast as possible to Split to deliver his yoghurt. Two weeks later, Kiro received the fateful letter, summoning me to a Magistrates' Court appearance, so I had to drive down from Zadar to go to court to await my sentence. Kiro came with me for moral and linguistic support and we sat waiting with the yoghurt lorry driver in the court lobby – a typically disgusting public space with peeling wallpaper. The only saving grace about this interlude was the moment when a pretty young lady in a stunning lemon dress swept into the room, greeted everyone and walked into the court. We had no idea who this was but Kiro had obviously taken a great fancy to her. When we were ushered into the court, it turned out that this lady was the judge. Kiro used all his charms to win her over and managed to get me off with a very light fine (perhaps £3.50 equivalent). The yoghurt lorry driver was extremely upset about the small fine but could do nothing about it. This was by no means the end of the story, for Kiro started an affair with the judge that lasted maybe two years. The real winners were Kiro and the judge with the lemon dress.

At the very end of the project, most students had started to make their way back to the UK and Maja and Eleanor had flown to Beograd to be with Maja's parents. I was left with one female student to drive back to the UK. We started off one early morning and I was driving Pretty Polly along the *magistrala* when there was a bump and I suddenly had to slow down sharply. I couldn't see what the problem was but it was clear that I was not able to continue to drive, so the student loyally left me in the road and hitchhiked all the way back to England. I found a local mechanic who looked at the engine but also couldn't diagnose the problem. Since I knew a good garage in Zagreb, I managed to start Pretty Polly in second gear and drive at 20–25 km per hour down the *magistrala* and over the mountains. I couldn't drive any faster for the whole of the day and I had to cross the entire Dinaric chain to reach Zagreb very late that evening. The most embarrassing times came in the foothills of the Dinaric Alps, when I was regularly overtaken by tractors. The next morning in Zagreb, the mechanic I knew from previous years found the problem immediately: a limestone pebble had bounced up from the road and lodged itself in the gearbox. It took a 10 minute repair once the problem had been diagnosed to save Pretty Polly for the trip across Europe at a slightly higher speed.

The experience of conducting a field-based project on the Adriatic coast in the 1980s was exhilarating and highly positive. In geopolitical terms, my exploratory reconnaissance occurred at a time when the Dalmatian tourist economy was still in full swing and many of those living in the narrow tourist coastal zone were still very prosperous. The project years of 1982–1986 saw an overall economic decline but this hardly affected our fieldwork. The project was welcome partly for bringing summer funds into the Zadar archaeological community and that was accepted by everyone concerned. For the British side, living on the coast and having the leisure opportunities which came with that was an unforgettable experience. I cannot imagine why more people in prehistory did not live by the Adriatic and Black Seas and benefit from the pleasures of swimming and fishing.

Chapter 7

The background to the Third Balkan War of 1991–1995

The creation of the multi-ethnic, religiously pluralistic federal state of Yugoslavia was a political task that relied on co-operation between formerly warring parts. The Yugoslavist ideology of '*bratsvo i jedinstvo*' ('brotherhood and unity') substituted a secular religion for the three main communions – Croatian and Slovenian Catholics, Serbian, Montenegran and Macedonian Orthodox Christianity and Bosnian–Hercegovinian and Kosovan Islam. The threat from the West in the years immediately after the Second World War and the threat from the Soviet bloc after 1948, when Tito distanced himself from Stalin, produced an internal unity which meant the 'Yugoslav idea' worked for many – perhaps most – citizens. This nationalist ideology not only covered up religious differences but also tacitly buried the genocides of the Second World War, which remained unresolved under the surface.

The country had a poorly developed market economy throughout the 1950s. My partner Šime Batović used to tell me stories about how he would go for weeks on end without a coin in his pocket, with barter being the principal economic mechanism in Zadar. In this decade, there were hardly any consumer goods, few people owned a car and there was a vestigial bus service. The lack of infrastructure once almost cost Šime his life. He was doing early morning fieldwork on the Radovin hillfort, 20 km north of Zadar and, as he climbed over terrace walls to reach the site, he stepped on a *poskok* (viper[1]) which had not yet woken up. The *poskok* drew its head back to strike at Šime's leg but was so slow that Šime managed to escape. If he had been bitten, there was no way Šime could have returned to get a serum in Zadar hospital in time to save his life.

The gradual Western acceptance of Yugoslavia as a Socialist state with a difference and the diminishing pressure from the Soviet Union after the death of Stalin combined with Tito's growing confidence as national leader, buttressed by his cult of personality. This combination led to the liberalisation of Yugoslavia in the 1960s and 1970s, with an increase in religious behaviour and a decentralisation of cultural and educational

[1] For other *poskok* stories, see pp. 98–99.

policy. Tito's major foreign policy triumph was the establishment of the 'non-aligned movement' of states not formerly tied to either the USA or the Soviet Union. However, a huge state borrowing programme made Yugoslavia increasingly dependent upon the West and, in particular, IMF loans facilitated by Yugoslavia's non-aligned status. This brought market development and a consumerist boom to 1970s Yugoslavs, as seen in personal possessions such as cars, fridges and TVs, but also in personal consumption. Only part of this spending was paid for by the now legal emigration of guest-workers (German: '*Gastarbeitere*' or the derogatory '*Jugoschwaber*') who sent money home to Yugoslavia. The economic boom of the 1970s was unevenly spread across the republics, with the Beograd region, Croatia and Slovenia making most money, together with the tourist centre of the Dalmatian coast. A major boost to Dalmatian tourism came through the construction of the Adriatic Coastal Highway (1961–5), which combined foreign loans with a huge volunteer effort in manual labour from coastal communities. Without this triumph of Socialist co-operation and international finance, Dalmatian tourism could hardly have taken off in the way it did.

The long-term difference between the Italian zone of the coastal cities and towns and the Slavic settlement of inland villages set the secene for 20th-century tourist realities. The prosperity of the tourist zone comprised a narrow coastal strip, between 2 km and 5 km wide, with far less development further inland. Our project was divided between the two zones: we lived in the prosperous tourist part but did fieldwork in the impoverished inland zone. The daily contrasts were enormous, whether in the range of dishes and alcoholic drinks in restaurants in most inland villages as compared to Zadar old town restaurants, or the narrow range of opportunities for social interaction in the villages as compared to those in the old town.

There was another aspect of Dalmatian tourism – the dependence of the locals upon tourists. After eight years of speaking Serbo-Croat, I could express myself competently but, during the first part of my 1980 trip down the coast, in the Quarnero, I felt resentment at my linguistic skills for the first time. Eventually, I realised that the locals had a binary view of people – you were either a local who spoke Serbo-Croat and with whom you remained on decent terms; or you were a tourist who spoke another language, whom you would rip off to the greatest possible extent. As a foreigner who spoke Serbo-Croat, I did not fit into this black-and-white worldview and that caused locals concern, if not resentment. The expansion of tourism on the coast offered many locals jobs in which they could earn in four months more than they could earn off the land in a year of hard work. But this economic reward came at a cost of a dependence on tourists, which locals bitterly resented. In contrast, those living inland – for example in a village on the Plain of Zadar – had no opportunity to make hard cash (Serbo-Croat: '*valuta*') and thus had no alternative to hard agricultural work.

Tito's over-borrowing and the oil price hike in the 1970s led to an economic crisis that was building at the time of the leader's death in 1980. Tito's immediate successor, the Croatian Milka Planinc, resolved the debt crisis of 1981–2 with admirable fortitude and reached out to ease the ethnic divide that the crisis had exacerbated. Thereafter, there was no comparable leader strong enough to maintain the union of the six republics. The tensions were felt worst in Kosovo, where the government struggled to control rioting in 1981. While football teams from different republics were always the foci of nationalist support, it was only in 1980 that the first major battles between fans from rival republics were fought at matches.

Meanwhile, in the mid-1980s, the Yugoslav economy was nose-diving, with greatly increased inflation and rising unemployment – unequally divided between the republics. In the last project season, the first 5,000 dinar note was issued, with a picture of Tito on it. The joke was that Mrs Tito was the only widow who could go to the market and buy a meal for that day in exchange for her husband. Power-cuts in Zadar were a daily event in the 1985 and 1986 seasons, with a fifth of the city without power for two or three hours in a cycle of hardship.

Another aspect of economic and political fragmentation appeared from 1985. Whenever I drove across the Dinaric Alps on the way to/from Zadar, I found villages in which barter rather than cash was the main form of exchange. In villages where there were many *Gastarbeitere*, the dinar was no longer the main currency – it had been displaced by the Deutschmark. It also became clear that there were little clusters of villages which you might call 'fiefdoms', run by local politicians who were not yet warlords but who were developing independent ideas of governance with not even the pretence of adherence to national laws. During these trips, I had the feeling that things were breaking down, especially out there in the countryside far from the reach of Beograd.

One of the long-term results of the de-centralisation of the 1960s was that the post-war generation (those baby boomers born in the late 1940s and 1950s) had developed different views about their cultural heritage, with a higher proportion of the new generation answering 'Croatian' or 'Bošniak' rather than 'Yugoslav' to the legitimate but loaded question, 'Who are you?'. At the beginning of the project, the Zadar archaeologists were perfectly aware of my wife Maja's Serbian roots, as well as my extensive network of Serbian archaeological contacts and this did not prevent our co-operation. However, by 1985, a lot of locals were feeling the pinch and inter-republican rivalries were growing. Whenever I was in Beograd, the Serbian archaeologists asked me why I was working with '*those Croatians*', while the Zadar archaeologists thought I was crazy to go to Beograd after the season and mingle with '*those Serbs*'.

In the towns and cities, the concentration of population meant greater chances for the formation of small nationalist groups. The Project had little contact with such groups, except through a person on the fringe of the project – a small, dark-haired bespectacled, bearded Croatian journalist whose name we never found out but who called himself 'Anonymous'. In the last year of the project, we began to learn more about Anonymous and the company he kept and realised why he needed to keep his anonymity. He staged an invitation to dinner for Maja and me somewhere in the centre of Zadar with six other people, all of whom turned out to be members of the far-right

Croatian nationalist group '*Oko*'. During the dinner, various political discussions were going on round the table, some of which I understood but most of which I didn't. At one point, Maja, who always fancied her connections to the occult, told the company that she could look into their minds and she knew exactly what they were thinking. The members of *Oko* did not take this well and we had to leave in a hurry. I'm still not sure what part the members of the Zadar chapter of *Oko* played in the wars that followed the project but I wouldn't be at all surprised at their tangential involvement.

The one major ingredient in this Balkan mix which we saw little of during the project was the religious divergence, which, when allied to ethnic differences, became a potential danger. The term 'ethnoreligious' has been coined to emphasise how divergent, nationalist identities in each of the three main religious communions were filling the vacuum left by the decline in Communist ideologies. Although our fieldwork in inland Krajina, as much as our living in the tourist centre of Zadar, made us sensitive to the other multiple components of people's identities – whether your clan, your village, your provincial place, your city, the dialect you spoke or the ethno-folklore you knew and told to your children – there were tendencies to reduce these complex aspects of identity to a homogenising ethnoreligious identity. In this way, all of the overlapping, cross-cutting aspects of identity that enabled diverse ethnic groups to live together for decades, if not centuries, could be replaced by a polarising duality. Such ethnoreligious identities were supported in rival popular cultures, often dominated by ethno-kitsch. The civil society and civic consciousness of Tito's Yugoslavia were not strong enough to cope with such threats to the federal notion. Even the celebration of the Winter Olympics in Sarajevo in 1984 as a pan-Yugoslav sporting event was insufficient to hold back fissiparous tendencies.

When populist nationalist leaders gained power in Belgrade (1986: Slobodan Milošević) and Zagreb (1990: Franjo Tudjman), they found that their populist politics gave them enormous power but at the cost of weakening and dividing the nation – indeed the entire Yugoslav project. Without Milošević and Tudjman, I have no doubt that the whole war would not have broken out in the early 1990s. It is the happenstance of archaeological fieldwork that our five-year project concluded in the same year that Milošević took control in Serbia.

In 1994, I published an article about the damage to the cultural heritage in the 1991–1995 war in the West Balkans.[2] In Perica's (2002) book *Balkan Idols*, the sum total of the damage done to monuments was updated to the end of 1995, by which time there was evidence for the destruction of 1,024 mosques, 182 Catholic churches, 28 Serbian Orthodox churches and monasteries and many historic bridges (Plate 11). While this destruction changed the landscape of the entire West Balkans, it is little in comparison with the genocide and ethnic cleansing practiced by all sides in what Misha Glenny has termed the 'Third Balkan War'.

---

[2] Chapman 1994.

The war had a serious effect on the Plain of Zadar and the city itself, since, in their battle for the Krajina, the JNA (Yugoslav National Army) had overrun the Plain of Zadar and had moved to fortify the Nadin hilltop where we had excavated in 1986. It turned out that we were actually doing war rescue archaeology before the event, for a tank regiment from the JNA dug into the Nadin hill, casing huge damage to the monument. The Nadin hill was 25 km from Zadar, bringing the city within range of tank-shelling. Zadar was often shelled and miraculously escaped major damage, with only one shell-hole in the medieval cathedral roof and the destruction of the clock tower above the Ethnographic Museum (Plate 12).

There are many tragic stories about the war, which affected our family in a very minor way. The flat that Maja had purchased was in a block of flats otherwise all owned by Croatian nationals. When Maja tried to visit the flat once more, in 1988, the neighbours made it very clear to her that, being a Serb, she had lost the title to this flat and she never went back to Zadar.

As a coda to the Neothermal Dalmatia Project, 21 years after the end of the project and 12 years after the end of the war, the Zadar archaeologists made their debut on the centre stage of European archaeology with their hosting of the Annual Meeting of the European Association of Archaeologists in 2007. By then, I was long divorced from Maja and my third wife was Bisserka Gaydarska, a Bulgarian PhD student whom I supervised in Durham and who later would marry me. During the meeting, I wanted to show the NDP sites and monuments to Bisserka and another Durham PhD student – Lyn Gatland. We rented a car and set off to see some of the most important sites. We started off with a clear warning from the Zadar archaeologists not to step off the tarmac roads because of the danger of mines. Indeed, some of the shepherds from the village of Nadin where we excavated in 1986 had been blown up along with their sheep, so we were very careful about where we walked.

We first drove to the *Pridraga* cairnfield, which we could look down on from the main road. The site consisted of lines of cairns on a number of terraces descending from the road right down to Karinsko More. We stopped in our traditional parking space and looked down to see the hillside completely covered by young Mediterranean forest trees – oaks and beeches. We overcame our disappointment in a restaurant in the village of Novigrad with a fantastic seafood lunch and then drove on to the other sites. We could not even go close to the Nadin hillfort because that was 2 km off the tarmac but we drove to a vantage point to get a distant view of the site. The main devastation caused by the JNA was to village houses, especially in the village of Tinj, where most houses were burnt, with shell-holes in the walls and the roof. All of the other sites we tried to see, except one, were covered in forest. The only site we actually walked to off the tarmac was the Mataci enclosure, since we had been told that no soldiers had operated in that area. That was a risk but we took it – but even that site was difficult to find in the young forest.

The re-afforestation process of the last 16 years was caused by three inter-linked factors, two connected to the war. First, mines were laid by the JNA all over the

Plain of Zadar, which certainly killed a number of people and animals and deterred shepherds from pasturing their sheep over the landscape. This meant, secondly, that there were very few sheep to eat the young growth so there was little to stop new trees growing. The third factor was the gradual replacement of wood stoves by Calor gas burners in local houses, which reduced the demand for firewood and stopped the felling of young trees. All of this meant that, within one human generation, the Plain of Zadar was re-afforested and it was impossible to see the sites that we had discovered. Indeed, it would now be impossible to conduct the kind of field survey that we had done – turning the entire project into a kind of war rescue archaeological operation.

Chapter 8

The Upper Tisza Project

By the late 1980s, it was very clear to me that Yugoslavia was drifting downhill into warfare – whether civil wars or inter-state wars still remains debated today. My position as a British archaeologist with close ties to both Serbs and Croatians made me a ready target for populist nationalists, so I took the cowardly but pragmatic decision to move my operations out of Yugoslavia. It seemed to me that Hungary would be the next best place for me to start up a long-term project. Why I didn't start a project with the prehistorian I had been working with for 15 years – János Makkay – is very simple and it relates to the fall of the Berlin Wall in 1989.

Through the autumn of 1989 and winter of 1990, all kinds of media developments occurred in Budapest, with an extraordinary mushrooming of publications expressing views that had never been openly permitted before. As many as 120 new journals started up, most of which collapsed within two years. Most publications were simply celebrations of being able to communicate freely in public. Many relied on a ground-swelling of Hungarian nationalism against everybody – especially Russians – but this virulent nationalism I found extremely difficult to cope with. It transpired that János became one of the most nationalist archaeologists I'd ever met in all my years in Hungary and the Balkans. So, although I'd been working for him on and off for more than a decade, I could not work further with János for personal reasons.

I had to make alternative plans and the other friend I'd known for a long time was Pál Raczky (Fig. 15), who was by then working in Eötvös Loránd University Department of Archaeology. Pali was the opposite of a Hungarian nationalist – indeed, very much an internationalist who had already started a collaboration with Walter Meier-Arendt from Frankfurt in 1989 to provide very sizeable grants to excavate the tell of Polgár-Csőszhalom. At that time, there were plans to complete several motorways that the former regime had started but failed to finish. One such was the M3 motorway, going east from Budapest for about 120 km as far as the town of Gyöngyös. The new plan was to complete the M3 motorway, with one branch going to Miskolc in the north-east and another branch going to the city of Nyíregyháza further east and close to the border with the Ukraine at Chop. The reasons for the M3 extension remained unclear, especially since County Szabolcs-Szatmár-Bereg was

Fig. 15. Pál Raczky excavating at Polgár-Csőszhalom

the poorest county in Hungary and had extremely little industry. It appeared to us that the main beneficiaries of the M3 motorway would be the Hungarian Mafia and their cousins, the Ukrainian Mafia. At any rate, the Hungarian law was such that fieldwalking and the excavation of any sites discovered on the motorway line had to take place before motorway construction. Thus, a cross-section of the Hungarian landscape 100 m wide and many kilometres long was fieldwalked. The part of the M3 fieldwalking around the town of Polgár was organised by the Déri Museum in Debrecen, with finance from the M3 motorway company, channelled through Eötvös Loránd University Department of Archaeology. While Pali himself didn't want to develop an international collaboration with me, since he already had one with Meier-Arendt and a full programme of M3 fieldwork as well, he suggested a collaborator from his Department of Archaeology – József Laszlovszky, a medievalist with an excellent command of Western archaeological theory and a good record in organising field projects. At the same time, Pali suggested that this collaboration should involve not only ELTE, with Professor Bóna its Head of Department, but also the Hungarian Academy of Sciences Institute of Archaeology, led by Professor Sándor Bökönyi. Sándor Bökönyi sealed the deal by proposing his then colleague Magdi Vicze as one of the main contributors to the project. Thus, in 1990 and very much behind the back of János Makkay, I regret to say, I worked on a project brief to develop fieldwalking in three survey blocks – the Polgár block, the Bodrogköz in the lowest-lying areas between the Tisza and the river Bodrog and the Zemplén block – an upland block north of Mount Tokaj. This outline plan was accepted by the Hungarians and we jointly decided on a five-year project in which we would have regular seasons of intensive fieldwalking in the three survey blocks, a trial excavation in Year Four on one of the lowland sites – to be decided the year before – and a Year Five trial excavation in a site in the Zemplén block – also to be decided closer to the time. The two sides agreed that the British side would fund the project, with financial support primarily from the British Academy but also from the Society of Antiquaries of London, National Geographic Society and Newcastle

Plate 1. The author at the Lion Gate, Mycenae

Plate 2. John Nandris with his cat Oedipuss

Plate 3. The Danube section, Vinča-Belo Brdo, Serbia

Plate 4. Sandy shore, Lepenski Vir, Serbia

Plate 5. Maja Martinović in local costume, Reşiţa, Romania

Plate 6. The author in local costume with the local cat, Reşiţa, Romania

Plate 7. The author's Morris Minor in concentration camp, the Niš Museum's outstation, Serbia

Plate 8. Pavel Dolukhanov (right) with Kevin Greene (centre) and Peter Fowler (left) at Castle Hill, Alnham, Northumberland

Plate 9. Velika pećina, Lošinj, North Dalmatia

Plate 10. Šime Batović at the Roman cistern, Nadin hill-fort, with Huw Evans (inside the cistern) and, from left to right, A. N. Other, Siniša Bilić, Branka Nedved and Ivna Anzulović

Plate 11. The Ottoman bridge at Mostar, Bosnia and Hercegovina, in 1980, before its destruction

Plate 12. The Venetian clocktower of the Zadar Ethnographic Museum, Croatia

Plate 13. Rob Shiel, with Robin and Diana Fursdon, Bükk Mountains, Hungary

Plate 14. Upper Tisza Project team, 1992

Plate 15. Mount Tokaj, with Tokaj wine inset, Hungary

Plate 16. Manor house, Újhuta, Hungary

Plate 17. Gheorghe Dumitroaia (left), Dan Monah (centre) and Mark Francis (right), Piatra Neamţ, Romania

Plate 18. Figurine of a big cat, Goljamo Delchevo, Bulgaria

Plate 19. Fragmented model of a 'sanctuary', Căscioarele, Romania

Plate 20. The Danube downstream of Călăraşi, Romania

Plate 21. Kristian Kristiansen casting his vote at the Maastricht Annual Meeting of the EAA

Plate 22. Henry Cleere, at an EAA Inter-ABM meeting

Plate 23. The author, supported by Bisserka, signing the Marriage Register, Durham Registry Office

Plate 24. Rocky landscape opposite Çayönü Tepesi, Eastern Turkey

Plate 25. Sacred mountain, Sevilla Basin, south-east Spain

Plate 26. Boyan's graduation photo, with Bisserka and the author

Plate 27. (from right) Anthony Harding, Burcin Erdoğu, Bisserka Gaydarska and Dan Monah at Tuz Gölü, Turkey

Plate 28. The author receiving a framed print of the University, on the occasion of his Honorary Doctorate, University of Alba Iulia, Romania

Plate 29. Ghiţa and Magda Lazarovici with Bisserka Gaydarska, Sofiyivsky Landscape Park, Uman, Ukraine

Plate 30. Experimental one-storey 'Neolithic' house with two-storey house burning, Nebelivka village, Ukraine

Plate 31. Nebelivka Project Travelling Exhibition, National Museum of Moldovan History, Chişinau, Moldova

Plate 32. Bisserka Gaydarska and other winners with their Shanghai Archaeological Forum Top Ten Fieldwork Awards, Shanghai, China, 2015

University. One of the principal benefits that the project could offer comprised two visiting scholarships for undergraduate and postgraduate students per year, with the fellows to come to the University of Newcastle for one term, help the project out with project research, provide Hungarian lessons for ther British side and have the opportunity to do targeted reading. I thought that this programme of 10 students coming to the UK over the five-year project to develop their skills in archaeological method and theory was a very positive step, which was very much welcomed by Pali Raczky. The three institutions made a formal agreement, with a starting date in September 1991.

There are at least four ways of finding archaeological sites in Hungary. The first is very simple and it deals with monuments. Look for a mound; if there are lots of sherds on the mound, it's probably a tell and if there are hardly any sherds at all, it's probably a barrow. The second traditional way is to find a good high first river terrace, preferably above a river well-stocked with fish, and walk along it and you'll be sure to find lots of sites. The third way is perhaps more *recherché*. Otto Trogmayer told me about this when he showed me around Körös sites near Szeged. He said that if you watch where hares lie down on the earth, you will find a Neolithic site. His reasoning was very simple: Neolithic sites have many pits and the pits would be filled with soil, providing an extra depth of soil, which means that the area above these pits tends to retain heat better than thinner soil, attracting hares who appreciate this warmth. The fourth method of finding a site is probably the riskiest and this has not yet been known to yield many new discoveries. When István Ecsedy was working in the Bükk mountains on a hillfort excavation in the 1960s, he would spend the week working on the dig while his wife was living in Pécs and she came to join him at the weekends. One Saturday morning, they went for a walk in the forests far from the hillfort so as to resume conjugal activities. It is not recorded who was relatively higher in this operation, so to speak, but the lower partner stopped the activity when they felt something very hard scratching their back. When they looked hard, they found that they were lying on top of a bronze axe. Upon further investigation, they found several more bronze axes and in fact had turned up a hoard of late Bronze Age socketed axes. So the fourth way to find sites is through copulation. Alas, it has not been tried sufficiently frequently to tell whether it's a successful way of finding new archaeological sites – but it must certainly be the most pleasurable way.

The 1980s were the time when Geographical Information Systems (or 'GIS') were starting to make an impact in archaeology. I was actually in America in 1985 when I first heard of this approach, when the American archaeologist Kenneth Kvamme gave the first conference paper about GIS that I had ever come across to a specialist meeting in Denver. In the late 1980s, this new technology was around but not widely used, even in America, and hardly used at all in Britain. One or two departments had made a one-year appointment for a spatial archaeologist to explore the archaeological potential of GIS (*e.g.*, Cambridge appointed Chris Scull in the 1980s) but no British department had really taken this technology on board. As part of my forward planning for the Hungarian project in 1989, I thought that GIS would be an important way of developing the project, so I made a small tour of American departments that had started working with GIS. The department of Anthropology that really impressed me was in the University of Arkansas in Little Rock, where Fred Limp had started up a GIS operation with three other colleagues, using free GRASS software based on American military products. Fred convinced me that GIS was really the way to go and showed me the potential of the software. I decided that I would try to set up a GIS lab with cutting-edge kit at Newcastle and persuade the University to back this scheme by providing funds for a three-year appointment. In 1991, we advertised the post and interviewed four candidates, of whom the outstanding person was Mark Gillings. Mark came to Newcastle and managed to stay for five years and, with his experience of GIS and the knowledge I'd collected on my American trip, we managed to equip a GIS lab with state-of-the-art kit and set up the first GIS-based project in British archaeology. Mark did crucial work in operationalising GIS and especially digitising dozens (he would say hundreds!) of Hungarian 1:10,000 maps and producing a project geodatabase – a really important step.

The first season was based on the village of Polgár and we would complete a field survey in as much of the Polgár Block as was possible given the one-month season and the number of participating fieldwalkers. For the first season, we had the loan of the University of Newcastle Land Rover but as soon as possible we purchased a project van – a white Ford Transit van called 'Seaview' in honour of the Hungarian's lack of a maritime zone. We drove project kit and some students to Hungary in our vehicle.

The accommodation in Polgár was based on wooden huts in the Polgár campsite. While some students brought their own tents, most of the team lived in the huts. The principal delight of the Polgár campsite was the presence of the thermal pool complex opposite the campsite. This consisted of a series of pools, the hottest of which remained at 35°C for the whole year, with slightly cooler adjoining pools. At the end of a hot, hard day's fieldwalking, there was nothing better than to plunge into the hot pool at the grand cost of a five-forint (then 16 p) entrance fee. The social structure of the village was mirrored in the spatial access to the inlet pipe in the warmest pool. Closest to the pipe were the old men of the village, next the older women, then the middle-aged men and women, further away the younger villagers and furthest away the excavation team. This unchanging social structure was frustrating for 90% of the bathers but no one dared to challenge gerontocratic primacy.

The field survey methods we used in the Upper Tisza Project (UTP) were similar to the methods that that we'd used in the Neothermal Dalmatia Project but with the enormous advantage of having detailed, 1:10,000 scale maps. The two reasons why we started the 1991 field season in September were the reduced heat and the agricultural schedule, which gave us access to many freshly ploughed fields. We were able to record a large number of field scatters across the whole of the Block, using 10 m or 25 m spacing between fieldwalkers. One observation that we made in the first season was that the notion of offsite scatters was hard to sustain. In most cases, concentrations of pottery indicated site scatters and it was quite difficult to work out what was going on between the sites. One important finding that echoed the results of other surveys in southern Hungary was that there were high concentration of sites in the same small area – that is to say that 80% of the sites were found in 20% of the landscape. We developed this idea through the idea of 'multi-community zones'.

The aerial photographs of Block 1 and the detailed topographical maps showed a profusion of hitherto-undated palaeo-channels, often cut off by other palaeo-channels. This gave us an excellent opportunity for working out a dated sequence of palaeo-channel development. For that reason, Pavel Dolukhanov (Plate 8), who had joined the department in 1990, came with us to Hungary, bringing a fine Dutch peat pollen corer with him. We were hopeful that the peat corer would be sufficient to take samples from the Polgár Block palaeo-channels. I had also made contact in 1980 with Professor Zoltán Borsy from the University of Debrecen Department of Geography, who had probably cored more sediments than anybody else in north-east Hungary. He drove over from Debrecen on the first morning of the palaeo-environmental fieldwork. He looked slightly askance at the Dutch pollen corer but didn't make any overt comments. When we went off to attempt the first coring in a nearby palaeo-channel, I think Professor Borsy was the only person in the group who was not surprised that, after 30 minutes, the Dutch pollen corer broke and could no longer function. Professor Borsy generously offered the use of a corer that was used to tough Hungarian sediments and I had to drive him straight back to Debrecen to collect such a corer, which he lent to us for the rest of the season. Zoltán's advice on where (and how) to core made a huge difference to the success of the palaeo-environmental programme.

The other environmental study was the soils research run by Rob Shiel (Plate 13). Despite being in a wheelchair following his accident in Zimbabwe,[1] Rob was able to carry on soils research on the flat Hungarian plain, with the dry-as-dust dirt roads quite adequate for Rob to move around on, even finding several archaeological sites by identifying lithic scatters. Rob had one or two soils students as his 'eyes' for soil mapping off the main network of tracks, enabling him to build up a project soil map.

Working conditions for the survey teams varied very much, from the first- and second-terrace ploughed fields with their lighter soils to the arduous heavy clays in the floodplain areas. These differences influenced the strategy of the sampling of those areas to be fieldwalked because most Hungarian teams ignored the floodplains, assuming, for the most part correctly, that there would be few settlement remains there. In fact, we found a few site scatters as well as quite a lot of single finds scattered across the floodplains and so this was one of the areas where we could contribute to survey methodology in Hungary – by looking intensively at where no one else had looked.

When we started out in 1991, Polgár was still officially called a 'village' and that was the sort of feel that it had as you went around the handful of shops in the 'centre'.

---

[1] See pp. 100–101.

It was also the impression I had when I went to the only bank in the village to cash travellers' cheques for project wages. I had made very sure that the travellers' cheques I brought had the very latest designs. Unfortunately, the Polgár bank would not accept travellers' cheques of any design and when I asked, 'Why can't you give me money for travellers' cheques – they're perfectly legal?', the teller looked at me with total amazement and said, 'But we are a bank' – as if giving out money was not something banks did. So once a week, I had to travel to the next town across the Tisza – recently renamed Tiszaújváros from the more formidable-sounding 'Leninváros' after the fall of the Berlin wall – where I found the only place in Block 1 that would change travellers' cheques – the Tiszaújváros tourist office. The other advantage was that next door was a café with really good espressos.

Although there was only one bank in Polgár, there were several restaurants, the finest of which was the 'White Raven' (Hungarian: '*Féher Holló*') – the place where people came for wedding receptions for miles around. It was impossible to eat in the *Féher Holló* at weekends but, on most other evenings, you would find the team there. The restaurant had a fantastic range of food, with only one blind spot. In the early 1980s, hardly anyone in Hungary had heard of vegetarian cooking – it was even quite difficult to find vegetarian options in restaurants in Budapest, so why would I expect a Polgár restaurant to have vegetarian options? The small number of students who were vegetarians had a narrow range of food, consisting mainly of toasted cheese sandwiches, baked potatoes, grilled mushrooms and a range of salads. There was one valiant attempt by the cook to prepare boiled broccoli for the vegetarians. Although I'm not a vegetarian, I thought this sounded extremely good and I tried it and it tasted extremely meaty. Before it was served to the vegetarians, I asked the cook how he had prepared it and he said that he had of course boiled the broccoli in meat juice to give it a good flavour. So it was impossible in that first season to get very far with vegetarian meals. To the credit of the *Féher Holló*, we did manage to train up the chef slowly and, when we came back to Polgár in 1994, vegetarian dishes were definitely on the menu.

The greatest attraction of the *Féher Holló* was the resident band – *Kiss Duo* – a bass guitarist and a keyboards player who also 'sang'. My most treasured possessions from the first season were the very first music cassettes that *Kiss Duo* had ever recorded. I bought 10 copies of the cassette and gave them to the most musical friends I had in Newcastle. *Kiss Duo* had a limited range of music, though wider than the gypsy violinist who played at my wedding.[2] They started with the same tune each evening, went through the same repertoire and finished with the same tune an hour and a half later. While some of us found this hilarious, some students who really couldn't stand *Kiss Duo* gave up meals in the *Féher Holló* and went off to a pub to steep themselves in Tokaj wine or *pálinka* (aka fruit brandy).

[2] See pp. 49–50.

The second season of the UTP (1992) was based on a low-lying area between the Tisza and Bodrog, well to the north of the Polgár block and east of the town of Tokaj. One of the lessons that we learned from the first season of the UTP was that fieldwalking of all parts of the Block was important, no matter the quality of the soil. We continued to fieldwalk widely, even in areas such as north-west Nyírség where there was a lot of relatively infertile sandy soil. The other method of investigation we were trialling was geophysical investigation, run by a Newcastle colleague from the Department of Physics called Clive Titman. Clive drove out to Hungary in his sexy red sports car, which caused quite a stir in his field visits to remote villages.

Accommodation was much harder to arrange, since campsites in the Block were few and far between. Our friends in the Jósa András Museum in Nyíregyháza had identified a campsite on the River Tisza north of the city but a long way outside Block 2. Camping Ibrány had just enough wooden huts to take the team, so we had a fantastic base right next to the Tisza, run by a cook who enjoyed fishing. We had the most amazing fish-and-chips dinner in Hungarian style – with carp or catfish – every night.

The team members that season (Plate 14) didn't come from only Newcastle or Budapest but also from Vilnius. I'd been in touch by email with three Lithuanian archaeologists – Giedrius, Algis and Zenonas – who had enquired if it was possible to join the team. When I agreed, they said that they would make their own way from Vilnius to whatever address we gave them. Equipped with the address of our campsite, the Lithuanians arranged to arrive on the Sunday before the season started. When the Newcastle group arrived in 'Seaview', the Lithuanians had beaten us to it and they were sitting in the campsite, drinking cold beer. They told us the story of their epic train trip. They had taken the first train from Vilnius to Minsk, the second train to Chop, the border town between Ukraine and Hungary, where they walked across the border to take the third train to Nyíregyháza and then had to find the narrow-gauge railway (fourth train), which took them to Ibrány, only 5 km walk to the campsite. It was a great piece of Central European navigation – we had three more very competent archaeologists on the team.

Another important project place near the campsite was the village of Nagyhalász, which, like most Hungarian villages, had Friday night discos. We would pile into Seaview, with nine or ten students, plus the three Lithuanians, and drive to the village disco. One evening, the music was so retro it could have come from the Bronze Age and everyone was dancing like crazy. But I had noticed from the corner of my eye that Zenonas the Lithuanian was flirting with the local village girls and this had also been spotted by the beefy Hungarian village blokes, who were looking askance at Zenonas. It was Zenonas the newlywed who made the first move on the dance floor and this slow, up-close dance almost led to all-out war between the locals and our team. It took all the skill I could muster, with the help of Giedrius and Algis, to get Zenonas, who was really drunk by then, off the dance floor and into the transit van. At this point, I said that I would bring the van back later to collect the team but Mark suggested that I had better stay with the Lithuanians, so he came with us to drive the van back. This was lucky because it took three people to hold Zenonas down in the back of the van. At one point, he escaped and pushed me so hard that I almost drove into the Tisza. I parked the van so that there would be a clear exit from the back door straight into the Lithuanians' hut. Zenonas leapt out of the van and did two forward rolls straight into his hut, where he fell asleep on the floor till the next morning. At least we had avoided a diplomatically disastrous village incident.

One of the really great places that Pali Raczky had introduced me to privately before the Bodrogköz season was the village restaurant in Tiszadob. The restaurant was run by a genial giant of a man called Dezső Galambos with his tiny redhead wife Pötyike. For a long time, Dezső had been the main chef in a Socialist party hotel in Nyíregyháza but he quit after two decades of cooking fillet steak and chips most days of the week for most of the visitors. He was in his early 50s and Dezső had saved enough money to buy a large village house in Tiszadob and convert the bottom floor into the village restaurant. Dezső had collected mementoes of the 50s from other old pubs, which he used to decorate the walls of his restaurant. He had a menu from 1955 with the top price for a drink being 3 forints. Another menu listed the kinds of *Spritzer* (white wine with soda water) on sale, varying from 20% soda (*nagy mester*), one-third soda (*nagyfröccs*) to a 50:50 (*kisfröccs*). Dezső ran his restaurant on the basis of three very simple policies. He would cook one dish for lunch and one dish for supper; he would charge a fixed price for drinks; and, most importantly, he had no set prices for his dishes but simply asked for what the customer thought they were worth. While this was a perfectly fine principle for most guests, this was dangerous with undergraduates and I had to be circumspect in ensuring that everyone paid a decent rate to Dezső. Once a week, we would call him to book enough tables for us to have a special meal. In fact, Dezső's cooking was so superb that we booked it for the end-of-season party, hired a coach so everyone could drink whatever they liked and had a fantastic meal. It was only many years later that I heard from Pali that Dezső had died. We raise a glass of *Kisfröccs* to a fantastic family and a wonderful restaurant.

The other centre that we visited once a week for a night out was the town of Tokaj, famous for its conical volcanic hill and its fortified wines (Fig. 15). I had long been visiting No. 25, Main Street, Tokaj, where a village lady with her own vineyard would sell me different kinds of Tokaj wines. On one of our evenings out, we went up the moderately steep other Main Street, Óvár utca, in Tokaj, calling at every restaurant on the way. Each restaurant had its own wine cellar and we would take Rob down into the wine cellar for a drink and then pull him and his wheelchair up the steps of the cellar. This wine cellar crawl got out of hand and we must have taken Rob to five or six. At a certain moment, he must have realised that we were not keeping as close an eye on him as we should and he started his wheelchair rolling down the hill. At the bottom of the hill, there was a roundabout and 30 m beyond that a patch of grass, followed by a steep drop into the River Bodrog. Five or six of us raced downhill after him and caught him just as he arrived at the roundabout. This was probably one of the greatest rides that Rob ever had, for his jailors never allowed him to escape from them again.

Preparations for the 1993 season started in Budapest, when it was agreed that the student team would meet me on the steps of the Hungarian National Museum at 10 o'clock on the last Saturday in August – an echo of the place where the revolutionaries were supposed to meet before starting the 1848 Revolution (they also arrived two hours late!). We drove up in convoy to the Zemplén Mountains, where colleagues in the Ottó Hermann Museum in Miskolc had found us a fantastic base in the centre of the Zemplén Mountains. In a small valley, there were three villages called '*huta*', meaning 'glassworks' – all founded during the expansion of Zemplén glass production in the 17th and 18th centuries. The first, or lowest, village was Óhuta ('*Ó*' means 'old'), the middle village was Középhuta ('*közép*' means 'middle') and the latest and highest was Újhuta ('*új*' means 'new'). Museum colleagues had found for us the manor house, or Palace, in Újhuta – also built in the 18th century and in extremely good repair (Plate 16). It had been fitted out as a youth holiday centre and had nice bedrooms, a dining hall, a basketball court in front and plenty of space for football. Everyone was extremely happy with their accommodation in 1993. It was especially impressive for important visitors!

The economics of Újhuta village, however, were in a dire state. Since it was one of those villages where most of the young people had already left for jobs in Miskolc, Debrecen or Budapest, I thought that buying food for the team would help the village economy a little. When I went around the village with Magdi Vicze, we first went to the bakers, where we enquired whether it would be possible to bake an extra 10 loaves of bread a day for the next 30 days. Much to our surprise, the baker turned us down flat, stating that there were 24 working houses in the village and he baked 24 1 kg loaves of bread a day and that was all. This was irritating because it meant a long drive to the village of Tolcsva every day to get fresh bread. There was, however, an upside to this trip. Next to the Tolcsva bakers was a wine shop which sold Tokaj Furmint – the early, non-vintage form of Tokaj that could be drunk six months after being produced. So as long as project members brought me plentiful numbers of empty 2 litre lemonade bottles, we could buy as much Furmint as the team could drink in a day. By contrast, the Újhuta villagers had no sense of economic survival and this also applied to tourism, in the sense that if they set up a small village tourist company with accommodation provided in village homes, the village could presumably have made quite a lot of money – after all, Újhuta was a beautiful spot near even lovelier places. However, this idea foundered on the hospitality of the residents, who thought it was wrong to charge people money to stay in their homes if they had a spare bed and they liked the visitors. So tourism really wasn't going to work in Újhuta. Nonetheless, for the project these were minor logistical problems that could be easily solved and we had a fine base in which we were close to the central parts of our Block.

The only places to do traditional fieldwalking in ploughed fields were the inter-montane basins and even there the amount of traditional fieldwalking was much reduced since ploughing was sporadic. Although we spent quite a lot of time walking over fallow fields, we didn't get many results. The other zone that was essential for us to cover was the forested area, in which there were two principal hazards – first, the poisonous common adder and, secondly and more seriously, ticks so large that they actually lived off the snakes much of the time. If someone was bitten by a Zemplén tick, they certainly knew about it and we would have to deal with it that same day – otherwise, there was a severe risk of encephalitis leading to hospitalisation. We had volunteer 'tick squads' who checked fieldwalkers in the evenings for a week until another 'tick squad' took over. Because of these precautions, no one was hospitalised.

Forest-walking produced a totally different set of results from anything we'd ever found in the lowlands but, because there was very little datable pottery, we found it very difficult to date the landscape features (technically called 'humps and bumps') which were prolific under the tree cover. One of the main types of feature that we encountered was the Holloway – the remains of an ancient trackway. We sometimes found small local holloways going from one place in the valley to another. In other places were multiple holloways, where the track had been repaired and regenerated because it followed an important route. But we also found fragments of longer-distance tracks leading from village to village. One of the great achievements of Mark Gillings' GIS research was to link up the fragments of inter-village tracks with the quantified shortest distance routes (least cost analysis) that could be constructed from digitised GIS maps. The other class of find that we made concerned industrial remains. I've already mentioned the expansion of glass-making, which could be tracked through the distribution of glass-production sites. There were also mills with their mill-races and a lot of other water-management features on the streams of the central Zemplén. Although we didn't have the resources to make accurate plots of all of these features, we could at least locate them accurately on 1:10,000-scale maps and produce publishable sketch plans.

The other type of feature that we found in the Zemplén inter-montane basins was the remains of ridge-and-furrow cultivation – something we'd rarely encountered in the lowland Block 1 but which formed well-preserved fields in the Regéc Basin. Here, the ridge-and-furrow cultivation was used certainly into the 19th century and possibly even into the 20th century. The Regéc Basin was akin to a well-preserved medieval landscape, with its ruined 13th-century stone castle built on a peak on the south-east side and overlooking the whole basin. The linear village with houses attached to long fields with extensive traces of ridge-and-furrow lay near a feature which the project discovered through a combination of topographical survey and archival research. This was the third, long-lost Pauline monastery of Regéc, which Jóska and his students had located in the archives and whose field remains – the stone walls of the monastic building, a fishpond and its field boundaries – confirmed it was the missing monastery. This was a very important and interesting find to which both fieldwalking and the study of medieval manuscripts made their contribution.

Another aspect of our fieldwork concerned lithic raw materials and it became very clear from the datable pottery scatters that two of the only three phases of occupation in the Zemplén Mountains were closely related to lithic raw material sources – the Middle Neolithic and the Late Bronze Age (the third phase was the medieval and post-medieval settlement of the upland villages). One of the great stars of Hungarian archaeology – Katalin (Kati) Biró – worked in the Hungarian National Museum and, along with colleagues in the museum, had created an internationally famous '*Lithoteka*', which consisted of the databases of all the lithic raw material sources that Kati and her colleagues had found in Hungary, along with large quantities of samples of the raw material from each source. While the Lithoteka had started in the 1980s, Kati expanded it into the 21st century to include more sources from Hungary but also from other countries in the Carpathian Basin. This was a fantastic database and Kati was extremely pleased to join the project and work with our own lithic specialist, Karen Hardy. The third, key member of the Biró-Hardy team was Kati's Trabant, which she'd used to enormous effect and which managed to climb virtually any hill in Hungary, no matter how steep, and helped Kati to reach a huge range of the Zemplén raw material sources. Over a two-week period, the Biró-Hardy team managed to locate over 40 lithic raw material sources in Block 3, including ones for which the Lithoteka had no previous raw material samples.

The other strand of our fieldwork concerned palaeo-environmental and specifically soils reconstructions with Rob Shiel, whose constraints on mobility in this Upland zone made it much harder for him around the Zemplén region and left much more work for his two soil students. They clambered over much of the uplands, taking samples for Rob after intensive early morning de-briefing. For one week, we were joined by a Zoltán Borsy student from Debrecen, Timea Kiss, who was a botanist wishing to core the only marsh with a published pollen diagram from the Zemplén area. Unfortunately, the coring lasted 30 minutes before we hit solid rock, so we could never produce a vegetation history for the upland zone.

The Zemplén season was a very different fieldwork season from those of the two lowland blocks, underlining the importance of doing this work. No one previously had devoted such an intensive fieldwork season to a Hungarian upland zone. In fact, the only intensive project-based reconnaissance previously done in the Zemplén was by Nándor Kalicz, John Nandris and Olwen Williams (later Williams-Thorpe) who were seeking to locate the Carpathian sources of obsidian. The main Slovakian source at Szőllőske was clearly defined, with large blocks of outcropping obsidian blocks, as we saw on our 1995 visit. But in the south Zemplén area, Nandris and Williams were dealing with the remains of a volcanic eruption in which obsidian balls were thrown up into the air and scattered very widely but in low density across an area of several square kilometres. Thus, it was never really a surprise that the

Carpathian 1 (Szőlőske/Viničky, Slovakia) source was the preferred source for 80 or 90% of all of the analysed obsidian tools. But this didn't stop us from making some interesting discoveries in the Zemplén region, with its extreme diversity of lithic raw material sources.

The fourth project season in 1994 was an excavation season, in which we returned to the lowlands and settled into a new civic entity – the *town* of Polgár. Many things had changed since our 1991 season there. The biggest change in Polgár was that it did been promoted from a mere village to a new town, the population threshold being more than 8,000 people. There was a new market area and many of the shops had become more prosperous, with a wider range of goods for sale. The biggest factor was the construction work on the M3 motorway, which brought large numbers of well-paid construction workers into town. However, some of the best features of Polgár had not changed. The campsite with its fantastic thermal pool was still working and the *Fehér Holló* restaurant was still the best restaurant in town, now doing more to cater for vegetarian students than it did in 1991. Some of the team were pleased to discover that *Kiss Duo* was still in musical residence at the restaurant.

Because of the flood of rescue excavations, Pali Raczky's Polgár-Csőszhalom excavations had paused and Pali and many other colleagues were excavating sites along the line of the M3 motorway. This was all part of a huge national rescue effort by all field archaeologists in Hungary, which included any colleagues who could come from neighbouring countries. Motorway developments were planned in fully 15 of the 19 Hungarian counties and it was the county museums that were tasked with organising the rescue work. The county museum of Hajdú-Bihar – the Déri Museum in Debrecen – was fortunate that Pali Raczky already had an excavation based in the county and was on excellent terms with the M3 construction firm. Pali had now established a rescue excavation base in Polgár, funded largely by the M3 motorway programme, for his team's accommodation and for post-excavation finds processing.

As our small part of the rescue excavation efforts, Pali proposed that we excavated the Middle Neolithic site of Polgár-10 in the bend of the Kengyel palaeo-channel 7 km east of the town. The fieldwalking plans of the site showed that the M3 crossed only the lowest, middle part of the site – an area of 650 × 70–80 m – with the site extending both north and south onto low hills. It became clear that we needed to scrape back the topsoil over the 5,400 m^2 area, so Pali organised for us his most experienced machine driver – a wizened man of the plains called *Pista bácsi* (*i.e.*, 'Old Uncle István') (Fig. 16), who had had decades of experience driving and was phenomenally skilled – he could remove soil depths of anything from 10 cm to 2 cm for a given area. The common practice in the other motorway rescue excavations was to excavate down until the first cut features, whether post-holes or pits. Unfortunately, this collapsed the cultural stratigraphy into a single level and it was not possible to tell the ground surface from which the cut features were cut. Our alternative method was to remove the topsoil down to the top of the cultural deposits and then select areas for excavation of the

Fig. 16. Pista bacsi *('Old Uncle István') with his machine, Polgár-10, Hungary*

upper cultural horizon and other areas where we sacrificed these layers and went down to the lower cultural horizons. This was, in effect, a sampling strategy for the different phases of the site occupation, which, on Polgár-10, all belonged to the Middle Neolithic. I still claim that this was one of the few rescue sites on the M3 motorway that was excavated stratigraphically.

Once again, we were living in the wooden huts of the Polgár campsite and continuing to enjoy the delights of the thermal pool after work. In 1994, it was the turn of the British team to organise the end-of-dig party – a huge *gulyás* party making use of the concrete hearths in the campsite. We borrowed two enormous metal cauldrons from the campsite manager and started to make the *gulyás* in the early evening. When the members of the Hungarian team started to appear, they asked us why we were cooking two *gulyás* dishes and we explained that this was quite simple: one of them was a meat *gulyás* and the other one was a vegetarian *gulyás*. 'A vegetarian *gulyás*,' said the Hungarians in total horror, 'you can't be serious!' But, by 1994, the number of British students who had vegetarian diets had grown to perhaps a quarter of the team, so vegetarian *gulyás* was essential, though never something that the Hungarian side accepted.

By the end of our four-week season, we managed to excavate all of the sectors of Polgár-10 down to the depths which we had targeted and, at that point, we abandoned the site to its eventual destruction by the motorway. It was only in 1997, after much discussion at both the national and the regional level, that the M3 motorway company had to change the route further away from Polgár so as not to damage archaeological sites. In effect, the motorway company couldn't afford to have them all excavated. So the M3 motorway never actually destroyed the Polgár-10 site at all. Nevertheless, the stratigraphic excavation of a Middle Neolithic site was still a very useful operation.

In 1995, the final major field season in Hungary was held back in the Zemplén Mountains, where we had decided to excavate the only multi-period field scatter that we'd found in our fieldwalking season. This was the site of Regéc-95 in the Regéc Basin, on a long sloping hill above the village of Regéc. Although we knew that there was Middle Neolithic and Late Bronze Age pottery on the site, we had no idea how to differentiate the two occupations. It was also not known whether the Late Bronze Age people were great users of the copious lithics that we found in the fields all over the site. Regéc-95 was also quite a large site by Zemplén standards, so we needed to choose areas for excavation within the total surface. Before the excavations started, Keri Brown and I arrived to set up a site grid of 10 × 10 m squares in which we would make a surface collection of sherds and also make a phosphate analysis to see if there were differences in the quality and depth of the soil. This helped us to choose where to locate our trenches.

The excavation went well but the key problem that we had anticipated was how to differentiate between Neolithic lithics and Late Bronze Age lithics. Often, there was very little stratigraphic difference between the two and the depth of soil was so small that quite often Late Bronze Age finds were found mixed with Middle Neolithic material. This was only solved through typological analysis in the 1998 post-excavation season.

The other aspect of the site excavation which was very difficult was that there were very few structural features that were left on either the Neolithic or the Bronze Age ground surfaces. In some of the trenches, we did find traces of stone lines on what we took to be the Late Bronze Age ground surface but, at the time, we couldn't link these lines in a plan of the whole excavation. Again, we had to wait until the lab season in 1998 before we understood that the parts of a structure that appeared in three different trenches made sense as a Late Bronze Age structure – probably a light, seasonal house. Such preserved upland site features were rare in the Carpathian Basin.

The accommodation for 1995 was organised in the lowland village of Boldogkőváralja (literally 'the meadow by the castle on the Happy Rock'). This village was located in the Hernád valley, on the western edge of the Zemplén mountains. This meant that the field team had to drive up to the Regéc Basin for excavation each day – a drive of some 25 km through the stunning autumnal colours of the Zemplén woodland. There were two kinds of accommodation available in the village: the eight members of staff were put in four village houses, while there was a less salubrious, former barrack block on the edge of the village for all of the students. I was not in favour of this social stratification of staff and students but there was no other way to accommodate the team since, unfortunately, the Újhuta manor house had already been booked for that season.

One of the delights of working in the Zemplén in September was that it was already mushroom season. In Regéc-95, several village workers who excavated with us were skilled mushroom-pickers and became aware that Keri Brown was very fond of fresh mushrooms. From then onwards, a small plastic bag full of fresh mushrooms appeared in Keri's trench, which she kindly shared with the rest of the team. One day when we were driving back to Boldogkőváralja, one of the students was caught short and we had to park the Transit while the student went into the woods to relieve themselves. They came out shouting, 'I've found an absolute treasure of mushrooms!' and indeed we had never seen such a dense growth of edible mushrooms in any part of the Regéc Basin. However, I made a policy decision that we should not interfere with the villagers' best woodland crop. The news reached the village mushroom-gatherers that, although we had discovered their main mushroom patch, we hadn't raided it, so their fungal generosity continued throughout the season.

There was only one really strange moment in what was perhaps the first crime in Regéc village that year or perhaps even longer. One of the students had brought a fancy camera to the site each day to take personal site photographs. The student had by mistake left the camera on site when clearing up at the end of the day, which he remembered when we had already returned to Boldogkőváralja. No one really wanted to drive back up to the site and we thought it was a fine evening and a nice night with no rain, so even if the camera-case might suffer a little bit from early morning dew, the camera itself would remain intact. This was a bad mistake, for when we returned to the site in the morning, the camera was no longer there. The Hungarian team leader Magdi Vicze decided to go to the police station in Regéc village to report the theft. The only village policeman took one moment to understand and said, 'Ah, that's probably *János*.'[3] He explained that János was one of the very few people living in the village with a police record for petty theft and said he was confident that he would be able to retrieve the camera. Which was exactly what happened. János came along to the site with a bag of mushrooms to apologise for his action, claiming that he was merely looking after the camera and making sure it wouldn't get wet overnight. After all, this was plausible *and* he did come up with the goods immediately when he was challenged by the policeman. So the student was lucky enough to get the camera back as well as all of his photographs and some mushrooms.

The Regéc-95 season was the last of the major UTP fieldwork seasons but, in 1996, a small team returned to Polgár to investigate intra-site pottery distributions on a sample of multi-period sites. This was a necessary step in estimating the size of each phase of occupation. We had managed to complete a small number of intra-site gridded collections over the years but we never had time to make this a priority for more than a few sites. Our plan was for a small team led by Josh Pollard – at the time a post-doc in Newcastle – to sample two dozen sites in the Polgár block in

[3] NOT Makkay!

September. I went out with Josh and the team to introduce him to the delights of Polgár town, to indicate the areas where collections should have been possible and to identify most of the main sites on our hit list. Unfortunately, September 1996 was the wettest September of the 1990s; it rained almost every day and it was clear that I had made the right move in going off for the first month of my three-month museum trip, in western Hungary. I cruelly abandoned Josh and the team to pick up the pieces during those occasional dry hours. It was greatly to Josh's credit that, despite the weather, he came back with a very precise and superbly-recorded set of intra-site gridded collection data. I was really sorry that I missed this season but I had to start my sabbatical year with a three-month museum tour.[4]

The research during my sabbatical year, which lasted from October 1996 to September 1997, also stymied work on the UTP post-excavation studies until the next year. In summer 1998, we held a lab season in ELTE thanks to Pali Raczky's hospitality. By that time, his Department of Archaeology in ELTE had been renamed the 'Institute of Archaeological Sciences' – a political move to rival the Hungarian Academy of Sciences Institute of Archaeology with its new focus on spatial studies and archaeological science. The ELTE Institute was the first Department of Archaeology in Hungary to set up a full-scale GIS lab, with an integrated geodatabase recording system for all of the M3 rescue excavations.

We had a small team of six people to complete the post-excavation recording of all six UTP seasons. The team included Steve Cousins who worked on the lithic samples, Leanne Stowe and Denise Telford worked on the ceramics and Steve Leyland who worked on the spatial aspect of recording, especially with the single finds. This was an immensely productive season because it was the first time that we were able to study and record the pottery peacefully and in much more detail than before. We had regular visits from our Hungarian colleagues who were period specialists who knew far more about the dating of prehistoric pottery.

One of the most important international visits I made that year was to Százhalombatta, which featured an Iron Age barrow cemetery as well as a Bronze Age tell on a hilltop overlooking the Danube. The museum benefitted from the location in town of the headquarters of the Hungarian petrol company MOL, who invested heavily in the museum and its activities. The director of the museum, Ildikó Poroszlai, had the vision to start up what at the time was the first experimental archaeological museum in Hungary, in which she not only reconstructed various prehistoric and early historic buildings but also developed summer schools with experimental programmes in pottery-making, metallurgy, glassmaking and other crafts. This was one of the most important museums in the whole of Hungary and it was great that the excavation of the Százhalombatta tell was chosen over the other Middle Bronze Age tells strung out along the Danube.

[4] For the fragmentation museum tour, see pp. 134 ff.

The Százhalombatta Project was a three-way international project, involving the Hungarian team from Százhalombatta, a Swedish team led by Kristian Kristiansen from Gothenburg and a Southampton team led initially by Jo Sofaer but which later morphed into a British team with a major contribution from Marie Louise Sørensen from Cambridge. One of my great summer pleasures was to visit the SAX project on their fun day (I didn't go along to the serious excavations, you understand). One feature was a triangular international football match between Százhalombatta, Southampton and Gothenburg, for whom Kristian Kristiansen played goalkeeper and, I have to admit through gritted teeth, let in remarkably few goals. I would go along and offer to play for the Southampton side, which didn't help them win any matches – as far as I remember, each season I played for Southampton, they were beaten in both matches.

The most memorable of the Százhalombatta fun days was Kristian's 50th birthday party, which was held not in the museum but in a nightclub/restaurant in a big wine cellar cut into the loess cliffs below the hillfort. The night-club benefitted from a cool atmosphere with a constant temperature, which was ideal for evening dinners. All the staff and the three teams of students and any guests went along to the nightclub. I couldn't help but notice that, at one end of the main room, was a stripper's dancing-pole, which I thought was a permanent fixture and I wondered if there was any significance to this feature. After a fantastic meal, some erotic disco music started and a blindfolded Kristian was brought into the main room and sat down on a comfortable seat. At this point, a very attractive black-haired lady with a stunning figure came out and stood by the pole and started to dance. She carelessly lost more and more clothes, until she had stripped right down to her panties (the bra went sometime before) and, at this critical moment, when the music was really getting hot, she sat down on Kristian's lap and offered herself to the birthday boy. Being a gentleman, Kristian knew exactly what he should do. I think the Gothenburg students, in particular, were embarrassed to see their professor with an almost naked stripper sitting in his lap but since he enjoyed it, why shouldn't they? Some felt that this was a fine way to celebrate the 50th birthday of a great archaeologist.

As you might imagine, there were many spin-offs from the UTP for future visits to Hungary. One of them involved a concentrated, short piece of fieldwork while I was staying in Hungary for a sabbatical year to finish off the UTP writing in 2001 to 2002. I had heard about an amazing palaeo-environmental site not very far from the town of Polgár from one of the leading young Hungarian palynologists, Enikő Magyari. Enikő had made preliminary corings in the Sarló Hát marsh (literally 'sickle back marsh') and the preliminary ^{14}C dates from two cores suggested that peat had been laid down through almost all of the Holocene period. It seemed to me that it was a very useful operation to do targeted fieldwalking around the Sarló Hát lake to identify how many Neolithic, Copper Age and Bronze Age sites existed around the lake, since it was very likely that the pollen cores would have records of human impact from such nearby settlements. So a small group of us, including my then partner Tünde, a Canadian

Masters student at Durham called Marg de Guzman and one or two students from Budapest, formed a team which stayed in a village house in Tiszagyulaháza organised by the village Mayor. Each day for a week, we drove the team out in the Saab 900 to do fieldwalking near Sarló Hát lake. The week was incredibly productive because we managed to cover all of the ploughed land around Sarló Hát and were able to define precisely the settlement pattern for sites relating directly to the human impact in the pollen core. The Mayor really hoped that we would be able to find finances for a future project based on his village. Sadly, we never managed to find the funding but Enikő's analysis of both of the Sarló Hát cores emabled her to produce two of the most detailed, best-dated pollen diagrams ever published for Hungary.

The main aim of my 2001–2 sabbatical year was to complete the writing-up of the UTP programme and prepare materials for publication. I found accommodation through a friend of a friend; an archaeologist who worked most of the year in the Hermann Ottó Museum in Miskolc but who had a flat in Budapest that he would use on his occasional trips to the capital. My friend persuaded István Paszternák that he would make a lot more money if he rented this flat to me for the year and he agreed to do this. It was a first-floor flat above a typical 19th-century courtyard on Hegedűs Gyula utca, just outside the Inner Ring and not very far from Nyugati Station. This was an area with good tram connections to many places – including west to Moszkva tér, with a short climb up the Buda Hill to the Institute of Archaeology. I would cross the Margaret Bridge on the way to Buda at a time when the Danube always showed wonderful colours in different lighting conditions – an outstanding way to start a working day. I could also take the tram east to ELTE, where the collections of the UTP were still stored, the National Museum, with its Lithoteka, the covered market near Szabadság Bridge and my favourite jazz club in Veres Pálné utca.

It was interesting to experience how the neighbourhood changed through this year. At the beginning, there were two or three corner shops which sold wine and a couple of quality supermarkets on the Inner Ring. But, by the end of the year, lots more corner and basement shops had opened, including two specialist food shops and three more specialist wine shops. The owner of one wine shop told me that this was a result of the opening-up of a lot of small, private vineyards, especially in the Balaton area, soon after the Fall of the Wall. Slowly, the products of those very early years became ready for drinking and started to come onto the market. But the quantities were never sufficient to interest large supermarkets or supermarket chains who would rather purchase 5,000 litres of *Badacsonyi rizling*, so the best possibility was for sale in small specialist wine shops. That area probably reflected the trend that was happening all over Budapest.

This was also the year when I visited for the first time the Communist Memento Park, now called the 'Sculpture Park' (Hungarian: '*Szoborpark*'), located on the south-west side of Budapest. In many parts of Central and Eastern Europe after the Fall of the Wall, there was a cataclysmic demolition of Socialist statues. Different countries had different attitudes to this rejection of the 40-year-long Socialist heritage. In Czechoslovakia, there was a father-and-son team who dynamited 93 Socialist sculptures before they were finally stopped by the state. They clearly rejected the argument that the works of some good sculptors of the post-war period could only be seen in public Socialist sculptures, whose *oeuvre* was virtually all destroyed. Hungary took a very different attitude to Socialist sculptures, which they thought should indeed be preserved. They were collected at great public expense and transported to a site outside Budapest, with a new museum building and a concert-quality sound system, which played great anthems of the Socialist period in Hungarian every quarter of an hour – an echo of Cathedral clocks. Some of the finest sculptures of the Socialist era have been transported to the sculpture park and it gives a wonderful impression of the breadth of work that was done – by no means only Soviet brutalism but a lot of very fine sculptures as well.

During my sabbatical year, I had been in touch with Staša Babić, who, like a lot of other colleagues in the University of Belgrade, had resigned their post when President Milošević had taken over the University in order to stop any independent academic research. Staša joined a number of other archaeologists to set up a Gender Studies Institute in the centre of Belgrade. Through the latter part of 2001, she negotiated with me to come and give a week-long 'Archaeology of Gender' course in Belgrade. In the course of a lot of my research and also through my university teaching, I had accumulated a lot of material on the archaeology of gender, so I was able to put together six lectures and present the framework to the new Institute. This framework seemed acceptable, especially a lecture on Queer Archaeology on the final day, to which leading members of the gay and lesbian community in Belgrade would be invited. This sounded like a grand climax to the course, to which I readily agreed. I took the train from Budapest on the Saturday and used the Sunday to catch up on seeing my old friends. This included Petar Popović ('Pera Whisky'), my best man who, for two years, was so affected by the Third Balkan War that he'd lost all powers of speech. The course was moderately well attended, with 20 to 25 people there – mostly students. The greatest disappointment was that the gay and lesbian group representatives decided they would not come to the final day's meeting, so we had a general discussion instead of a targeted discussion on Queer Archaeology.

The Belgrade that I'd known as a PhD student was gone, with the final hammer-blow the NATO bombing in March–June 1999. I was not only a foreigner but also a foreign citizen of a fully paid-up member of NATO and Staša advised me to be careful where I went in the evenings, with whom I met and what I said to strangers. As I sat in a restaurant near the university, I ate my *leskovačka mučkalica* (a speciality of the town of Leskovac in South Serbia) in silence, not daring to talk to any of the strangers in that place. This was not how things had been. But with the signs of the impact of the bombing in several public places in the centre, it was clear that there would be no early forgiveness for the bombing. Even when I talked with good Serbian friends, I found that my justification for the NATO bombing – that no local resistance could ever overthrow Milošević because his Secret Service was too effective – was angrily rejected out of pride in potential local achievements. So there was no chance of talking to strangers about this subject on that trip.

Once the course was over, I was planning to take the 8 am train from Belgrade back to Budapest, since I had tickets for my partner Tünde and me for a concert in the Grassalkovich Castle near Gödöllő, some 35 km out of Budapest. A taxi had been ordered to take me down to Belgrade Station, which I knew very well. I went towards the platform from which international trains usually left and saw to my horror that a train was moving away at the far end of the platform. I had either been given the wrong time or – hardly credible – the train had left 10 minutes early. I really had only one choice – to try to catch up with the train. I complained long and loud in my Serbo-Croat to a railway attendant, which, as was my intention, attracted the attention of the local taxi drivers. I offered $25 to anyone who could drive me to the next station at Ruma, 40 km away, and if they missed the train at Ruma, $40 more if we had to go to Novi Sad, 75 km away. For any taxi driver, the attraction of $25 was sufficient to seal the deal and, within five minutes, the driver was speeding past the Socialist blocks of Novi Beograd and up the 19th-century cobbled roads into Zemun, before climbing up onto the loess plateau above the Danube. On a Sunday morning, there was very little traffic and, in any case, a taxi was able to go much faster than an international Balkan train. Long before Ruma station, we spotted the train heading steadily west along its track and so the taxi driver got me to Ruma and he got his $25. I caught the train and managed to get back to Budapest in time to take Tünde to the concert.

I wanted to share with Tünde some of the places and sites I knew and loved in north-east Hungary and so we made a three-day excursion to UTP-land. On the last day, we made a trip to east Slovakia for an emotional return to Košice. As we were walking down the main street from the cathedral towards the Archaeological Museum, Tünde made a suggestion that ordinarily I would have dismissed out of hand but, because we were in love, I took her challenge seriously. She bet that I couldn't carry her all the way to the Archaeological Museum at the other end of the main street. I did manage this but with a huge effort. I did not feel the ill effects of this lift for two weeks, by which time it became obvious that I'd got a real medical problem. My friends Laci and Alice had very good medical contacts – Laci's father was a rheumatologist who worked in the Railway Hospital in the centre of Budapest – probably the best hospital in the capital. They managed to book me in for a hernia operation, which went very well until the post-op phase. The most painful part was the two days in hospital in recovery, when the nurses made me walk up and down in the ward and along the hospital corridor to get my meals. While this exercise was no doubt essential to my recovery, it was the most painful part of the whole procedure. In short, the operation was a success and the patient didn't die. When I saw Tünde, I explained that, in all probability, I wouldn't be carrying her anywhere else any time soon. She looked suitably devastated.

Tünde's former husband was a jazz musician, so she was really into jazz and this was one of the great features of my sabbatical year. We would go to concerts in the Jazz Garden Music Club in Veres Pálné utca, to the Budapest Jazz Club and to jazz concerts in the Musical Academy. One of the great developments in Hungarian music was that, in the post-war period, the Musical Academy, with its mainly classical and folk orientation, was extended to include a Jazz Music Academy, which proved to be the fertile ground for an entire generation of Hungarian jazz players. The next generation – the children of these early players – formed a new cohort in the 1990s and 2000s and these were some of the players whom we most appreciated that year, including older players like Aladár Pege and Sándor Benkó, the Lakatos dynasty (Béla, Tony and Roby) and younger players like Elemér Balázs.

My sabbatical year in Budapest ended in August 2002 and I had been planning to drive to the EAA conference in Thessaloniki that year but, because of my hernia, I was unable to drive such a long distance. My Durham PhD student Bisserka Gaydarska, whom I had shamefully neglected except for regular internet discussions throughout my sabbatical year, was extremely kind and agreed to fly over to Budapest and drive my Saab 900, along with me in it, all the way to Bulgaria. This was a kind of personal transition, as I would later realise.

Before my visit to Thessaloniki, I had been invited to spend 10 days in the summer house of my great friend Kostas Kotsakis, who had filled the fridge with food and wine and let me stay there on my own. The house was far along the first finger of the Chalkidiki peninsula, in an area of mature pine forests with trees over 50 m tall. The first thing that I noticed about Kostas' house was the constant buzzing of what I supposed were bees. Yet I couldn't see any bees, although there were beehives on the road to the house. When I talked to one of the locals in the nearby hotel, he explained that the bees lived in the pine forest all year and they made particularly delicious honey but they stayed right at the very top of the pine trees, well out of the reach of humans. You could hear them but you could never actually see them until they swarmed down to the beehives at the end of autumn. I had a very fine 10 days, by which time I'd more or less recovered from my hernia and I was able to drive the Saab around. In one excursion, I wanted to drive to the second finger of Chalkidiki, from which I could look across to Mount Athos on the third finger. Although I'd seen pictures of individual monasteries before, I had never actually seen the Athos landscape. When I drove over, I still didn't get the full impact of the landscape because there was low cloud covering most of the peaks. But, as I waited, the low cloud slowly lifted off some of the peaks to reveal a natural Gothic castle with turrets. There were so many peaks, large and small, many with monasteries on them. If ever you wanted an example of the sacred power of a rocky landscape, Athos was *the* example.

The Upper Tisza Project years

For me, the Upper Tisza Project was primarily an escape from the Third Balkan War – from a catastrophe that was unfolding in parallel to the project and uncomfortably close at hand. For me, this was a schizophrenic time, with my heart often back in the Balkans and my head in the Neolithic of north-east Hungary. I could not reveal this dilemma to project partners or students at the time – it was not the project's problem and there were no Yugoslav partners or volunteers on the project with whom to discuss the war. It was like a close-up scene with much realistic detail, yet whose true meaning stemmed from the reverberations of distant thunder when you paid attention to the rumble.

There were two immensely satisfying personal experiences during the project – both personal friendships. The first was the evolution of my friendship with Pali Raczky. We had met on János Makkay's excavations at Bicske in 1973 and immediately felt a mutual attraction of character and archaeological interests. I could tell that here was a future leader of Hungarian prehistory. When we next met in the late 1980s, we were both university junior lecturers, with our careers just beginning to take off. When it was clear that I was going to develop a project in north-east Hungary, with two seasons based on the village/town of Polgár, there developed a closer relationship, based on a tension between my dependence on Pali (if we fell out, my project would hardly have survived) and our independence in each working out new and exciting ways of doing archaeology in that region. Moving out of Polgár in the second, third and fifth seasons was essential to the long-term relationship – it reduced the tensions arising from proximity. Mixed in with the friendship and mutual respect was a rivalry between a Central and a Western European – someone who knew local sites and material culture better than I and someone who had a stronger hold on archaeological theory than Pali. A sense of complementarity emerged between us. As the local landscape, monuments and sites took hold of me and shaped my understanding of Hungary, so the theoretical reading that Pali immersed himself in stimulated new interpretations of the familiar sites – especially his home base of Csőszhalom.[5] But there was also a different power dynamic in our careers in the 1990s. Pali was heading towards the head of department's role at ELTE, in effect presiding over the growth and modernisation of his Institute while building a fine research library, while I was avoiding as many administrative positions of responsibility as I could in Newcastle. The demands on his time grew with the expansion of Pali's powerbase, preventing him from publishing as much as he wanted, while I published more but hit severe funding limitations. It was fortunate for both of us that our rivalry never transformed itself into a deeper, zero-sum competitive game – the friendly rivalry is still there but within bounds.

The second experience was becoming closer to Laci Bartosiewicz, his wife Alice Choyke, their daughter Ana and their pet labrador. Laci and Alice's flat on Sas hegy

[5] See in particular Raczky's writings in the late 2010s: Raczky 2018; Raczky and Fülesi 2018.

('Eagle Hill') became a sanctuary for me whenever I came to Budapest – usually at the start and finish of UTP project seasons. Their kindness and tolerance of anything I said did much to remove the pressures of the project and its political overtones, while their encyclopaedic knowledge of matters Hungarian was freely shared. I owe more to them than they could ever possibly guess.

The structure and capacity of archaeology in 1990s Hungary was on a totally different level from that of Dalmatia in the 1980s. It was not just the contrasts in the available topographical maps – it was also the sheer number of specialists involved in any period and the totally different investment in scientific archaeology in Hungary, whether ^{14}C dating or palynology. These differences meant that the two projects made very different impacts on their regional archaeology. The NDP established a new synthesis for Dalmatian prehistory, with the greatest impact on our understanding of the Bronze Age, with its earliest drystone-walled monuments. In Hungary, so many new motorway rescue excavations were being published that it was hard for the UTP to create a new synthesis and the excavation reports often made a much bigger splash than the fieldwalking results. So the UTP never left its mark on Hungarian archaeology in the same way that the NDP affected later Dalmatian research.

Chapter 9

The fragmentation breakthrough and other broken stories

Fragmentation research originated for me quite by chance in 1996. That year, Vicky Peters, the archaeology editor for Routledge, offered me a contract to write a Balkan prehistoric synthesis. My plan was to use my sabbatical year from October 1996 to September 1997 to make three museum tours of one month each in Hungary, Romania and Bulgaria and then spend the rest of the sabbatical writing the book in Warszawa with my second wife, Bożenna Szwejkowska. I started the research visit in Hungary by abandoning Josh Pollard to the September rains of Polgár town[1] and spent a month in Budapest and western Hungary, catching up with recent Neolithic developments. I drove on in October to Romania, where I visited several centres and collected a large amount of material.

My visit to Hungary helped me to extend my previous knowledge of groups that I knew already quite well rather than showing me totally unknown material. In a visit to Pécs to meet István Ecsedy, he showed me a good selection of the material from the famous Lengyel cemeteries in the Pécs Museum which I knew from the literature. But it was in Romania that I came upon most material I had not studied before. One of my most revealing visits was to the Romanian Museum of National History in Bucureşti, with its fine collections of Gumelniţa and Cucuteni material. The late Mirel Popovici showed me great generosity in preparing a one-and-half-hour PowerPoint presentation on the new Romanian–French excavations at the key sites of Hârşova and Borduşani.

Another main centre of archaeology in Bucureşti was the Institute of Thracology, which I visited one morning to meet the director, Petru Roman (not the Prime Minister of the time!). Quite by chance, that was the time of the PhD viva for Georgieta El Susi, an archaeo-zoologist who had focused mostly on the Vinča group but also other groups in western Romania. Improvising superbly, Petru Roman invited me to join the PhD viva as an international adviser. Realising that I hadn't even read the thesis, Petru trusted in my general knowledge of the Balkans – in fact, I knew enough about Georgieta's articles to be able to make some sensible comments.

[1] For the wet September story, see above, pp. 125–126.

Another member of the panel was Marin Nica from Craiova. Marin was late for the viva and arrived puffing and panting, carrying two enormous bags each containing three 2 litre lemonade bottles of homemade *ţuica* (plum brandy). Marin sat down, rested a bit and waited his turn. When he was given the word, he stood up and took from his attaché case a fat script, which must have been 30 pages long. He started reading the commentary in his inimitable peasant dialect. It was after only two pages that Petru Roman stopped him and said, 'Yes, absolutely, we agree with everything you say, Marin – thank you very much for your precise summary.' Marin was so astonished that he could not think of a reply fast enough and was forced to sit down. Thus Petru stopped a viva that lasted an hour and a half from continuing for at least three hours. Naturally, Marin's main contribution was his homemade *ţuica*.

The first provincial museum I visited was on the Romanian Black Sea coast in the city of Constanţa, to which Ovid had once been exiled. There was, indeed, a statue of Ovid outside the National Museum of History, where the senior archaeologist was Puiu Haşotti, a Neolithic specialist who had recently written a book about the Neolithic of the Dobrogea. He showed me all of the Hamangia pottery and figurines in the collection, which later turned out to be crucial for fragmentation studies.

Puiu was a rarity among Balkan prehistorians in having a healthy scepticism for pottery typology. He particularly distrusted Henrieta Todorova's 5-stage typology of Hamangia pottery, so he set up an experiment to test her. Puiu labelled from 1–15 three sherds from each of the five stages and gave them to Henrieta as a blind test, for her to place in the correct stage of her own typology. Puiu was delighted to announce the result – less than 40% correct determinations. Even though Puiu had made his case, Henrieta continued to use the typology!

Another of the great provincial museums in Romania was the main museum of the Neamţ County Museums complex in Piatra Neamţ. The museum had one of the all-time great high-delivering teams in Romanian archaeology, if not anywhere in the Balkans (Plate 17). Dan Monah was the ideas man, while Gheorghe Dumitroaia (Ghiocel) was the consummate fixer who had all the right political contacts and could fund Dan's ideas. This pair formed a formidable team who developed some of the most stimulating museum exhibitions in the country, including reconstructions of prehistoric houses and a magnificent collection of figurines. Dan and Ghiocel were kind enough to show me around some famous sites, including Cucuteni itself as well as some of the famous Neolithic salt sites in the area. Ghiocel was also happy to show me figurine collections. It was clear that there was a very high fragmentation rate amongst Cucuteni figurines and Dan later became one of the first Balkan prehistorians to accept the deliberate fragmentation hypothesis.

I then went on in November to Bulgaria – the country that I knew least about but where I'd already made some friendly contacts with Ana Raduntcheva and Tsoni Tsonev. I had spent a week in Sofia, looking at museums and collections and talking to prehistorians and, on my last morning, I wanted to say goodbye to my new friends and colleagues. I parked Seaview the Ford Transit van close to the National Museum, which was then in the old Palace of Justice in the centre of Sofia. When I came back after half an hour, to my total horror the Transit van had been broken into and all of my clothes, my laptop with two months of notes from Hungary and Romania and much other kit had been taken. The only things left were three boxes of books and the Transit van, which was, according to plan, too decrepit to be stolen. I called Tsoni Tsonev to come and help me and we called the police, who said that they would of course look for the stolen items. The only positive suggestion came from Tsoni, who informed me that the Bulgarian Mafia had expanded into the insurance world and may return my stolen things if I were to take out vehicle insurance with a Mafia-linked company for a year. Since I didn't want to throw away good money after bad, I turned down the suggestion. Two days later, I was called to the police station nearest the crime scene and I drove there with Tsoni in Seaview to give a detailed statement. After an hour and a half, we emerged from the police station and walked to the van. We both became aware of a car with darkened glass windows parked quite close to the Transit. As we climbed into Seaview, the men in the car were looking at us very closely. My impression was that, if I had been wearing my Armani suit that day, I could easily have been kidnapped. So I told Tsoni that I was leaving Sofia at this point to let the trail go cold and said I'd see him later that month. That was a scary moment and I needed to put some space between the Mafia and Seaview.

My first stop outside Sofia was the Archaeological Museum in Vratsa, the home museum of Dr Bogdan Nikolov, who had unfortunately retired by the time I arrived. Dr Nikolov had come to Britain on a British Academy–Bulgarian Academy Inter-Academy exchange in the 1980s. He paid a visit to Newcastle and I showed him around the sites in the city and also Hadrian's Wall. He hinted that if I ever wanted to send him a book, his address was simple: Bogdan – Museum – Vratsa. I was sorry I couldn't find him on this visit but the new archaeologist, Georgi Ganetsovski, was extremely kind to me and showed me a lot of Bogdan Nikolov's materials, including figurine collections, which I noticed had a a very high fragmentation rate.

Bogdan Nikolov was a legend in Vratsa, with the most amazingly tolerant wife who allowed him, maybe not every year but certainly every couple of years, to go out into the town centre and 'pick up' the prettiest, dirtiest gypsy girl he could find and bring her home to wash her. He would then go out to buy new clothes for her and lived with her for a few months until he got bored. Bogdan did this with a string of gypsy girls, for which he was famous in the town. It was a strange legacy for a prehistorian.

There was also a story concerning Bogdan and one of the Biggest Fishes (cf. Polish: '*grubi rybe*') in Bulgarian archaeology. When Bogdan was excavating the Copper Age site of Gradeshnitsa, he was turning up such amazing finds that the then director of the Sofia Archaeological Institute, Dr Georgi Georgiev, was minded to see the site and the finds for himself. On the day of the state visit, the barouche arrived at Gradeshnitsa and Georgiev got out of the car, walked to the trench and asked where the excavation director was. When the diggers said, 'I'm sorry – we don't know,' Georgiev, who was a stickler for form, was most upset by this breach of protocol and walked over to a large tree to shelter from the blazing sun. This was a bad mistake for, a short while later, Bogdan, completely naked, leapt out of the tree and knocked Georgiev to the floor, before running off into the woods. Georgiev was so astonished that he didn't know how to respond other than to brush himself off, get into the car and return to Sofia, never to visit Bogdan Nikolov again.

Another museum I visited in late November, when there was already snow on the eastern part of the Stara Planina, was the Museum of Targovishte, where Ilka Angelova was the principal Neolithic specialist. There were two museums at the time – an old museum, which had a very fine display showing many of the best artefacts that Henrietta Todorova had found during her complete tell excavations at Poljanitsa and Ovcharovo. There were also the finds from Ovcharovo-Gorata, excavated by Ilka. But the old museum display was eclipsed by the new museum, with its beautifully displayed materials. By now, 10 weeks into my study tour, I was beginning to notice fragmentation in every museum I visited. Ilka Angelova had managed to re-fit fragments of the same figurine from different trenches – suggesting to me that re-fitting could be an extremely important aspect of fragmentation studies. The other aspect of fragmentation that Targovishte shed a light on was that of human remains. Although I may not have necessarily agreed with the interpretation of the scattered human bone remains as evidence for cannibalism, I realised immediately that there was real potential in studying partial human remains and incomplete burials.

One of the greatest Bulgarian museums is the National Museum of Archaeology in Varna. The museum had to be moved to a top-security building that was previously a bank after the excavations at the Varna cemetery had revealed a mass of golden grave goods that has to this day never been equalled in prehistoric Europe. On my first visit to Varna, I met the excavator of the Varna cemetery, Ivan Ivanov, who was a leading figure in Varna society. He was kind enough to take me to a nice hotel, where he asked his friend the owner to put me in a good room at a reduced rate and so I had a pleasant stay in Varna. Ivan was kind enough to show me not only the great exhibition with most of the gold finds from the cemetery but also all the other material in the storeroom – the flints, the polished stone, the shell ornaments and the pottery.

It was with the Varna pottery that I was able to complete my first fragmentation analysis of funerary ceramics. The argument was that, in a well-excavated cemetery, the discovery of parts of objects in a grave meant that the missing parts were somewhere else – in another grave or perhaps outside the cemetery altogether. This could demonstrate links between the land of the dead (the graves) and the land of the living, where the other parts of the pots must have been deposited. Many of the Varna graves had incomplete vessels and also parts of shell bracelets – an important part of the costumes of the dead at Varna. This inference was important for demonstrating links between the land of the dead and the land of the living.

It was the then director of the museum, a Romanist called Alexander Minchev, who pointed out a stunning example of deliberate fragmentation. Alexander was showing me around the main exhibition and I had mentioned my interest in fragmentary objects. He looked at me and said, 'Well, you'll be interested in the Goljamo Delchevo panther.' Indeed, there was a dark grey, apparently complete figurine of a big cat (Plate 18) and Alexander explained that, actually, it wasn't what it seemed. He was a student on the excavations with Henrieta Todorova and he remembered very well that the body of the big cat was found in one pit and the head was found in another pit, maybe 70 m away across the tell. It was only after both parts had been found that Henrieta decided to re-fit the head to the body and displayed the panther as a complete figurine. Once again, the museum display was presenting a different story from the excavation account. This was a classic example of re-fitting within a site which must certainly have resulted from a deliberate decision to deposit one part of the figurine in one pit and the other part in another. The Varna Museum experience made a big difference in how I approached what was clearly emerging as deliberate fragmentation.

Some 50 km from Varna across the loess plateau of the Dobrudzha was the town of Dobritch. The first time I visited the Town Museum, Todor Dimov was the principal archaeologist and his lack of English made him enlist the aid of Sonja, a local translator. Most of the Neolithic and Chalcolithic exhibition featured finds from the Durankulak complex, comprising a flat settlement beside the lake, a tell settlement on an island and a huge cemetery on the shore of the lake. This was the biggest Neolithic cemetery known in the Balkans up to the discovery in the 2000s of the Alsónyék cemetery in western Hungary. Todor and Sonja took me to the Durankulak complex and showed me the whole site. At the time, the tell on the Big Island was in extremely good condition, with little grass hiding the dry-stone wall houses up to 18 m long and 8 m wide. It struck me that this would be a great site for archaeo-tourists to visit.

Todor also explained to me how the cemetery had been found. As with all her tell sites, Henrieta was keen to find the associated cemetery and she dug many trial trenches without finding a single grave. One evening, Todor and Ivo Vajsov (Henrieta's son) had been sent off to a local State pheasant farm to bring back four pheasants for dinner. Because both of them had been drinking before this expedition, they made far too much noise when they entered the farm and several pheasants ran away up the hill. Todor had never looked at the site from this angle before and he realised that the hill slope over which the pheasants were escaping was an extremely promising place for a prehistoric cemetery. Although everyone else was greatly disappointed to lose their pheasant dinner, Todor was very happy and explained that he'd like to have two workers the next morning to put in some trial trenches on Pheasant Hill. Henrieta was typically dismissive of this idea but acceded to Todor's request. This was just as well, since each worker found a grave in his trench – the very first graves to be found in the Durankulak cemetery. As far as I am aware, this is the first Neolithic cemetery discovered by a combination of archaeological intuition and a search for pheasants.

On the way back to Sofia, I called in at two more museums. The Archaeological Museum in Plovdiv had a rather poor public display because it had recently been vandalised and some of the best objects stolen. The one thing that stood out from the main exhibition was the hoard of 25 greenstone axes from the village of Svoboda – apparently a genuine Neolithic or Copper Age hoard, which would play an important role in studies of extra-Balkan exchange in the 2010s.[2] There was also a prehistoric outstation in a Bulgarian Revival house from the early 19th century on one of the five hills of Plovdiv. The museum archaeologist Bistra Koleva was a great friend of Ana Raduntcheva, so I went up the hill with the two ladies to see the finds from the completely excavated tell of Dolnoslav, which included an amazing collection of mostly broken figurines and pottery. I made a mental note to return to Plovdiv one day to study the Dolnoslav figurines.

These visits to sites like Durankulak, Yunacite and the Ai Bunar copper mine, as well as fantastic museums such as Varna, Targovishte and Dobritch planted in my mind the idea of a visit by the British Prehistoric Society, which organised an annual summer study tour abroad. Before I left for London, I discussed this idea with Ana Raduntcheva and Tsoni Tsonev and they both thought that this would be a wonderful opportunity to showcase Bulgarian archaeology at a time when they had some of the most spectacular sites and finds in the whole of Europe.

At the end of November, I drove back not to Warszawa but in fact to London – the first big change of plan in my sabbatical. I had made good friends with the director of the Institute of Archaeology and Ethnology, Romuald Schild, and I already had a very good friend in the Institute – Jacek Lech. Professor Schild had kindly offered me a desk in a shared office in his Institute, which was truly generous given the pressure of space there. I thought that it would be an opportunity for Bożenna to spend nine months in her homeland, since she'd never spent that much time since she left in the 1970s. However, at the very last moment, she decided she didn't want to go to Warszawa or confront the ghosts of her past there. It was true that three members of her family had died recently and she felt it was not right to spend the whole year there. So I had to cancel my sabbatical year in Schild's Institute and think of another plan.

The idea I came up with was to go to University College London to the Department of Anthropology, where my friend Mike Rowlands was working. He talked to the head of department, Leslie Aiello, who confirmed that the year's visit would be possible and she too offered me the use of a desk in a shared office in the department. I didn't want to go to my *alma mater*, the Institute of Archaeology just over the road from UCL, because Peter Ucko was by then the director of the Institute and I had no intention of spending much time with him.[3] UCL was also enormously helpful in setting up this very late change of direction, not least by offering us a Highgate flat that was rented out to visiting academics. This was the most fantastic London flat I had ever lived in, near the top of Highgate Hill, opposite a side road to Hampstead Heath. So,

[2] The 'greenstone' axes from Svoboda proved to have been made of jadeite, exchanged from as far away as the French Alps.
[3] For the reason why, see pp. 86–87.

instead of a year in Warszawa, we had a year in Highgate and in the Department of Anthropology.

The second great change in my sabbatical year was in the topic of the Routledge book. As I went around the museums of Central and South-east Europe day after day for 90 days, it began to dawn on me that most of the famous objects that were published were, for the most part, fragmentary. To take a classic example, the large house model from the Romanian island site of Căscioarele displayed in the Romanian National Museum of History in Bucharest was, on close inspection, only 20% complete (Plate 19). The rest of the model had been very beautifully restored – so well that it was impossible from publication photographs to tell that it was markedly incomplete. If this was just a single example, it wouldn't have made any difference to my writing of a general synthesis. But when you see similar patterns of fragmented objects for almost 100 days, you begin to realise that something was going on. I didn't know what it was and I didn't even know how much of the fragmentation was deliberate, though this was sometimes obvious. I had never considered the topic of fragmentation for research before. But there were so many examples of fragmented objects, including many of the most important objects in Balkan prehistory, that I decided to change tack and write a book about fragmentation instead. I was fortunate that Routledge, and Vicky Peters in particular, were open-minded enough to agree to a change of topic, so in autumn 1996, we rewrote the contract and I started to investigate fragmentation.

What happened to the Balkan synthesis? Vicky Peters was always quick off the mark and she immediately turned to another Balkan Neolithic specialist working in Britain at the time – Doug Bailey, a lecturer in Cardiff. Doug signed a contract with Routledge for a Balkan prehistoric synthesis, which he published in 2000 as *Balkan Prehistory* – in the same year as my first fragmentation book.

The great thing about working in the UCL Department of Anthropology was that there were colleagues who may not have known directly about fragmentation but who were deeply knowledgeable about social relations involving material culture. It became clear that the Cambridge specialist Marilyn Strathern had written about Melanesian ethnography in ways that may have been relevant to the fragmentation idea. One of her major books was *The Gender of the Gift*, in which she discussed the notion of 'dividuals' – the idea that we are not all 'individuals' in a 20th-century capitalist sense but that what makes us people are all the links we share with other people, other places and other things. Her other key concept of *enchainment* was a concept by which people were chained to each other through material exchange. Thus, if I have an axe and I give that axe to Bożenna, Bożenna gets the axe and part of me. And if she gives the axe to her daughter Caroline, Caroline gets part of Bożenna, part of me and the axe and so on, in the form of a chain of gifts. The two key concepts of dividuals and enchainment, from Melanesian ethnography, became the basis for a theoretical appreciation of object fragmentation in the Balkans. The major difference between modern Melanesian and ancient Balkan enchainment was that Melanesian entrainment connected dividuals through complete objects whereas, in the Balkans, the enchainment worked partly through complete objects but also through fragments of objects. While archaeologists since the 1920s had made the empirical observation that objects were broken, apparently deliberately, it was not until the 1990s that there was any real social development of this idea. I was able to use important research by Laurie Talalay and some others who were starting to put deliberate fragmentation in archaeology into some kind of theoretical perspective. My aim in writing the first fragmentation book emerged through the desire to place fragmentation in archaeology in the context of general anthropological theory.

Because of the theft of my Romanian notes from Sofia, I had to return to Romania in the summer of 1997. The colleagues I'd met the previous autumn were very happy to show me the same material again, although I couldn't blame Mirel Popovici for not wishing to repeat his 90-minute Hârşova-Borduşani PowerPoint. One of the greatest field trips I've ever had in the Balkans came about through the combination of Silvia Marinescu-Bâlcu and her contacts in south-east Romania with the company of Dragoş Gheorghiu and his partner Cornelia Catuna. We drove off in my Saab 900 to the mighty Gumelniţa tell, which so dominated its micro-region. We then drove to the nearby town museum of Olteniţa with its superb Neolithic exhibition, where there were Cucuteni imports into the Gumelniţa tell and a superb block of Bulgarian flint, which must have been shipped across the Danube and brought to the same tell. Hidden away in a cupboard in the director's office was a group of gold tabbed pendants, though quite how many had excavation contexts was not explained to me. The next place we went to was Căscioarele, where the site lay on an islet in the middle of a lake. It was not easy to reach this site because the village was desperately poor and there were no fishing boats to be found. I spotted two half oil-barrels by the shore of the lake and I suggested that we re-ran the Cambridge Boat Race, with Dragoş and Silvia in the light blue boat and Cornelia and me in the dark blue boat. Silvia was as competitive in this race as in any other aspect of archaeology and she made sure that her boat got to the islet first – what a great way to visit the site! We then moved on for lunch to the town of Călăraşi, which was made famous in Tony Harrison's film-poem *Prometheus*. The poem starts with an account of the 1984 miners' strike in Britain, after which a golden statue of Prometheus was driven across Europe, stopping at some of the worst polluted places on the continent. One of these was, sadly, Călăraşi where, in the 1960s, the Russians had built a factory using 19th-century Russian technology, which belched out red fumes 24/7. This made Călăraşi the least healthy town in the whole of Romania, infamous for birth defects and sick children. The excellent exhibition in Călăraşi Museum was organised by Marin Neagu and, at the time of our visit, there was a temporary exhibition of Neolithic figurines – particularly important for me because it included some of the Hamangia figurines which I hadn't seen in Constanţa. Marin Neagu had organised something really special for our afternoon – a speedboat trip down the Danube almost as far as the last bridge. This trip gave an amazing impression of how magnificent a river the Danube was close to its delta (Plate 20). The only blott on the landscape was that, after looking at the Hârşova tell, we arrived too late to take a fishing boat from the village of Borduşani across to the island where the tell was located. Otherwise, it was a perfect Balkan expedition.

The Prehistoric Society accepted my idea of a summer visit to Bulgaria and the 1998 trip was led by Tsoni Tsonev, as the local specialist, and myself, as Vice-President of the Society. In addition to the 'students' on the tour, who were mostly senior citizens and long-term amateur archaeologists, often members of the Society for decades, the President of the Society, Tim Champion, and his wife Sara came along too. The group met in Sofia Airport and next day drove off to look at the Temnata cave before going on to spend the second night in Veliko Trnovo – one of Bulgaria's former medieval capitals. We were staying in a hotel I'd never visited before and, when I looked at some of the exhibition cases in the foyer, to my horror there was a number of quite obviously Neolithic polished stone axes. I discussed this with Tsoni and we thought it best to say nothing, since clearly somebody was looting archaeological sites and selling axes through a prominent hotel. This was certainly not a good start to the trip but fortunately nobody else noticed the axes. At an early stage of the tour, the six or seven seasoned drinkers of the group decided that it would be a good idea to have a 'Bulgarian *rakia* of the tour' competition, in which we would each evening try to identify the best *rakia* (brandy) in our hotel. Since we stayed in several different hotels, the competition continued right up until the very last night, when we came to a vote for a '*Burgaska 63 perla rakia*' we'd tasted in Varna. This tour was a particular pleasure for me because I had visited all of the museums and the sites the previous year, so everything was really fresh in my mind and there was really no problem about writing up a tour guide or guiding people around the sites. The one thing that fitted in with my latest research was the 'Fragmentation Song' which I'd written one evening. In our Plovdiv hotel, there was a piano in the lounge and Sara Champion, a great blues singer and piano player, accompanied me on the world premiere of the 'Fragmentation Song', which went to the tune of the standard 'All of Me, Baby, Take All of Me', re-titled 'Part of Me, Baby, Take Part of Me'.

The publication of what we call the Frag 1 book – my solo-authored book – took place in 2000. I had been encouraged by the Durham Department to finish and publish this as one of my main submissions in the next Research Assessment Exercise in 2001. It was an enormous pleasure to offer a general account of fragmentation and how it might relate to past social developments.

It was an attractive possibility to set up an experimental project to see whether objects had been accidentally or deliberately broken. This became feasible with Dragoş Gheorghiu's invitation to join his experimental season in Vădastra village in 2002. Alex Gibson also came out to work with Dragoş on the building of a lookalike Copper Age kiln in which we would fire objects for fragmentation. The idea was that the students from Dragoş' University of Fine Arts in Bucureşti would be given clay of the kind used by Vădastra potters and make 10 copies of a number of different artefacts, including four or five pottery types, several figurine types, stamp-seals and a variety of other

Fig. 17. The author treading a clay floor with Seth Priestman and Gina Stancu, Vădastra fragmentation experiment, Romania

fired-clay objects. Out of these 10, one would be kept complete for the reference collection, five would be dropped accidentally on five different surfaces and four would be broken deliberately. We prepared 1 m^2 areas of grass (!), a wooden floor, a stamped clay floor, a fired clay floor and finally a cobbled floor[4] (Fig. 17). The object was dropped from the same height of 1 m onto each surface. There were four ways in which we broke the objects deliberately: one with a large stone, one with a bone, one with an antler and the last breaking it apart with our bare hands. The idea was that we would study the remains of the fragmentary objects to see if deliberate and accidental breaks could be differentiated. For this plan to work, the fine arts students would need to make 10 copies of each object. The immediate problem was that they were *artists* and artists did not make multiple copies – they made individual, unique artworks. Dragoş had to use all his skills of persuasion to get the artists to agree to make copies. At this stage, we didn't dare tell the artists that we were going to smash their artistic *oeuvre* – they would certainly have refused to make the objects if they knew this was their fate. But at the end of a week, we had over 150 objects, which we fired in the experimental kiln along with a lot of other pots. The kiln took a day to

[4] I should say that it was quite rare to find cobbled floors in Neolithic houses but they do occur.

make and by evening we filled it up with the experimental objects, loaded the base of the kiln with fuel and started the firing. The firing went on till midnight, reaching 980°C, at which point we reverted to our single malts, eventually going to sleep. When we opened the kiln at noon the next day, we were delighted to see that there were remarkably few breakages- only three of our objects were broken. We left the objects to cool down and, next day, we started breaking them – to a stream of protests from the fine artists. After two days, the artists realised what fun it was to break objects and so they eventually joined in the fragmentation activities, happy to break anything that they had not made themselves (!). Seth Priestman, a Durham undergraduate with experience of potting, came along with me to help in the experiment. He proved very skilful in recording the breakage patterns of a large number of fragments and we recorded perhaps 20% of the breakages that we'd made.

The most memorable night for me in Vădastra village, where I was staying with a family, was utterly unexpected. Normally, my family would have dinner early, chat a bit and go to bed by 10 pm. This evening, people started to come round after 10 pm and no one was going to bed. It transpired that one of the householders had organised a rabbit hunt with his three friends and two hunting dogs. The hunters would drive around in an estate car, with four in the car with the dogs and a searchlight operator on the roof rack, trying to spot rabbits. The leader asked me if I'd like to come along and, since I'd never been hunting before, I thought this would be quite exciting. I sat inside on the back seat, with a man and two dogs. We drove around until the torch-man spotted a rabbit, when we released the dogs. But the first rabbit was too far from the hunting dogs and escaped in a maize field. The dogs returned, panting and sweating profusely, and sat inside the car next to me. The smell was offensive but it seemed a small price to pay for the excitement of the hunt. The next three rabbits also escaped and the dogs by this time smelt utterly disgusting. At this point, simply to avoid the smell of the dogs, I insisted that I would take over as the torch-man. I spotted two more rabbits but, by then, the dogs were feeling really tired and could hardly keep up with the rabbits even in the first 50 m, so the rabbits were safe for the night. We returned home feeling very sorry for ourselves. The dogs slept for the next two days. Next morning, I was walking down to the village market and I spotted a young lad on a bicycle, who was part of Dragoş' figurine-making session in the school. When I pointed out how perky he was looking, he replied that he had gone hunting rabbits on his bike last night and caught three! I didn't bother to tell our householder.

As the 2000s progressed, it was becoming clear to me that there were some extremely large samples of heavily fragmented material sitting in Balkan museums and which could form the basis for detailed case studies in fragmentation analysis. In the Frag 1 book, I had cleared the ground by examining a series of examples of fragmentation of different materials and different types of objects but what I had not done was to look closely at a series of well-defined case studies of large assemblages. I realised that this could be the main focus for a second fragmentation book. By this time, people had started to discuss fragmentation more and smarter university

Archaeology departments had invited me to give research seminars on the topic. Each seminar produced the same conflicting responses – deep scepticism from some colleagues and new examples of deliberate fragmentation from others. It was also becoming clear that, alongside the numerous examples of intra-site re-fitting, there was now a smaller number of examples of inter-site re-fitting. This phenomenon was to prove extremely difficult to study but my research showed a wide range of examples, starting in the Upper Palaeolithic. The second fragmentation book required collaborative research, so, after the submission of her PhD in 2003, Bisserka Gaydarska accompanied me on a visit to Plovdiv to study the Dolnoslav figurine assemblage.

The collection of Dolnoslav figurines, numbering some 800, was curated in the prehistoric store in a Bulgarian Revival house. Architecturally, this was a wonderful house but the storage and workspace was extremely cramped. There was one room in which the curator, Bistra Koleva, would sit and chain smoke through the whole day. In the other room, we had six small desks to lay out all of the figurine fragments for re-fitting. We soon realised that a system based on body parts was essential: in other words, no left leg would re-fit with another left leg. This involved putting all of the right legs together on one table, all of the left legs together on another table, and so on. Once we had divided up the material into groups that would not re-fit with one another, we could try re-fitting each leg with every other potential match. This was a stressful week but we stuck at it and, to their credit, so did Bistra. The result was many re-fitted figurine parts, often between different houses or pits or middens (Fig. 18).

The success of this re-fitting study led to a British Academy-funded project, with Bisserka as post-doctoral research assistant,[5] with a second major data collection trip to the Balkans. The main aim of this trip was to collect information on large site samples with supposedly high fragmentation rates. In parallel to this, we wished to make one attempt at inter-site re-fitting. The inter-site re-fitting operation took place in the East Rhodopes of Bulgaria. Ana Raduntcheva had excavated the Copper Age levels of the Sedlare tell, near Kardzhali and, while most of the material was in Kardzhali Museum, a smaller part was curated in Momchilgrad Museum. Even though Ana had good friends in both museums, the real problem was the relationships between the two museum directors. Delicate negotiations were needed to persuade one museum director to allow us to take his figurine fragments to the other museum to try re-fitting. The obvious question 'Why can't the other museum bring their figurines to me?' was answered with the argument of preponderance – 'There are 200 figurines in the other museum and only 50 in your collections'. We managed to unite the two collections in one museum only once and we didn't find a single 'inter-museum' re-fit (!) but we still somehow managed to remain friends with both museum directors. Thinking on a wider scale, the obvious museums for inter-site re-fitting experiments were national museums in small states (*e.g.* Slovenia) and museums on islands (*e.g.* the Manx Museum on the Isle of Man, or Valletta Museum on Malta).

[5] Bisserka and I were later married (see p. 160).

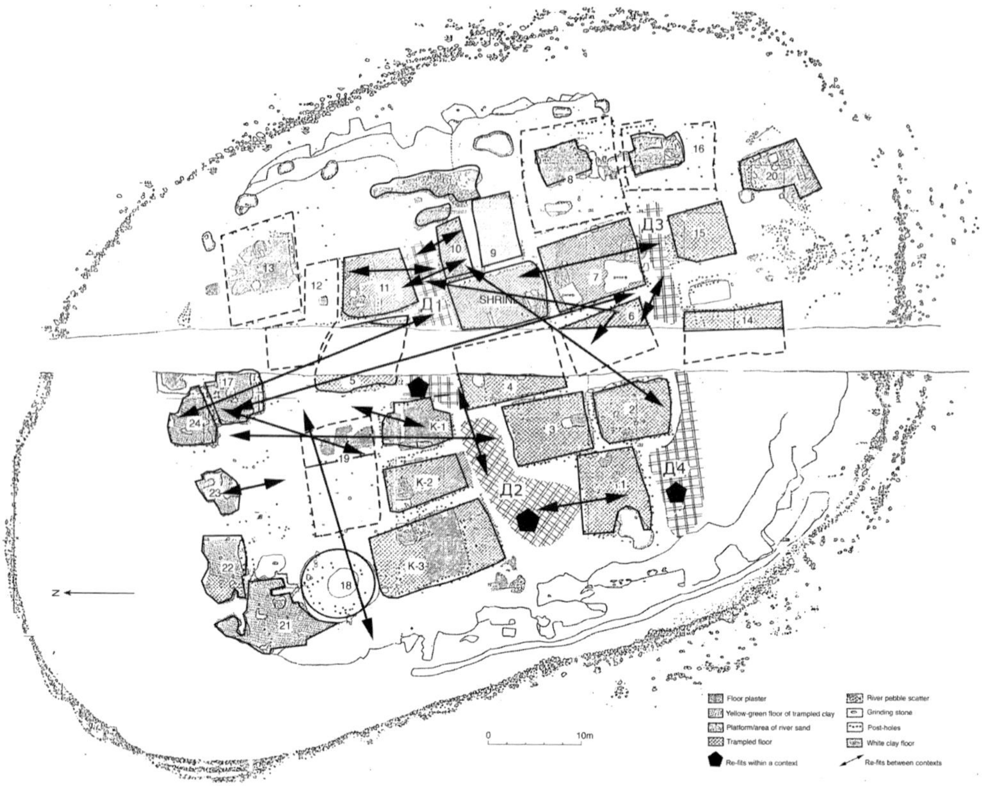

Fig. 18. Figurine fragment re-fit map, Dolnoslav tell

We had our eyes on three Bulgarian samples for detailed case studies: two large samples of shell bracelets from the cemeteries of Varna and Durankulak and the large collection of fired clay tables ('altars') from the Struma valley site of Sapareva Banja. We made agreements with close colleagues to study the Varna and Durankulak shell bracelets but, unfortunately, the then director of the National Institute of Archaeology, Vassil Nikolov, was preparing a general book on fired clay 'altars' and, although our study would have complemented his own research, he blocked our access to the Sapareva Banja collection *in perpetuo*.

We had to extend our search to Greece to try to find a site that had a large group of shell bracelets from a settlement context. The only site that we could find for this was Dimini in central Greece. We had to jump through five administrative hoops before we could study the Dimini assemblage. This started off with informal contacts in the Archaeological Museum of Volos, where we were encouraged to believe that the museum would support the research. The next step was to gain the consent of the British School at Athens by applying for one of the three British permits per season offered for the study of material in a Greek museum. This application was approved, translated and sent to the Greek Archaeological Service for general approval and then sent to the local Ephorate in Volos for their approval. Fortunately, the director of the Volos Ephorate was the director of the museum and, with the help of our friend Stella Souvatzi and her friend the museum curator Litsa Skafidi, we managed to clear these hurdles too. The fifth and last hurdle, which I could only clear thanks to my friendship with Kostas Kotsakis, was to gain the consent of the last excavator of Dimini – Georgios Hourmouziadis, a senior prehistorian who had given up archaeology in favour of politics. Without Kostas' help, I would have found it very difficult to locate Hourmouziadis but Kostas managed to contact him and persuade him to write a letter of support for our study to Volos. We had managed to navigate the five steps of the bureaucratic jungle – all that now remained was to study the shell bracelets.

The first re-fitting study formed part of a two-pronged archaeological sciences approach to the Varna Cemetery. Ever since the failure of Axel Hartmann's spectrographic analysis of the Varna gold, for which he had taken samples from almost 140 gold objects, Ivan Ivanov had decided that he would allow very few scientists to take samples from the Varna materials (as one exception, the copper objects were subject to lead isotope analysis) and certainly not from the gold objects. At the time when Vladimir Slavchev took over the collection following Ivan's untimely death, scientific investigations had not been given priority for Varna for over two decades. When we returned to Varna in 2003, there were two opportunities. The first was to collect samples for an AMS dating programme; unbelievably for such an important cemetery, we had no AMS dates at all. The second was to make a complete study of the Varna shell ornaments, with particular attention paid to a full re-fitting study of the bracelets.

A successful AMS dating programme depended on discovering the location of all of the Varna human remains and there remained one huge problem. Nobody knew, or admitted to knowing, the location of the human remains from the first 60 graves. Varna claimed the bones were in Sofia, Sofia was sure they were in Varna. The Varna curator Vladimir Slavchev (Vlado) did at least search long and hard for the remains from the first 60 graves, yet the only bones in Varna were those from later seasons (graves 61–310). The director of the Sofia Institute for Physical Anthropology and Experimental Morphology, Professor Yordan Yordanov and his assistant, Dr Branimira Dimitrova, also denied all knowledge of these human remains. At least the Varna Museum agreed that we could take all of their Varna human bone remains to the Sofia Institute, where they would be sampled by Tom Higham from the Oxford Lab. We realised that this would be a logistical nightmare, since the only transport we had was my Saab 900. We loaded all of the cardboard boxes containing the bones into the back of the car and Bisserka drove it to Sofia – there were so many boxes that there was no space for my long legs to drive! But we arrived late and it was pouring with rain, so there was no way we could unload the material at the Institute that Friday. We reluctantly accepted that we would have to disguise the materials in the back of the Saab for the whole weekend, hoping that the police wouldn't notice there were bits of human femur sticking out and calling us to account for storing 6,500-year-old human skeletons in a Sofia residential district. It was still pouring with rain and we had to use a very conspicuous orange blanket to cover the materials and leave the Saab in a paid parking area near Bisserka's flat. Luckily, nobody realised that the human bones were there and Monday was fine and bright, allowing us to unload the skeletons in the Institute.

It was only when we had unloaded the Varna materials in the Institute that we were allowed to see the store in which other human bones from the whole of Bulgaria were stored, including the Durankulak human remains which we wished to sample. This storage area was located in the Institute loft, which had holes in the roof and which was regularly used by pigeons. There was an enormous jumble of wooden military crates and cardboard boxes scattered over the loft and there were only three days to go before Tom Higham was due to arrive. We contacted the New Bulgarian University and asked if they could find two students who would be prepared, for a decent daily rate, to move boxes and crates around in the Institute for three days. There were plenty of students who were happy to take on this heavy work for cash. They started to move things around and slowly came upon more and more of the Durankulak human remains. Then, on one miraculous morning, the students found the first of the Varna human remains from the missing 60 graves. Halfway through that day, they came upon perhaps the most significant skeleton in the whole cemetery – the human remains from Grave 43. It was an amazing re-excavation of the Varna skeletons and we were extremely pleased to have all the material ready for Tom and Noah Honch when they arrived the next day.

Back in the Varna Museum, the re-fitting of the Varna shell bracelets was carried out in the storeroom of the Varna Museum where all of the non-gold material was kept. The storeroom was dark and dingy but we managed to commandeer two desk-lamps and two large tables in which we could spread out the shell bracelets and try the re-fitting. The curators Olga Televina and Vlado Slavchev were extremely helpful in all of this and we managed to do a complete re-fitting analysis. The findings were interesting but not devastating, in the sense that all of the re-fits of bracelet fragments we found occurred within a grave but not between graves. Nonetheless, we still managed to demonstrate the enchained links between the land of the dead in the Varna cemetery and the land of the living in some other site, yet to be discovered.

A similar story unfolded in Dobritch Museum, where we were given decent if small facilities: again, we had to use a few small tables to look at the Durankulak collection of shell bracelets. The results duplicated those at Varna – re-fits within graves but none between graves.

The third re-fitting study we did concerned the collection of exactly 100 shell bracelets in the Volos Museum that came from the settlement of Dimini. The museum provided us with as many large tables as we wanted in a very well-lit room with lots of space and NO SMOKING! The Keeper of the Neolithic finds from Dimini was Litsa Skafida, who had worked in the Museum for some time and was finishing off a PhD on the Dimini figurines and who took great interest in our stories of the deliberate fragmentation of figurines. She introduced us to all of her colleagues as well as to a restaurant in the harbour area, where a Volos speciality was a particular combination of seafood meze and alcohol. The *tsipouro* was served in small flasks and, every time you finished a glass, the waiter brought you a new side-plate with a different seafood delight. There was an obvious incentive to drink a lot and we went there as often as possible. Litsa also persuaded the director, Mrs Vasiliki Adrymi-Sismani, to take us to the site of Dimini, partly because she had done a great deal of work on the Late Bronze Age (Mycenaean) remains next to the Neolithic tell. It was Vasiliki who alerted us to the presence of what appeared to be Neolithic rock-art in the Dimini Mycenaean palace; there was a decorated boulder which had clearly been brought in from outside. This led Litsa to introduce us to an amateur archaeologist whom most of the Greek archaeologists would consider as beyond the fringe but who had developed a passion for rock art and had done a huge amount of fieldwork. Stelios Papanikolaou had funded a private publication of rock art motifs from 600 sites, each with GPS co-ordinates. Stelios took us out one afternoon to the landscape where the rock art was located. It was difficult to explain to Stelios that, just because a rock art site is close to a Neolithic tell, it doesn't mean that the rock art dates to the same period as the tell. But here in Thessaly was a fantastic corpus of rock art, which remains to be studied through more advanced archaeological methods. The other person to whom Litsa introduced us was a colleague from Larisa, Giorgios Toufexis, who had carried some of the most important excavations on the Greek Late Neolithic. While most archaeologists thinking of Thessalian tells would think of a world of clay, in fact at a certain point in the Late Neolithic, communities started building in the dry-stone technique, best exemplified at Toufexis' site of Palioskala.

We had a successful time in Volos Museum, in which we identified a decent number of bracelet fragment re-fits, some of which connecting houses that were as much as 50 m apart and others connecting adjoining houses. There was a very clear difference between the shell bracelet re-fitting results on the Dimini settlement and those from the two Bulgarian cemeteries. The good number of inter-house re-fits in a settlement and the total lack of inter-grave re-fits in the cemeteries of Varna and Durankulak suggested that it was the settlement context that was important in this different re-fitting pattern, just as it was with the Dolnoslav figurines.

We completed the comparative analyses to publish the second fragmentation book (or 'Frag 2'), which came out in 2007 with Oxbow Books. Many colleagues appreciated the complementary nature of the two Frag volumes.

However, there were still more aspects of fragmentation which we had scarcely touched on. Perhaps the biggest gap in our studies concerned 'normal' settlement pottery. In the Frag 2 book, each of the case studies targeted a particular category of rather special artefacts. We had not studied the ordinary settlement ceramic assemblages, which were usually so vast as to be off-putting. Many excavators would have the materials spread out in the pot shed to find re-fits between sherds from different contexts. However, their analysis was almost entirely related to chronological questions of stratigraphic links and, in our view, this completely missed the point that inter-contextual re-fits might have something to say about the social as well as about the chronological. But neither Bisserka nor I had the opportunity to look at a large assemblage to study this.

It took the beginning of a new phase of fragmentation analysis, with the appointment of the Marie Curie fellow Antonio Blanco González in Durham in 2012, to look at bulk settlement pottery. Antonio had long studied assemblages of Bronze Age pottery on the Meseta, in central Spain, where he had already identified several sites suitable for bulk ceramic re-fitting. But before the data collection in Spain, I wanted to run a training session in which we worked out clearly definable protocols for the closeness of the relationship between two potentially re-fitting sherds, within the range 'physical re-fit' to 'same general appearance, probably from the same vessel'. I set up a one-week training session in the Newcastle Department of Archaeology, which curated the largest Neolithic pottery assemblage in the north of England – the Thirlings site in Northumberland. Andrea Dolfini kindly provided us with a large lab in which we could lay out the whole of the pottery assemblage and work out a graded series of criteria for re-fits. This training gave Antonio a solid grounding for his study of Beaker assemblages when he returned to Spain for data collection.

The next advance that Antonio made was to involve a ceramic technologist from Hungary called Attila Kreiter, who worked in the Hungarian National Museum. Attila agreed to make thin sections of pairs of sherds that exemplified each of our different re-fit criteria and compare those with the visual assessment that Antonio had made. The consensus from Attila's results was that the re-fitting criteria for each pair of sherds matched the similarity as shown by the scientific analysis. This was a useful study, in which fragmentation was dragged kicking and screaming into the world of modern (2010s) archaeological science.

Even before the publication of the Frag 2 book, deliberate fragmentation had been accepted, if not as a definite fact of prehistoric life, at least as an idea worth further exploration. I was invited to give the keynote address in Adam Smith's Eurasian archaeology conference in Chicago in 2005. We were also invited to contribute an archaeological perspective to Will Tronzo's inter-disciplinary workshop on 'The Fragment' at the Getty Research Institute in 2006. There was even recognition from my home department, when Marga Díaz-Andreu suggested that I presented a paper on fragmentation in archaeology at the 75th anniversary conference of the Durham Archaeology Department in 2007. Bisserka and I had the chance to explore fragmentation and enchainment in the *longue durée* of human evolution, after a long-time supporter of the fragmentation project, Clive Gamble, invited us to his 'Social Brains, Distributed Minds' British Academy conference in 2008. But perhaps the kindest, most positive comment about our work came from our good friend Andy Jones, who had already identified the notion of enchainment as central to all interactions in prehistory. Andy dedicated his new book, co-authored with Marta

Díaz-Guardamino, *Making a Mark*, to us, remarking that, 'The very idea that artefacts are worthy of study owes much to Chapman and Gaydarska's pioneering work.'

The latest chapter in the fragmentation story concerns two planned events still at risk from Covid-19. The first was a session at the Theoretical Archaeology Group conference planned to be held at Leicester in December 2020 but then postponed for a year because of the Covid-19 virus. Here, Helen Chittock and Matt Knight have organised a session entitled 'Fragmentation Theory in 2021' – an assessment of what fragmentation research has achieved (and not achieved) in the 20 years since the publication of the first Frag book. The second was a post-doctoral workshop based in Stockholm entitled 'Fragmentation in Archaeological Context – Accidental Breakage, Deliberate Gesture and Beyond', organised by Anna Sörman, Astrid Noterman and Markus Fjellström. Let's hope that both of these sessions happen soon.

Chapter 10

Working in the European Association of Archaeologists

The European Association of Archaeologists (henceforth 'EAA') started in a very interesting and not at all obvious way. The EAA began not with the organisation itself but with a journal. In the late 1980s, Kristian Kristiansen (Plate 21) had the insight to realise that there was no journal for European archaeology as a whole and so he proposed to start one, even before the Fall of the Berlin Wall. The name he chose was a no-brainer – the *Journal of European Archaeology* (or *JEA*). He had strong support for the idea from a small working group, including Ian Hodder, but could find no publisher willing to publish it until he met Ross Samson, who ran a small private press, the Cruithne Press. A number of Kristian's buddies were happy to write peer-reviewed articles for a new journal and so, after one year of preparation, the first volume of the *JEA* was published in 1993. At the time Kristian and Ross published Volume 1, there was neither an editor nor an editorial board, nor yet an Association!

JEA Volume 1 was so well received that, in the light of the changes in European politics after the Fall of the Wall, Kristian began a discussion of the idea of creating an association of archaeologists for Europe. At the 1992 EUROTAG conference in Southampton (a Europe-focused conference of the Theoretical Archaeology Group), Mike Rowlands gave a paper 'Why do we need a European Association of Archaeologists?' Initially, the name of the organisation was a problem: the name that Kristian originally wanted was the AEA – the Association of European Archaeologists – but the acronym had already been taken by the Association of Environmental Archaeologists. Hence the second-choice name was adopted – the EAA or 'European Association of Archaeologists'. Holding an inaugural meeting was entirely the inspiration of Kristian and the 'provisional' EAA Organizing Committee, who invited bids from Ljubljana and Poznań and who ultimately favoured Ljubljana. Ljubljana advertised widely for the meeting of the EAA, which was held in September 1994.[1] I knew of the meeting but was unable to attend because I was in the middle of a UTP rescue excavation season at Polgár 10. But the central purpose of the Ljubljana

[1] For a hilarious account of the preparations for the inaugural meeting, see Predrag Novaković (2013).

meeting was to organise the first business meeting, where Kristian appointed the first executive board of his trusted friends. That is how the EAA started.

Kristian and Ross Samson managed to publish the second *JEA* volume in 1994 but Kristian had realised that a fully effective journal needed an Editor and an Editorial Board representing all regions of Europe. Moreover, he simply could not keep pressurising friends into writing top-notch articles indefinitely. At some point in the spring of 1995, I was working at home when I got a phone call from Kristian. To my great surprise, he offered me the chance to become Editor of the new journal – which I immediately accepted. Thus, the Kristian–Ross duo became a trio and I joined the EAA. Volume 3 of the *JEA* was more or less ready for printing, so I didn't have much to do. But I was fully in charge of the next journal volume – *JEA* 4 – and I remained the editor for eight volumes – the last four volumes of the *JEA* (volumes 4–7) and the first four volumes of the *EJA*.[2] I stepped down from the editorship at the Lisbon Annual Business Meeting.

The first time in which my job as Editor of the *JEA* could be confirmed officially was the first Annual Meeting of the EAA in Santiago de Compostela. The Annual Meeting was also the time of the first Editorial Board meeting, when the EAA appointed a number of members to the new Board. I have not been to all of the EAA Annual Meetings but of the 15 annual meetings I have attended over the last 25 years, the Santiago Annual Meeting stood out for hospitality. The wonderful food on the excursions and the fantastic quality of food and wine, especially seafood, every night of the conference, was the result of Felipe Criado Boado's energy in finding a different sponsor for each feast. This was really a standout achievement by the meeting organiser, Felipe, who at the time had been appointed to the Executive Board of the EAA. Many congratulations to Felipe for setting such a high standard for annual meetings. The other great thing about Santiago was that events happened on a Spanish timetable, so everything was timed to start late. We had a late dinner, after that a late party and the conference started at 10 am the next morning. Everything was extremely relaxed and produced the most successful EAA that I ever attended.

One of the most exciting days was the day of excursions to see rock art in the mountains south-east of Santiago, with the day ending at a lowland 'hillfort' on a small island joined to the mainland at low tide. After the group had inspected the hillfort, we came back to the car park and were immediately ushered into a restaurant where, of course, Felipe had organised a seafood reception. It turned out that the owner of the restaurant was an amateur archaeologist who kept an eye on the hillfort, so he was happy to provide us with the most spectacular seafood buffet we had eaten so far, even exceeding the standards of all the other EAA buffets at Santiago.

I also visited the famous angel sculpture near the West Door of Santiago Cathedral. The stone angel had such sumptuous breasts that an 18th-century archbishop rightly considered them an enormous temptation to his priests, so he instructed a stonemason

[2] For the change of name of the journal, see below, p. 156.

to cut off the angel's breasts. While the priests were upset, they could do nothing to express their regrets. But the townsfolk were so furious that the bakers decided that they would remind the Archbishop of this sacrilege by baking breast-shaped bread rolls in honour of the disfigured angel. Bakers still make them today.

As Editor of the *JEA*, I became an ex-officio member of the Executive Board. There was an inter-Annual Meeting Executive Board meeting and in those early years they took place in Paris, thanks to the support of Alain Schnapp, who organised the use of the Maison des Sciences de l'Homme, which used to be the social anthropologists' main meeting-place. The timetable consisted of an all-day Executive Board meeting, to be followed the next day by a half-day Editorial Board meeting, which I would chair. It was at these Executive Board meetings that I first realised the enormous energy and determination, scope and vision of Kristian Kristiansen, who was the driving-force behind the growth and development of the EAA. Using the experience he had gained while running what is now called the 'Danish Agency for Culture and Palaces', as well as his committee experience gained from being a professor of archaeology in Gothenburg University, Kristian set about creating an organisation with long-term prospects. It was an amazing sight to see Kristian at full throttle, moving the EAA onwards and upwards. Nevertheless, there were difficult moments in these long, often six- or seven-hour meetings and I have to pay tribute to my fellow Englishman, Henry Cleere (Plate 22). I had to sit next to him to make sure that we would keep each other awake with strategic nudges or whispered jokes. It was only through Henry that I managed to survive the meetings; unstoppable energy can be quite exhausting.

Despite my best efforts and those of Ross Samson at Cruithne Press, we didn't manage to publish *JEA* volume 4 in time for the Riga Annual Meeting in September 1996. It came out a few months late and this was indeed a sign of the times. I was watching carefully to see what would happen, since a backlog of journal articles was beginning to pile up.

The preparations for an annual meeting always involved several meetings between the president, the treasurer and the local Organizing Committee. In the Riga meetings, Professor Janis Graudonis – an old communist professor steeped in the ways of the old system and chair of the local Committee – wanted to have a large advance and the entire EAA email list but the president and treasurer insisted on certain conditions being met. Eventually, the conditions were met and the treasurer produced old brown-paper envelopes full of dollars for the Riga advance! A sign of how deals were clinched in Eastern Europe.

During the Riga Annual Meeting, the members of the Executive and Editorial Boards were put up in a rather fancy hotel – the Europa Hotel – on the edge of the new town. This hotel that had been built in the years following the fall of the Berlin Wall to match the style of any other fancy Western European hotel, with identical breakfast buffets to those found in the Mercure Hotel chain. What was different about the Europa Hotel was the number of ladies of the night – mostly Russian prostitutes – who waited around in the evenings and made it difficult to avoid them. A good walk into the centre of town to the conference venue was the best way to remove the stench of Euro-sleaze.

The conference was exciting and unusual for the large number of delegates from Central, Eastern and Northern Europe. Everything ran like clockwork until the evening of the Annual Dinner. Following the success of the annual dinner at Santiago, the Executive Board had decided that, on the last night of each Annual Meeting, there would be a self-funded dinner in which the local organising committee would select the finest local specialities that they could provide within their budget. The Riga organisers were happy to plan the dinner, for which every delegate would pay €20 – a princely sum in 1996 for a Baltic State. But, unbeknown to everyone else, Professor Graudonis had unilaterally decided that a large part of the €20 would be best spent on Latvian fieldwork in the next summer. Nearly 200 of us turned up for dinner in the Riga Latvian Society Hall, a very fine 1909 timber building next to the Town Hall. We climbed the grand wooden staircase to a large first-floor reception room, with tables laden with large quantities of vodka, fine salami and cheese. We started off in high spirits, thinking this was a great way to start a Latvian dinner but, after a while, there was a dawning realisation that this was the only food we were going to get. There was no main course and no dessert – just vodka, salami, bread and cheese. As this realisation spread through the 200 guests, people started to express their disapproval of how they had been cheated by the Latvians and quite a number of members left for a pizza next door. At this point, we were facing a mutiny and things were looking extremely bad for the EAA, until Kristian realised there was a honky-tonk piano in one room and persuaded Ross Samson to go and get his trumpet. So Kristian started playing jazz and blues piano to improve the mood. Then Ross arrived with his trumpet and the Ross–Kristian duo saved the evening. There was strong criticism of the EAA at the Annual Business Meeting next day, as well as strong demands for refunds for the Annual Dinner. Astoundingly, Professor Graudonis never actually turned up to this meeting. But it may not be an exaggeration to say that Kristian and Ross may well have saved the EAA with their jazz improvisation that night.

After the Riga Annual Meeting, the issues over the publication of the *JEA* were becoming increasingly serious, with up-to-date versions of corrected texts being lost and the absence of a timetable critical. One of the biggest problems was that Ross was *incommunicado* much of the time. Ross was probably away from his office a lot and, in these pre-mobile phone days, this was problematic. When things got out of hand, I discussed the communication problems with the vice-president, Willem Willems, because it was difficult to discuss Ross with Kristian because of their close friendship. Eventually, even Kristian accepted that things could not go on the way they were going and he agreed to hold an open competition for a new publisher of the journal. Of course, Cruithne Press would be invited to enter the competition as well as one other small press, the Archaeolingua Press based in Budapest, together with two large commercial publishers who wished to enter the competition – Routledge and Sage. Each of the four presses made a presentation at the inter-annual Executive

Board meeting in Paris in spring 1997. Kristian was deeply unhappy to lose Ross but the vote in the Executive Board went in favour of Sage, who had impressed us with a good financial deal that no one else could match and with their plans for marketing the journal with a new name. So the last of the *JEA*s was volume 7 for 1997 and the plan was to start up a new *European Journal of Archaeology*, with the first edition in 1998 and three editions each year. Sage had made the case for higher sales of journal with the first name of the title being 'European'. I suspect that the only unhappy professionals were librarians, with a new title and a new book size. These changes meant a lot of work for me and also for Miranda Nunhofer, my main colleague in Sage working with the *EJA*. I'd like to thank her for everything she did to smooth the transition and for managing the first four volumes of the *EJA* so well.

The next annual meeting was held in Ravenna in 1997. Not only was this a great city with fantastic historical monuments but also most of the conference sessions were held in rooms in 17th- and 18th-century *palazzi* – spectacular settings that most speakers had never experienced before. The one really weird moment was a late morning session, when I was sitting in the first floor of one such *palazzo*. I was listening to a talk when the chandeliers in the room began to sway gently. This really worried me because I knew this was the first sign of an earthquake. Since the second sign would be if the door started to move, I ignored the speaker and started watching the doors very carefully. Fortunately, they didn't move, so this was only a moderate shock. Most of the audience in the *palazzo* hadn't even realised what had happened. It was only in the evening that we learnt that there had been a sizeable earthquake in Assisi (Richter scale of 5.6–5.8), some 160 km from Ravenna and what we felt was the outer shock from the Assisi earthquake. Luckily the historic buildings in Ravenna suffered only minor damage – some losing cornices – but it suddenly brought you very close to Assisi and the scale of damage there.

The Ravenna Annual Business Meeting (ABM) was the moment of truth for me: if the Executive Board wanted to reappoint me or if I would be fired. The ABM confirmed my re-appointment for another three years. ABMs had turned into normally quite staid affairs, bordering on the tedious, but this ABM was dominated by an exchange between the Italian Professor of Prehistoric Archaeology, Maurizio Tosi, and President Kristian. An emerging trend in the EAA was that someone from the home country hosting the ABM stood for election to the Executive Board. Being a consummate politician and seizing his opportunity, Tosi offered himself for election to the Executive Board but his reputation had preceded him amongst many of the members of the EAA, not least the Italian members. Tosi failed in his bid for election – a result announced at the ABM. With hindsight, it might have been preferable to explain the result to Tosi in private before the ABM. This defeat prompted a furious speech from Tosi, who denounced the EAA as a neo-capitalist, borderline-fascist operation which had failed in all of its major aims. He was extremely critical of the Executive Board and especially President Kristian. This speech continued for 10 or 12 minutes and, eventually, like a volcano whose eruption had burnt out, Tosi dried up. At this point, Kristian stood up, smiled in Tosi's direction and said, 'Next question', moving on immediately without even confronting Tosi or any of the issues he raised. This was one of Kristian's finest moments – a superb piece of political management.

After my re-appointment as Editor, it was clear that I needed to make some improvements to the Editorial Board. In general, it was difficult to keep a balance between three categories of people on editorial boards: the 'names' – the people who are appointed to bring glory to the journal; the 'workers' – those people who do what's really needed to be done working with the editor; and the 'pretend workers' who claim that they're doing a lot but in fact do little or nothing. Fortunately, it was EAA policy not to appoint any 'names' at all to the Editorial Board[3] but we had very good examples of both the 'workers' (for example, Teresa Chapa de Brunet) and the 'pretend workers' (for example, Peter Biehl). I tried hard to encourage every 'worker' on the Editorial Board to do more by setting out guidelines for each member to review each of the submissions and to encourage the 'pretend workers' to stop pretending and start working. These efforts worked only to a certain extent; the EAA Constitution made it very hard to remove freeloaders from the Editorial Board.

It was in the year leading up to the Gothenberg Annual Meeting in 1998 that I had my first and only serious battle with a member of the Editorial Board. The dispute concerned an appalling review of a Mike Rowlands–Susan Frankenstein book by the German prehistorian Louis Nebelsick – a task that was handed to Nebelsick by the reviews editor Peter Biehl. The latter was quite prepared to accept the *ad hominem* nature of the review, which was such a disgraceful criticism that I simply refused to publish it. I emphasised to the Editorial Board that this decision was not because of my friendship with Mike Rowlands (although I was friends with Mike) but because of the principle that such a personal review had no place in an academic forum such as the *EJA*. With the exception of Peter Biehl, the Editorial Board backed me unanimously. Since Biehl had voted against this motion, I suggested he might like to consider his position on the Editorial Board – an option that he decided not to take.

The issue of peer review also raised its head around this time. Although common in America and Western Europe, the practice of peer reviewing papers for journals was not widespread in Central and Eastern Europe and indeed in some quarters was deeply resented. One case concerning a salt paper that Nenad Tasić had written in 1999 and which I rejected for what I considered perfectly good reasons soured our relations for many years; indeed, Nenad occasionally complained about his rejection as recently as 2019. The worst problem of the peer review system concerned a paper offered by the Czech archaeologist Rotislav Pšenko, which was turned down following peer reviews from three other specialists. At this point, and without actually discussing the peer review comments that I had included in my polite letter of rejection, Pšenko sent a series of protest emails to every member

[3] Cynics would suggest they were serving on the Executive Board already!

of the Executive and Editorial Boards under the strap headline 'DOWN WITH JOHN CHAPMAN'. Mark Pearce has a folder of all of these letters, which certainly describe me as a fascist and the worst journal editor in Europe. The Pšenko file is one of Mark's most treasured possessions and served him well when he became Editor of the *EJA* in his turn.

In the inter-annual meeting of the Executive Board in spring 1998 and indeed at the 1998 Annual Meeting in Bournemouth, the EAA had to confront head-on an issue that had been getting worse for the last few years and which they had struggled with for some time – its own internal finances. Although more money than ever before was coming in from Sage from improved journal sales, at the same time the EAA finances were hanging by a thread and the problem was simply the continuity of membership. Like most such organisations, the EAA depended heavily for the members' subscriptions to keep going. At each new annual meeting, we both gained members, since those wishing to come to the meeting had to register for membership – a Kristian Kristiansen innovation at the time of the Gothenburg Annual Meeting – but also lost almost all of the members who weren't coming to the next annual meeting. One poorly attended annual meeting could wreak havoc with the entire EAA budgeting process. Modelling showed that, if we were not to get at least 1,200 members at the Bournemouth Annual Meeting, the EAA would be in serious deficit and the organisation might have to close. This was also a personal financial issue for the members of the Executive Board, since we were joint guarantors of the EAA budget. In fact, because the meeting was held in Bournemouth and because a high proportion of members came from Britain, the EAA managed to hit the target number. The instability of the finances had certainly been an issue for four or five of the last years in which I was sitting as an ex-officio member of the Executive Board. It was not for some time until a radical solution was put into effect.

After two terms of working as Editor for the EAA, it was my turn to step down at the 2000 Annual Meeting in Lisbon, when I was replaced by the new editor, Mark Pearce, from Nottingham. I have made my feelings very clear about the challenging, exciting, delightful and wonderful time I'd had with the *Journal of European Archaeology* and then the *European Journal of Archaeology* in an account in my last editorial (issue 4/1). At the Lisbon Annual Business Meeting, the new president, Willem Willems, who had just taken over from Kristian Kristiansen, kindly offered both Kristian and me lifetime membership of the EAA. Although I was totally delighted by this honour, I made a short but stunningly inappropriate speech wondering why I hadn't been told about this before I paid €75 for my next year's membership a mere two hours before the kind offer. Willem Willems said the only thing he could have said, which was simply to pretend that he hadn't heard this. Why did I say such a thing? This intervention undoubtedly stopped me from ever being approached by the EAA for any kind of future office, which was perhaps why I said it. Inside me was the feeling that I'd done a fascinating job that I was happy with and I didn't want to continue in any other job in the Association.

It was certainly a politically inept move and, in some ways, I regretted it. But, in other ways, I'm happy not to have become a member of the Nominations Committee checking on the credentials of those standing for future elections. I was happy with my time and it had reached an end. I want to thank the EAA not only for making me their Editor in such an interesting time of growth and change in the journal but also for honouring me with lifetime membership.

At one of the last EAAs that I attended, in Barcelona in 2018, my perception of the EAA was that it had become what a lot of societies become in their middle years – an established club where some people kept getting jobs by rotation and where there was a desperate lack of new blood and new ideas. The cutting edge of the *EJA* in research terms has been dulled and the battles for equal gender and regional representation have still not yet been won – even after 25 years. I am happy that the new president Felipe Criado Boado – at the time of writing in his third year of office – did what he did at the Santiago Annual Meeting and more recently helped the EAA recover from the Fritz Lüth presidency. It is also a tribute to Felipe and his team that the EAA managed to weather the first year of the storm caused by the coronavirus (2020).

Chapter 11

Life in Durham

A full life in Durham started rather later than the start of my job in Durham, since I was still living in Newcastle in Heaton, near the Corner House jazz pub. For the first two years, I was car-sharing with Mike Goldstein, a professor of Mathematics. We would go in to Durham four days a week, with a research day at home on the fifth day. The most exciting aspect of our morning commute through the Newcastle, Gateshead and Durham rush-hours was the construction of the Angel of the North, which we saw gradually growing into its full majesty. As many long-term car-sharers find, it's difficult to find new things to talk about after a year or two. Some car-sharers watch their partner's favourite films or TV programmes but I didn't want to go that far. So after two years, we decided that our car-sharing days were over. In any case, I had spent a research year in Hungary and, on my return, moved to a small flat near Forest Hall. This year, I had a solo drive four days a week.

The major change in my life in Durham was that my relationship with my former PhD student, Bisserka, was growing into something serious. I eventually returned to Durham, first renting a house in Gilesgate before we decided that we wanted to live together. We moved into a rented house in Church Crescent in Meadowfield village and were married on 18 February 2006. Our wedding took place on a bright and sunny February day. Our neighbour Brian Nelson had very kindly offered his own *barouche* to drive us to the registry office in Old Elvet. Bisserka, her son by her first marriage Boyan and I rode in this car, while Laci and Alice, our best man and maid of honour who had flown over specially from Hungary, drove with other friends. The group met in the Durham Registry Office – at the time, an elegant but compact place that seated a maximum of 20 people. After the ceremony, we went into the little garden of the registry office for photos in the sun (Plate 23). It was a gloriously sunny day for the short walk along Old Elvet to the Market Square and Claypath, where we had reserved the upper room of Oldfields restaurant. We had a wonderful wedding lunch, with a hilarious speech from Laci, who of course knew far too much about me (luckily Alice did not know quite so much about Bisserka). Vintage champagne and the wedding cake marked the climax of the meal and the start of a new life together.

We very much wanted to buy the rented house in Penryn Way but the owner refused to sell, so we looked around for a house with a ground-floor bedroom and ensuite facilities so that Bisserka's mother Penka could come to stay long-term – we were worried about her since the death of her husband Ivan in 2006. Having looked at maybe 80 houses, we found a house in Red Courts in Brandon village that had the right configuration of rooms. We bought the Brandon house in September 2006 and still live there. Penka came over twice to stay with us in the winter months. In the winter of 2006/7, she was in good health but the second time, sadly, her health declined and she died in the Queen Elizabeth Hospital Gateshead in February 2008. The Critical Care Unit at the QEH holds an annual memorial service for those who have died in their care and we still attend, more than a decade on.

Two of the three other big changes in my life were musical. It had been a long time since I'd learnt a new instrument and I thought I'd like to try a brass instrument in one of the local bands. One of our neighbours in Church Crescent, Brian Yates, played horn in the Spennymoor Youth Brass Band and he persuaded me to join the band. When I met the conductor, George Nicklin, he explained that youth bands needed older people to play the big instruments. When George said that they had a spare tuba and would I like to learn it, I replied, 'Yes, if you can teach me'. The main challenge was to adjust my breathing technique and *embouchure* from a clarinet to that of a tuba but, after two years, I was playing reasonably well. I regret that I haven't made much improvement since but I could at least help the bass section in the Spennymoor Youth Brass Band. Being used to committees, I volunteered to be the band secretary and this introduced me into a whole new dimension of inter-necine council struggles which I won't go into now. Suffice to say that, after a protracted dispute between the Spennymoor Senior Band and our Youth Band, our group resigned *en masse* and migrated to Fishburn to become the Fishburn Academy Band. I kept playing for Fishburn until 2018.

The other great musical experience I had came about through a friend, Kate Sharpe, then a post-doc in the Archaeology department, who persuaded me to join the Durham Choral Society. I hadn't sung much since school choir and wasn't sure if my voice was up to it but, since the choir didn't have voice tests, I joined the bass section, which was small and composed mostly of people who'd been singing together for 10 or 20 years. I joined for two concert seasons, primarily because the first winter concert in Durham Cathedral was the Verdi 'Requiem'. I never thought that I would have the opportunity to sing the 'Requiem' – an amazingly passionate piece. Comparing it to the Fauré 'Requiem', with its stillness, calm and elegance, the Verdi 'Requiem' is like a storm, with the most thunderous part of the storm the *Dies Irae*. To sing the *Dies Irae* with the whole choir and orchestra playing to the maximum possible volume was one of the most exhilarating musical experiences I've ever enjoyed.

By the time of the second concert, we had changed choral directors and appointed Mike Summers. Immediately, there was a new, more dynamic atmosphere in the choir; even the warm-ups were different, with lots more active singing and even a smattering of yoga breathing. It was quite a challenge to work with the new music director, since his standards were much higher than those of the former conductor. He chose two pieces for his first concert in the Cathedral. The first was William Walton's 'Belshazzar's Feast', which we practised in the first half of our rehearsal. The choir found this a difficult piece and the conductor was often very critical – especially of the altos! We then had a coffee break and returned to the delightful balm of the Fauré 'Requiem', which was conducted not by the new director but by Clare Lawrence-Wills, who gave us a much easier time. We were all struggling with the Walton right up to the fortnight before the concert and things looked bad. I'm sure that most singers were practising the Walton hard at home because, miraculously, the Walton came together on the night. We had never sung the 'Feast' so well and the audience confirmed later that it had really worked well. That was an unexpected triumph; the Fauré 'Requiem' was so relaxing to sing after the challenges of the Walton.

After two winter concerts, I had a really difficult decision to make, because at the same time as the Durham Choral Society rehearsals, a yoga class led by the uiversity chemistry lecturer Ritu Kataky had started up. My wife persuaded me that my body needed the yoga more than the choir needed my voice. Although I often wanted to go back to the choir, once I started yoga lessons, I realised that this was something I should have started a long time ago. So the needs of my body took precedence over the pleasures of singing. I hardly dare suggest that music's loss was yoga's gain, for I have consistently been the worst-performing member of the yoga class for 10 years.

The Hatha yoga class was a beautiful affair – a contemplative form in which the aim is to integrate your breathing, your bodily position and your mental state so as to come into a mental state of calm and peacefulness. But this learning process takes time and I was a complete Yoga beginner, whereas Bisserka had taken some yoga classes before; moreover, her body was much younger and more supple than mine. My body would just not perform even the simplest of stretches at all. My very first yoga class was an enormous shock – a revelation that my body had not been treated kindly for a very long time. If there is one thing about my life I regret, it's that no one had introduced me to yoga when I was much younger. Our teacher Ritu is extremely patient with all of us, especially with the worst performer in the class, and found ways for me to tackle positions that I found difficult. My body was initially unresponsive to many yoga positions, whether the plank, the downward dog or the Cobra position. My favourite position was the bridge. Ritu's instruction about coming down from the highest bridge that you can manage was to 'come down notch by notch, vertebra by vertebra'. The motto for my yoga class was 'notch by notch'.

One of the great things about the EAA Annual Meetings was that the local organisers put on excursions to see some of their most stunning archaeology both before and after the conference. Before the September 2014 Annual Meeting in Istanbul, a trip was organised to the monuments of eastern Turkey and, since we'd never been so far east in Turkey, we booked on this trip, which took us to places that would have been extremely hard to reach otherwise. It was a fantastic trip, with the stand-out sites being the Göbekli Tepe complex, the early site of Cayönü and the great Chalcolithic and Bronze Age tell of Aslan Tepe. For their own protection, the carved menhirs had been removed from Göbekli Tepe and placed in a newly built museum in Şanlıurfa. Although the museum wasn't officially open yet, the EAA group was allowed to spend a couple of hours looking at the fantastic Göbekli carvings – probably the earliest ritual site in the Mesolithic world. The visit to Çayönü Tepesi took us on a 2 km walk past a spectacular, if small-scale rocky landscape replete with weird shapes and strange rocks. Although the report on the Çayönü excavatipons is a model of precision and detail, no one mentioned the rocky landscape (Plate 24), which may have been why the tell was founded just 50 m opposite. The Aslan Tepe visit was also special because the excavator, Marcella Frangipane, was there to show us around the superbly preserved wall paintings and palace buildings.

After the Istanbul Annual Meeting, we organised a private holiday in north-east Turkey centred on the town of Trabzond (formerly 'Trebizond'), a place I'd been wanting to come to since I was a teenager and seen its Seljuk bridges. We rented a flat in the western suburbs, 20 minutes' walk to the centre of town. It was easy enough to find fantastic food in the local fruit and vegetable shops and there was a magnificent fresh fish shop with its own restaurant next door, which we found hard to resist in the evenings. There was only one thing it was impossible to do and that was to find alcohol. This was a very strict Muslim community, with a strictly observed prohibition on the sale of alcohol in shops and restaurants. It took several rather embarrassing questions before I found a fruit seller who pointed to a small building with black shutters on both windows and a black painted door. We waited until the evening before knocking on the door and entering the Holy Grail – an off-licence. The owners were trained to camouflage their sales of Efes, our favourite Turkish beer, in a black box inside a black plastic bag and we escaped with our loot back to the flat.

Instead of renting a car in Trabzon, we made several coach trips. The most intriguing was to Batumi just over the border in Georgia. This was the rainiest trip we'd ever been on, in which the guide valiantly took us around the Roman fort at the entrance to town, followed by mosques and cathedrals. But this was really a losing battle, with too much wind to allow the umbrellas to function. Despite missing a trip to the Botanic Gardens simply to warm up with Georgian tea and rum in a tea house, we all came back totally soaked and freezing cold. The other trip was to the Sümela monastery cut into the rock faces of a limestone gorge, with tiny cells providing both living accommodation and chapels. Further up the gorge was an old Ottoman cemetery with standing stones similar to those we had studied in Bulgaria.[1] The only

[1] For the Forest of Stones project, see p. 183 ff.

sad thing about the trip was that I never saw the Seljuk bridges which prompted the trip in the first place.

The most amazing treat that happened came in the middle of the winter of 2010/11. It had been my habit since I was a teenager to watch the New Year's Day concert from the Vienna *Musikverein* and I'd certainly done this every time that I could when I was with Bisserka and Boyan. We were approaching Christmas 2015 and we hadn't made any special plans for New Year's Eve but it occurred to me that it was our turn to invite people around. Bisserka is normally extremely sociable but downplayed the idea. I thought this was rather odd but accepted her decision. By the 27th December, Boyan and Bisserka looked at each other rather guiltily and she admitted that the reason we couldn't have a New Year's party in Durham was that she'd booked three tickets for the Vienna New Year's concert and that we were flying on the 29th. I was absolutely astonished, not so much at Bisserka's organisation – although she had to book the concert tickets on 2 January 2015, one year minus one day before the concert – as that Boyan, who was 17 at the time, had kept this secret for the whole year.

We flew off to a bright, sunny, cold and snowy Vienna and, after two days of sight-seeing, walked from our hotel to the *Musikverein* and had the concert of my lifetime. We still had two more days in Vienna to see many other great music venues, including the House of Music, where dancing in different ways on the floor produced different rhythms and where Boyan could spend time as the conductor of the Vienna Philharmonic. We also went to Haydn's *Wohnhaus* – much more modest than Mozart's house – and saw the Christmas exhibitions at the Kunsthistorisches Museum. A truly wonderful surprise trip!

Eleanor's birthday in 2016 was her 40th, so we really had to do something special. This time, I suggested that we could make a trip to Scotland. Eleanor had always believed in the Loch Ness Monster and suggested that we go to Loch Ness and see the monster. This led to a very entertaining month or two in which I was reading up about the history of the monster story and about all the attempts to find the monster and why most of them – perhaps all of them – had failed. But Eleanor was convinced that this was a great idea. After a five-hour drive from Tyneside, we arrived at the Drumnadrochit Hotel on the north side of Loch Ness. Right next to it, a new Loch Ness Visitor Centre had opened, so we were in exactly the right place. We spent an hour or so each day, sitting on a bench with our binoculars, watching and waiting to see the monster. Twice Eleanor cried out and said she thought she saw the monster moving but I could sadly never confirm these sightings. We did, however, have a wonderful birthday dinner in the loch-side Dores Inn restaurant.

The other thing about Loch Ness is that it's actually very close to the Isle of Skye, which is now more accessible than before because of the bridge. I had long wanted to see Loch Coruisk, said to be one of the most beautiful lochs in Scotland. When I was 15, I read a *Guardian* article about the way that the locals had protected the loch and its beautiful scenery against the army, who had wanted to build an unsightly bridge over the neck of the loch. The loch was so special to the locals that they blew up both the first and the second bridges, even though they would have helped mountain rescue on the Black Cuillin.

I had tried twice to see Coruisk but each time was foiled by appalling weather. Maybe this time, I would be luckier. We drove down the Loch Ness road to Fort Augustus and made our way to the Kyle of Lochalsh and over the new bridge. Once on Skye, we went to the Sligachan Inn, driving on all the way down a very narrow one-track road with passing points to Elgol village – the closest village to Loch Coruisk. There was little to do at Elgol except for talking to the fishermen and I asked how often boat trips went to Coruisk. They said there was a 2 pm boat with the return trip lasting two hours. But I couldn't persuade Eleanor to come with me and I didn't want to leave her at Elgol for such a long time, so I failed once again to get to Loch Coruisk. As a consolation prize, we went to Ashaig for Isle of Skye cod and chips.

After our last night in the hotel on Loch Ness, we spent our final hour looking for the monster before we left and drove through Inverness to see the recently opened battlefield centre at Culloden, which told the battle story very well. We then had a five-hour trip back to Newcastle in the rain and, because Eleanor couldn't resist smoking from time to time, we had to keep the windows of the car open to get rid of the tobacco smell. It was a cold and wet ride back but we survived the ride and we got back after a memorable 40th birthday trip.

One of the best things about retirement, which began on September 2017, was that you can choose the times you go for trips rather than just university holidays. We were able to book the first cruise I'd ever been on in the middle of Term 2 – a trip to see the Northern Lights. The ferry company Hurtigruten was recommended to us by Per and Vanessa – Per a Norwegian who knew his country's ferry lines very well and Vanessa who spent a lot of time with Per in Norway.[2] In fact, a cruise was the *only* way to go to see the west coast of Norway, taking us to the Northern Lights and the Arctic Circle. Hurtigruten boats were not simply tourist liners but working ships that took the locals, the mail and commercial baggage up and down the coast.

We had made friends in previous EAA Annual Meetings with Knut-Andreas Bergsvik but we hadn't met his wife Gitte. When we told Knut that we were coming to Bergen for the start of a Hurtigruten cruise, he replied that they knew where the berth of the cruise liner was and invited us to stay with them. So we came three days early and had a fantastic time with Knut and Birgitte. On one day, we went on a full-day trip to see Knut's rock art sites and, on another day, we made a half-day trip to see Grieg's house, the wooden Fantoft stave church and the medieval monastery of Lysekloster. On the other day, we played tourist and looked around

[2] It was with deep sadness that we record the death of Per before our Norwegian trip.

Bergen town centre with its beautifully restored warehouses and superb museums, so we really had a wonderful start to our holiday before we even got on the boat just before midnight.

The Hurtigruten boat was extremely comfortable. The dinners were the only meals where you sat at a table with assigned seats – every other meal was a buffet meal where you could choose your partners. We were assigned to a dinner table with two retired ladies from Kent and Surrey, who came on trips together and proved to be extremely versatile raconteurs. The thing about the Northern Lights is that, however dazzling they look on a promotional video, it is extremely rare to find them looking so spectacular when you see them with your own eyes. Hurtigruten were quite upfront about the risks that we may not see the Northern Lights at all but, since our cruise was the last weekend in February 2018, we had a fair chance of seeing the Lights. Passengers had to respond quickly to the captain's call for action; if the captain saw the Northern Lights, an announcement would go out into every cabin. On the second night, our dinner companions responded to the call and went out and saw the Northern Lights, faintly but quite distinctly, for about half an hour. We were so tired from intensive eating and drinking that we did not go on deck – thinking there would be many more chances. That was the last time that the Northern Lights appeared for a week.

We slowly headed north up the Norwegian coast, stopping at a succession of fascinating small harbours (maybe only for an hour) and towns where we could look around. As we crossed the Arctic Circle, the scenery became even more dramatic, especially the deep fjords of the Norwegian coast. At one point, we went to North Cape, which was the closest point on the coast to the North Pole and saw stunning sea cliffs (Fig. 19) and a series of Sami summer sites. The final stop of our cruise was the town of Kirkenes, where we went for a husky ride and stayed in an ice hotel. The ice hotel was really exciting (Fig. 20); ice hotels don't last long – they are built in November using a centrifuge to create blocks of ice from fresh snow and stay up till they melt in the spring. We had booked a room in the ice hotel and were supplied with Norwegian Army Arctic division survival gear – the warmest sleeping bag you've ever climbed into. After the recommended solid dinner, we went outside and, to our utter delight, the Northern Lights appeared. We stayed outside watching them as the diffuse green and slightly light blue light moved across the night sky. After half an hour, Bisserka checked the temperature on an outside thermometer and it was -24°C, at which point we thought probably it was a good idea to go inside. But at last we had seen the Northern Lights. Our night in the ice hotel was absolutely amazing. We settled down inside the sleeping bags and slept very soundly.

We had a free morning in the town of Kirkenes, where we saw the town museum with a dramatic display of the battle between the Germans and the Russians in 1944 and another room displaying Sami culture illustrated by their own paintings and etchings. Our return trip took us to Edinburgh via Oslo. A breathtaking trip!

Another chance to add trips onto the main event was the EAA Annual Meeting in Barcelona in 2018, what with local cuisine, beautiful conference spaces and brilliant

Fig. 19. North Cape, northern Norway

Fig. 20. Ice hotel, Kirkenes, north Norway

conference organisation by Margarita Díaz-Andreu. Before the Barcelona meeting, we booked into an EAA excursion to the island of Menorca, the great rival to the bigger island of Majorca but full of amazing megalithic monuments built in a stunning rocky landscape. We went on this five-day trip in which the price partly reflected the beautiful accommodation in the Sant Ignasi eco-hotel just outside the capital but also included lunches and dinners where you could drink as much as you wanted. Since this was late August and very high temperatures for site visiting, it was easy to consume litres of cold lager at lunchtime to be energised for the afternoon programme.

After the Barcelona Annual Meeting, we had planned to go to Sevilla, so we contacted Leo Garcia, with whom Bisserka had worked on Alasdair Whittle's 'Times of their Lives' project. We had discovered that, on the way it was possible to stop in Almería for six hours to visit the famous Copper Age fortified site of Los Millares before taking the evening flight on to Sevilla. This was a great plan but we made one mistake – not to include a SatNav with the car. When we drove off from the airport, I had an old map and we wasted half an hour on wrong turns. We knew that we should aim to arrive at the monument at 1 pm, because the site was due to close at 2 pm on a Sunday. We blew it by arriving only at 1.50 pm. We hoped that playing the 'British professors of Archaeology visiting a famous site' card would persuade the guard to let us see more of the extensive site. As was within her rights, the guard refused; maybe she had a family lunch planned for 3 pm? So we set off, noticing two elderly visitors who were moving so slowly as to give us extra time. We ran around three of the main parts of the site, seeing two of the cairn groups and one part of the defensive wall. At 2.02 pm, we started to run back to the gate, where the guard stood, looking extremely angry and threatening to lock us in. As we walked back to the car park, I took a photo of the guard on my camera, because she was so rude not only to us but to other visitors too and showed no sympathy for our predicament. This so enraged her that she insisted that I delete the photo and threatened to call the police if I did not. I replied, 'Call the police!', so the Guardia civil delayed her departure by another 20 minutes, arriving at 2.30 pm. When the police arrived, we explained the story and they asked if we wanted to make an official complaint about this lady. We replied, 'Of course – she won't even give us her name!' The form-filling in triplicate took more time and the policeman decided that no further action would be taken against *us* (!) provided that I deleted the photos. I agreed on condition that the police gave us her name, to which he agreed. The guard stormed off 45 minutes after she wanted to close the site. After lunch, we returned to Los Millares to walk around the perimeter fence and found some excellent vantage points over the east gate and the fortification walls with their bastions. We also gained a very good sense of the general landscape of Los Millares, which we couldn't have understood from within the site. But we did get a really good impression of how the Spanish archaeological 'service' treated their foreign tourists and a very good impression of Los Millares. This experience was in sharp contrast to the laid-back Spanish way of living. We managed to get back to the airport in time for the evening flight to Sevilla.

In Sevilla, we reached our rented flat in the centre of the city late by British time but early by Sevilla time and had a really pleasant meal seated outside in a restaurant five minutes from our flat. After two days, we met Leo who took us to one of the most famous megasites in Iberia – Valencina de la Conceptión. This turned out to be an all-day trip because, unlike our Ukrainian megasites, there were several major mortuary monuments forming the main architectural foci dispersed across the site. The tomb of La Pastora was open for viewing, giving us a sense of monumental megalithic construction in south-west Spain. Later that day, Leo took us to two of the major megalithic complexes in the Sevilla basin – Soto and Matarrubilla – both tombs overlooked by a striking mountain whose main ridge looked exactly like an Native American brave in costume (Plate 25). It was not surprising that both monumental complexes were oriented on this extraordinary natural feature.

Next day, Leo drove us 80 km to the town of Antequera to show us a rocky landscape covered with rock forms that took on all kinds of shapes. This would have been a landscape entirely suited to Ana Raduntcheva, who loved such natural shapes. We ended this great day with a celebration meal in one of the best tapas bars in the centre of Sevilla. We spent the next day on a train trip to Cadiz. Our last day in Sevilla was a tourist day in the city, when we visited the Monastery of Santa Maria de las Cuevas, where Leo's wife Silvia worked. In the evening, we had the largest sangrias we had ever drunk in Spain to celebrate the trip.

2019 was a remarkable year for two reasons. First of all, in March, we celebrated Bisserka's 50th birthday. I organised a ceilidh party for the occasion in Spennymoor Town Hall. From my time in Spennymoor Brass Band, I realised that the town hall was a great party venue for ceilidhs and also provided simple dinners with copious alcohol. Lots of friends came and the dancing was spectacular. I think it was a fitting party for her 50th. Then, in July, Boyan graduated with a good Law degree from University College London (Plate 26).

The major celebration of the two events of 2019 was a trip that we organised for the Australian cool season – in June. Because this was such a long way to fly, we decided to go for a month's trip. We spent a week in Melbourne, where Bisserka's great Bulgarian friend, Mimi, showed us around, then a week at Uluru, a few days in the north near Darwin, visiting Kakadu National Park and seeing salt-water crocodiles, then a few days on the east coast in Port Douglas to see the Great Barrier Reef and ancient rain forests, and a last week in Sydney, with side trips to the Blue Mountains with Kirrily White and to Canberra. What was so striking was the variety of the continent; every single day produced wonderful events or scenery and each day was different from all of the others. It was a truly magnificent holiday and a fitting reward for 50 years on the planet and three years of (occasional) hard work getting a law degree in London.

One of the pleasures of living in Durham is the biennial Lumiere Festival, which happens on odd-numbered years. It started in 2009 and the idea was to display the works of 'light-and-music artists' to produce a series of spectacles across the city.

In the first Lumiere, the most amazing spectacle was a 40-minute history of the cathedral projected onto the north wall of Durham Cathedral. On a smaller scale, an inventive idea was to fill one of the old-style red telephone boxes in the market square in Durham with water, also adding several goldfish. The telephone box was sealed and left for the entire Lumiere week. The university's best contribution in 2013 took advantage of the opening of the new Ogden Centre for Fundamental Physics, when a 30-minute cosmological sound-and-light show was projected onto the strangely angled roof of the building. Every year has its stand-out events and there were two particular ones in 2019. The first was a virtual reality show of a whale swimming in the River Wear, which you could see near the Radison Hotel. The university contribution featured the Botanical Gardens, where there is a mixture of a formal garden, well-kept woods and hirsute forest. For the Lumiere show, there were 20 different places in the orderly forest, with lots of virtual electric birds flying above your head and many different illuminated flowers and bugs crawling along your path. It was the sheer variety of these presentations that made this one of the best events in the 2019 show.

Moving to Durham brought me into a much larger department than at Newcastle, which meant a lot more specialised teaching. While in Newcastle, I was teaching all of later European prehistory from the Mesolithic to the Iron Age, in Durham there were specialists for each period and so I was teaching Neolithic and Copper Age Europe only. While this was an enormous pleasure, it was bad for my overall archaeological development since I didn't keep as up-to-date with what was happening in the rest of European prehistory as I used to. The other feature of the Durham teaching system was the emphasis on team teaching for general courses at all levels. Sometimes I would lead the team-taught module, while, at other times, I would contribute a few lectures. I was also encouraged to teach a Level 3 special topic, which I alternated between two Balkan Neolithic and Copper Age modules – 'Landscape, material culture and society' and 'Social communities and networks in Balkan prehistory'. This teaching was pure pleasure and occasionally a student would be inspired by those lectures to write a Masters paper with me. This meant that my teaching was kept within certain limits and there were very few years when I taught eight hours a week, with mostly five or six hours of teaching per week.

The size of the Durham department meant it was well-known and attracted our other researchers in addition to the research staff employed on other colleagues' research projects. This certainly helped in two successful applications to the EU for Marie Curie fellows. The first one was Enikő Magyari, a stellar palaeo-environmentalist from Hungary, who also worked with Brian Huntley and Judy Allen in Biological Sciences. Eni and her partner Áron took us on a successful pollen coring trip in Bulgaria and Turkey. The second Marie Curie fellow was Antonio Blanco Gonzáles, whom you have already read about in the context of fragmentation studies.[3] He published several high-profile papers as a result of his time in Durham from 2012 to 2014. Marie Curie

[3] See above, p. 150.

supervisions were really stimulating and enjoyable, as were some of the Durham PhDs. I supervised three successful PhDs who finished their doctorates more or less on time. The first was Burcin Erdoğu from Turkey, who risked the ire of the Istanbul Big Boss Mehmet Özdoğan by coming to Durham. Burcin wrote about Neolithic and Chalcolithic landscapes in European Turkey. His input was important at the start of the 'Forest of Stones' project[4] and we later collaborated with him on salt research.[5] The second PhD student was Bisserka Gaydarska, who started in late 1999. She had written to five British universities suggesting a PhD on a Balkan prehistoric topic and I was the only person to reply, so she came to Durham. She completed her PhD with a six-month extension, despite the fact that she was looking after her son Boyan for three years, as a single mother for the last year, so she was incredibly well-organised and dynamic. What she hadn't realised when she came to Durham was that I would ask her to re-shape her PhD entirely because the database she had for the Maritsa Iztok rescue excavations was simply incapable of sustaining a full-scale contextual analysis. This meant much more landscape work for Bisserka, who learnt GIS and performed a 'rescue GIS analysis' to re-create the Maritsa Iztok landscape, which had been devastated by open-cast coal mining. The successful use of GIS enabled her to reconstruct Neolithic, Copper Age and Early Bronze Age settlement patterns in her study region.

The third PhD student was Elena Sulioti from Greece. Her topic of 'Symbolism in Minoan Crete' was a little outside my field of specialisation but, since I knew a lot about symbolism and Minoan Crete was one of the places that brought me into archaeology in the first place, I thought that I would be able to find a co-supervisor who was a Minoan specialist to manage this PhD together. Unfortunately, Oliver Dickinson, Durham's leading Aegean Bronze Age specialist, had just retired from the Classics Department the year before and Anthony Harding had moved to Exeter, so there was no one else in Durham. I contacted Sheffield but the Sheffield department clearly felt I was superfluous to the arrangement and tried to persuade Elena to go to Sheffield full-time. But since her close friend at that time had won a scholarship in the Classics Department, Elena insisted on living in Durham. In the end, I approached Nicos Momigliani, a Minoan specialist teaching at Bristol but living in Oxford to be an external co-supervisor. Nikos got on very well with Elena, so the joint supervision worked effectively. Elena's highpoint was organising a 'symbolism workshop' in University College Durham in her third PhD year in February 2014, which showcased her energy and enthusiasm. I was very pleased when she completed her PhD a year late in 2016.

I inherited two PhDs – one from Bradford via Charlotte Roberts, who had transferred from Bradford to Durham but felt unable to continue with Anastasia Tsaliki, whom she considered to be a difficult student. Anastasia's topic was a

[4] See below, p. 183 ff.
[5] See below, p. 179 ff.

specific form of burial treatment in Greek prehistory and history, in which rituals to prevent the body and the soul from escaping from the tomb used either boulders or stakes through the body. This was almost fringe archaeology but Anastasia was very determined to do this. I persevered for two years, offering advice on how to make her work more rigorous. Eventually, the relationship with Anastasia became unsustainable after a conversation in which I explained the important Albanian component of the 'Greek' city of Volos right up into the 1940s. She considered that I'd insulted her and her country, refusing to work further with me. The then head of department, Chris Gerrard, came up with the solution of arm's-length supervision of Anastasia until she submitted her PhD, which happily passed.

The other student I inherited from Anthony Harding when he left for Exeter was Bruce Albert, a garrulous Texan who wore shorts and t-shirts all year round. Bruce had done an enormous amount of work in the Czech Republic, coring several sites and completing some extremely good pollen analysis but Bruce seemed incapable of writing things up. Bruce was also a great talker and a half-hour supervision could easily turn into a three-hour marathon chat if the supervisor allowed it. When Anthony left Durham to go to Exeter, I took over Bruce. I tried to standardise his approach, attempting to get him to formulate his strong methodology. Eventually, after much blood, sweat and tears, he submitted a mammoth PhD which passed. Later, he went on to work very successfully in my Ukrainian project, producing one of the best pollen diagrams in Ukraine.[6]

We also had a visit for a three-month CACEE fellowship in St Mary's College for Ivana Radovanović and her daughter at Mila.[7] I had known Ivana for many years from times in Belgrade and she was then the greatest living Serbian authority on the Iron Gates Mesolithic before the processual phase of Serbian archaeology developed using archaeological science in this region. Ivana actually saved me by putting me up for a week in her flat while I was recovering from the collapse of my second marriage. I was and remain immensely thankful to her for taking in a marriage refugee when she herself was a refugee from war-torn 'Yugoslavia'.

Another real pleasure was the annual visit – at least for three years – to Trevelyan College of Alison Wylie the archaeological philosopher and her partner Sam. Alison had an agreement with her University at Seattle that she could teach for one term a year in the Durham Philosophy Department. She didn't teach as much archaeological philosophy as we should have persuaded her to do but, instead, she taught ethics and applied ethics on heritage research. We went on several expeditions; perhaps the one that Alison and Sam found the most interesting was the visit to Wallington Hall, a National Trust property in Northumberland that had been owned by the Trevelyan family and displayed close connections to their college. It was a great shame when

[6] For the importance of the Nebelivka pollen diagram, see below, p. 209.

[7] For the CACEE research centre, see p. 86.

Alison changed universities to Vancouver, who would not agree to the continuation of part-time teaching in Durham.

The size of the Durham department was an important element in attracting interesting researchers but it also meant a heavy administrative load to be shared among the large staff of between 20 and 25 full-time teachers. The rotating three-year headship in Durham was a notoriously difficult job to look after a large and often unruly department. The continuing influence of Rosemary Cramp long after her retirement was best seen in the group known as 'Rosemary's Babies' – all of whom became Heads of Department in Durham or elsewhere.[8] I know that three of the heads who served while I was in Durham had associated health problems, one of them having to step down after two of the three years after serious issues. I had realised early that this was not a job that I wanted at all, even though it may be that my appointment brought with it the expectation that I would develop leadership and admin skills and become Head of Department in time. However, from the very beginning, I had absolutely no political ambitions in Durham and felt that any promotion would be based upon my academic research. I think Colin Haselgrove realised this quite early at a well-known feature of Durham academic life – the 'political dinner', in which Heads of Department would invite Deans and colleagues to arrange things. Colin was a master at these dinners and, quite soon after I arrived in Durham, he arranged a dinner for the Deputy Dean of Social Sciences, Joy Palmer, and her philosopher husband, my partner and me. I managed to spend most of an extremely pleasant evening talking philosophy and hardly said a word – certainly no strategic discussions – with the Deputy Dean. This gave the intended signal to the Decanate and to Colin.

Any thoughts that anyone harboured of me becoming Head of Department disappeared one weekend in 2000. This was an examination fiasco concerning the 'Introduction to Archaeology' Level 1 module taken by up to 100 students – not only archaeologists but first-year students from other departments as an external subject. The exam had been timetabled for a Monday morning at 9.30 am. On the Friday afternoon before, I had sent out a message about the format of the exam to all the students, which was in fact incorrect. I'd been sent an email by the Chair of the Board of Examiners, Ian Bailiff, which I'd misinterpreted, so no blame attaches to Ian at all. Later that afternoon, Ian received emails from a handful of students, stating their confusion at my recent, contradictory instructions and asking what was going on. This was a perfectly reasonable question on a Friday afternoon before the weekend before the exam and it led the head of department, Jenny Price, to move into overdrive. She collected as many members of staff as possible to go to all of the Durham colleges and notify all of the students in person or, failing that, by message of the correct conditions of the exam paper because the Chapman email

[8] The principal 'Rosemary's Babies' were Colin Haselgrove, Anthony Harding, Martin Millett, Chris Morris, Martin Jones and Ian Bailiff.

was incorrect. I am sure that Jenny Price put a very large piece of paper with a very large black mark in my personnel file in her office filing cabinet, stating this man is unreliable and he should never be appointed to a significant post. Indeed, my certainty was based on the meeting she had with me on Friday afternoon after the students had been notified. One more humiliation was that I was to be one of five members of the Archaeology staff – the other four resenting me enormously – who had to turn up at 9 am in front of the Maiden Castle exam room to make sure that all of the students sitting the 'Introduction to Archaeology' paper were indeed informed about the format of the paper, even at the very last moment. In fact, all of the students had received the message. This incident would have closed the door on any executive ambitions I had in Durham. But since I didn't have any at all, I never let this incident dishearten me.

A reader in Durham is usually given quite a lot of admin. In my case, the admin grew a little as my teaching load declined. On a sliding scale starting at the most boring and ending with the most interesting, I served on the Faculty Ethics Committee for more than four years, with meetings of excruciating boredom since 90% of business related to NHS ethics in medical research and teaching. As vice-chair of the Departmental Education Committee, I was put in charge of 'student progress', which meant chasing students who failed to hand in work, who did not come to lectures, seminars or tutorials or who were generally in a bad way. For most of the time, I had to listen to lies, damned lies and preposterous excuses for late work or absences. One student tried to convince me that both of his grandmothers had died within a term and that was why his essays were late. The worst case that I came across was a first-year student whose unique achievement was to fail every single module of his six Level 1 exams. I happened to be waiting with Anthony Harding's son Nicolas outside the Head of Department's office when the student came in to discuss his disastrous results with Anthony Harding, then Head of Department. This student was shaking when he went in but, when he came out, he was crying and howling that he would never get a commission in the army with these results. Nicolas was most impressed, believing this was one of the finest moments of his father's time in Durham.

I served on the Departmental Education Committee for many years, which was interesting at first but, as the University's demands for ever more specific details for each module grew and as the University's timetable for changes to modules became ever shorter, this Committee's work became more of a box-ticking exercise than a discussion of module quality. The Research Committee was, for many years, more interesting than the Education Committee because it enabled me to keep in touch with the research that other people in the department were doing. But as more of the Research Committee's time was spent on the strategic implications of the Government's successive Research Assessment Exercises, the boredom quotient soon began to rise. Another way of keeping in touch with departmental research was the annual Postgraduate Review Panel (PRP) procedure, which started off as a three-day exercise involving the supervisor, co-supervisor and two other members of staff interviewing PhD students after nine months, 21 months and 30 months. Keeping track of different postgrads' research was fascinating because, again, it led me to appreciate research I wouldn't have known was happening in the department. The PRPs were an ordeal for the students, especially the first performance. The operation was tricky because it was so difficult to take three days out of a busy May. Eventually, the Panels were streamlined so that each person had to be available for the whole of a single day, when all of their panels were scheduled.

Another interesting part of Durham admin was an invitation from Rosemary Cramp, the doyenne of archaeology in Durham, to serve as chair of her Research Fund Committee. When she retired from Durham, Rosemary made a generous bequest to the University, with interest accruing as a research fund for Durham postgraduates and members of staff, as well as the occasional outside applicant. The fund was mostly focused on Durham and, at least at the beginning, concentrated on Rosemary's research interests in early Christian Britain, with specific reference to the north-east. For many years, the Research Fund Committee consisted of Rosemary herself, her great friends Roger Mercer, the Edinburgh prehistorian, Richard Bailey, an Anglo-Saxon historian from Newcastle, and period specialists from the department – usually the Romanist Richard Hingley and the medievalist Pam Graves. I was chosen as chair when Anthony Harding moved to Exeter. Each winter, the committee would consider requests from between 20 and 30 applicants. The committee's job was to decide how much money each would get. Since the amount of money available was usually a quarter of the total sum applied for, there were some extremely tough decisions to be made. Each of the three senior members – the Three Rs – was extremely sharp in spotting the weaknesses of an application. But the main benefit of the meetings was to provide a platform for the Three Rs to tell old stories, with Roger often delivering his tall tales in an Edinburgh fishwife's accent. It was hilarious to listen to the gossip of the 1960s and earlier.

The most exciting – even pleasurable – admin job I held in the department also included a major social element. This was to chair the research seminar series, for which I had to decide on the seminar programme for the year and also take speakers out for dinner after the seminar. Most members of the department were extremely selective about the research seminars that they attended, as indeed, I confess, I was as well when no longer seminar supremo. The speaker was invited to a wine reception in the department, followed by a good meal in a Durham restaurant. There were some wonderful seminars from friends and colleagues. Sometimes, the desired event didn't happen. I was hoping to host a head-to-head discussion about Stonehenge between Tim Darvill and Mike Parker Pearson. Their totally opposite interpretations would have led to a great discussion but Mike claimed he didn't have the time.

One thing that the department was not great at was strategic thinking, especially in terms of the appointment of new staff. In such a large department, it was always difficult to press for a new member of staff in your area of interest. Once this had been achieved, there was absolutely no guarantee that the person appointed would fit the criteria. This was one of the strangest aspects of the Durham approach – the idea that, whatever the job specification, the best person on the day at interview would be awarded the position. This led us into some bizarre appointments, the most curious of which was when a Romanist's position was advertised and, out of sheer bloody-minded cheek, the Palaeolithic specialist Mark White applied for and got the job. Although he subsequently became one of the leading Palaeolithic specialists for the UK, he really had no business applying for the post and the Romanists were spitting blood for many *kalends*. In a more recent case, the department had recognised the long-term weakness in its coverage of GIS teaching and advertised for a GIS specialist, of which three applied, as well as Ben Roberts, a Bronze Age specialist working in the British Museum. Although Ben was certainly not a GIS specialist and has never taught GIS to anyone, Ben was appointed to the job on the strength of his Bronze Age archaeology, heritage and museum studies. But for the strategic importance of GIS teaching and research, he was not the person to be appointed. Indeed, to this day GIS is a weakness in department teaching, mostly because Big Data researchers like Dan Lawrence have never shown any enthusiasm for teaching GIS.

The worst example of a Durham appointments policy came with the failure to appoint a Chinese specialist. Bisserka and I had been invited to the second Shanghai Archaeological Forum in 2015[9] and we had made good contacts with a number of Chinese specialists, the brightest of whom was Janice Li, who at the time was working part-time in the Terracotta Army Research Centre in Xian and part-time in University College London researching the Army with Andy Bevan. The department had also developed its own Chinese links through the connections of the new Vice Chancellor, when Robin Skeates went to Beijing and the department set up an excavation project led by Derek Kennet in the Forbidden City – the only foreign department to do so. The obvious development was the appointment of a Chinese archaeologist to the Durham teaching staff and, after the normal struggle, the university agreed. Many applications were received, including one from Janice, and there were also three archaeologists who were not Chinese but who had worked in China as archaeological scientists. Despite the obvious benefits of Janice's networks as a Chinese archaeologist who spoke excellent English and had researched on the Shang Bronze Age, Janice didn't even get an interview. At the interview, I asked some basic questions about Chinese prehistory and about the origins of Chinese Shang civilisation, which none of the archaeological scientists was able to answer. At this point, it became obvious that none of these candidates could attract a large cohort of Chinese students if they knew so little about Chinese archaeology – indeed, possibly less than the Chinese students who came to Durham. The university recognised this objection and made no appointment. When the department failed to meet some administrative targets set by the centre, the Chinese archaeology post disappeared, so Durham missed a

[9] For an account of the SAF, see p. 209.

great opportunity to appoint a Chinese archaeologist. Three months later, Oxford appointed the second Chinese archaeologist (after UCL) to become a lecturer in Chinese archaeology in British universities.

My own position in the department as Reader since my appointment in 1996 had become anomalous and it became embarrassing that a number of my friends and colleagues – especially those with whom I'd served as external examiner in Reading and Bristol, Sheffield and Newport – began to ask me why I had not yet been promoted to professor. This was probably something to do with the 'Introduction to Archaeology' fiasco but also with my lack of political engagement in the university. But eventually, Robin Coningham, then Pro-Vice-Chancellor, proposed me to the Promotions Committee on the basis of my winning the largest AHRC grant ever awarded to a Durham academic. It was clearly the money I had brought to the university rather than my research publications over 35 years that won me a professorship in 2014.

One obvious trend in Durham through the 2010s was the move away from treating archaeological theory as a holistic framework essential for all archaeological research towards thinking of archaeological theory as a toolbox, like GIS, parts of which you would use for a specific research question. There was a widespread tendency in British archaeology towards the fragmentation of theory. It was a battle that several of us were fighting in the department, including Bisserka, who had taught in several undergraduate modules. But it was a battle that we were losing against the empiricists, especially those in the archaeological science wing of the department. Another complementary move away from archaeological theory came with the increased interest in the collection of Big Data, much of which was methodologically interesting and innovative but which had severe theoretical weaknesses which remain to be addressed. Instead of developing as a great centre of European prehistory, Durham chose to be the leading Archaeological Science Department in Britain, competing with rivals in Sheffield, Bradford and York. The most obvious sign of this was the department's successful attempt to persuade the Vice Chancellor to invest £1.5 million in a new ancient DNA lab, with one new member of staff appointed to run it. This contrasted with the increasing centralisation of the other big labs in Jena and Harvard, each with dozens of staff. It left the Durham DNA lab exposed to strong external competition which depended upon new technologies and economies of scale that the Durham lab could never match.

These disciplinary trends, allied to a growing weariness with teaching similar kinds of material to students for over 35 years, made me view retirement as a potential opportunity. I stayed on for an extra year after the year of my 65th birthday to consolidate the family finances and retired in September 2017 at the age of 66. Instead of having a public celebration of my career and retirement – perhaps Durham remembered the fiasco at Newcastle in 1996 (?) – Head of Department Robin Skeates organised a small dinner for 15 in a Durham restaurant, where I made a short speech, full only of compliments. Even before I retired, I was faced with converting the loft in our house in Red Courts to take my library since I was certainly going to lose my room. My post as a European prehistorian was sacrificed to appoint another archaeological scientist – a geo-archaeologist called Karen Milek. So I left the Durham department and have not regretted it. I have friends who still work in the department and I used to see them regularly pre-Covid-19. I rarely go into the department, since research seminars are all on Zoom and my university visits usually take me to the library. In the year after I retired, I was appointed as Emeritus Professor and still use that title at conferences to add to the reflected glory of the university. But I cannot say that I feel close to the department anymore, because my feeling is that the kind of archaeology promoted now has moved away from the one that I really enjoyed doing.

Chapter 12

Research in the Balkans in the 2000s

My research in the East Balkans – specifically Bulgaria and Romania – carried on through the 2000s up to the start of the Ukrainian project (see Chapter 13). It was a patchy affair, zigzagging from place to place, country to country and topic to topic, without the kind of major focus that I had found in my earlier projects in Dalmatia and Hungary. I wanted to start a major project but nothing ever quite came to fruition. While I had several ideas for projects, the funding climate of the 2000s had changed. It appeared to be much easier to get huge six-figure grants rather than small grants, although there were very few big grants available. This meant a drastic reduction in the diversity of research, from which I suffered all the way through the 2000s.

The first project concerned the prehistoric exploitation of salt (2001 to 2004). When it started, there was a rare convergence of interest from several people who were working on salt in different countries. The starting point was Dan Monah's salt research in eastern Romania, based on the salt sites of Lunca and the tell of Poduri. I followed this up with fieldwork in Bulgaria with my former PhD student, Bisserka. Another former PhD student, Burcin Erdoğu, was starting salt-related research in central Anatolia, while Anthony Harding was doing his own salt research in Romania in Transylvania with Valerii Kavruk. This rare convergence constituted a natural research network and we applied successfully to the British Academy for network funding. This network funded a visit to Turkey, where the group was shown around Central Anatolian sites by Mihriban Özbasarsan and Burcin. We started our trip with a visit to Tuz Gölü (Plate 27), a vast salt lake larger than Luxembourg, that is liquid and blue for most of the year but in the three hot summer months turns solid white as the salt crystallises, so you can (miraculously) walk on salt water. It transpired that there were five villages that still exploited the Tuz Gölü salt for their own local requirements, quite apart from the huge state extraction of salt, which has carried on since the Ottoman extraction of Tuz Gölü salt in the 17th–19th centuries. The modern villagers were using technology that was not at all out of place in the Bronze Age. When we visited a Bronze Age tell on the edge of Tuz Gölü, we made surface collections of sandstone grinders encrusted with white salt. The salt was picked out from the solid salt with stone or bronze axes and then ground down to a powder on grindstones – very much as is done in modern villages today. We also had the chance to visit the impressive excavations at *Çatalhöyük*, meet Ian Hodder and discuss Malcolm Todd's idea, published in the 1960s, that the prosperity and longevity of Çatal was partly based on their exploitation of Tuz Gölü salt. This was an argument that we were never able to prove during our visit to Anatolia.

The other activities in the project concerned small-scale excavations, which I ran with Dan Monah in Moldavia. We opened a small trench on the periphery of the Lunca site (2002), probably 50 m away from the Early Neolithic mound, which led to disappointing results. A more interesting trial excavation was at Prohozeşti (2003), where Mark Francis' geophysics survey of the site revealed several features that we investigated, including a large, lined pit, which appeared to have been filled with brine and was probably used for the processing of hides. Later, Karsten Mischka from Kiel completed the geophysical survey of the site, finding a much more extensive settlement that fitted into the seasonal exploitation of salt based on the Poduri site – the only tell known in the entire Cucuteni–Trypillia distribution.

As part of the British Academy network, we held two Round Tables – one in Durham for Dan Monah and the group and one in Piatra Neamţ, organised by Dan and Gheorghe (Ghiocel) Dumitroaia (Plate 17). The Piatra Round Table was much more extensive and resulted in a publication. In our salt research, we had a team of specialists covering three different countries, in each of which salt was exploited in manifestly different ways. This seemed to form the ideal basis for an application to the AHRC for a major grant, which was turned down, astoundingly, because, in the words of the rejection letter, it was 'too ambitious'. We felt deeply frustrated by this, even more so when in the following year the AHRC opened up a new funding stream called 'speculative research', which was probably an accurate description of what we were trying to do. But by now it was too late – the team had moved onto other projects and the chance to develop an integrated salt research project was lost.

I have to say that my own contribution to the salt research in Romania in no way matched that of Olivier Weller, who made an extremely thorough survey of all the salt sources in the Carpathian foothills and continued to do extremely interesting excavations with Ghiocel at the Lunca site. In Bulgaria, Bisserka and I managed to find a small number of salt sources, which, with one exception, were hitherto unknown to prehistorians, demonstrating that large parts of the country, including the densely occupied southern part of Thrace, lacked local salt sources and that there was really no alternative to salt exchange from east Bulgaria, Romania or Serbia. There were, however, small deposits along the Black Sea. We realised the potential of the evaporation of Black Sea water from the site of Pomorie, which was a major Greek and Roman salt exploitation site in which sea-water was concentrated in a sequence of ever-increasing salinity to produce high-quality brine. There was a series of '*tuzlas*' (the Turkish for 'salt' is '*tuz*', so 'salty places') along the Black Sea coast, which we visited. The first was Balchiska *tuzla*, near the town of Balchik, where there was a salt-water lagoon surrounded by magnificent haline vegetation. Further north, a *tuzla* in Taukliman formed part of a Nature Reserve of outstanding natural beauty on the Black Sea coast, which certain individuals were attempting to privatise to build tourist complexes along the road leading to the salt lake. Moreover, there were many caves in the limestone cliffs overlooking the salt lake, which we were keen to visit. Eventually we managed to get in contact with the owners through our friend Mariana Filipova, a palynologist working in the Varna Natural History Museum. Mariana helped to arrange a meeting at the site entrance. We drove down from the Dobrudzha plateau to the heavily fortified gate, where we were met by two huge German shepherd dogs showing no sign of friendliness. Some ten minutes later, a Mercedes drove down behind us and a man with the marvellous name of Gospodin Gospodinov ('Mister Mister') joined us at the gate, explaining how important it was to have top security for the site for the protection of 'their' site.[1] We assumed that Gospodin Gospodinov would have a key but in fact he didn't; instead, he phoned headquarters inside the site, who told him where the key was hidden. He went up the hill to a prominent rock on the right-hand side of the road and there underneath the rock was the key. Top security indeed! When we finally got into the site, we didn't have time to visit the caves but saw the potential of another salt lagoon for exploitation.

Another salt source that we visited was near the city of Burgas. In the Historical Museum, we asked our colleague Todorka to introduce us to the director, a historian who had contacts in the Burgas constabulary. We needed to talk to the police because one of the key sites near the salt source was a tell which lay within the boundary walls of Burgas prison. The director helped to organise an official visit led by an inspector of criminology in the Burgas police force, who was the first port of call for the investigation of murders in the city. He didn't tell us many stories about his work – just sufficient to whet our appetite for Pontic homicide. With the inspector to vouch for us, we were readily admitted to the prison grounds and, flanked by two prison officers, we walked to the Burgas-Zatvor tell, inspect it and look around for potential access to the salt lake at the bottom of the Zatvor slope. This site seemed an ideal possibility for excavation, with free local labour provided by the prison, but we never followed it up.

The other salt sources in Bulgaria were small and located at some distance from moderately remote villages. It was impossible to find the salt springs without the help of elderly villagers, who were the only people who remembered the exploitation of the salt sources. In both cases, at Braknitsa and Solnik, we were taken through forested landscape to salt springs on the side of small basins. It became clear that these sources were quite restricted – perhaps sufficient for local animals' drinking water – although perhaps larger when recorded in the Ottoman period. One other like this was located some 100 km inland, west of Omurtag near the village of Ivanski

[1] There appeared to be no such interest in protecting the natural beauty of the locale.

but again this seemed to be a small source that would scarcely have supported a prehistoric exchange network.

The largest salt source in Bulgaria was also located in a carefully protected area inside the company land of Provadsol, a Bulgarian–Swedish joint company exploiting a massive salt dome buried under several metres of sediment but which reached a depth of 80 m–100 m. This source of underground rock salt was Bulgaria's largest modern source of salt. The Provadia source was known and used by animals since the 19th century. In 1917, a Bulgarian soldier was walking across the landscape near the village of Mirovo and saw animals drinking from the spring. He was surprised to find that it was a salt spring and this was when the salt source was brought to wider attention. However, right next to the spring was a Copper Age tell surmounted by a huge Roman burial mound. Thus we had the combination of an important salt source and a Copper Age archaeological site. When we presented the results of our salt explorations at a seminar in the Sofia Institute, the director Vassil Nikolov pulled the same stunt that he'd pulled over fragmentation in claiming that he'd already invented fragmentation and he'd already been interested in salt research when he was an undergraduate student and had written essays about both topics (which regrettably have not survived). When Vassil tried to steal the credit for two of our research ideas, he could hardly stop us from maintaining our fragmentation research, although he did stop us in a small way.[2] But in the salt research field, he was able to capitalise on our discoveries and started excavations at the Provadia tell and the adjacent cemetery in a multi-year project in which he found what he claimed to be the remains of a large-scale brine-processing operation on the tell.

The person who went on to work in the most innovative way on prehistoric salt research was undoubtedly Anthony Harding (Plate 27), with his colleague Valerii Kavruk, who produced a magnificent monograph on their upland Transylvanian Bronze Age salt exploitation site of Băile Figa. Later, Anthony Harding wrote a book on the European prehistory of salt exploitation. So despite the failure of the AHRC to recognise the potential of salt research, some extremely valuable findings have been made to put the Balkans onto the map of European prehistoric salt exploitation.

Landscape archaeologists rarely come across a major class of field monuments that has been so completely neglected by both archaeologists and historians. During a field expedition to European Turkey in 2002, Burcin and Rabia Erdoğu had shown us some spectacular megalithic monuments near Kirklareli. One of the monuments consisted of over 250 standing stones. The stones were worked but un-inscribed and resembled north-west European Neolithic menhirs, ranging in height from 50 cm to over 3 m. When Burcin and Rabia took us to Kirklareli, they explained that each time they'd visited the mayor, he had showed them an additional site, usually with hundreds of standing stones. They were able to take us to three such sites – the

[2] Vassil Nikolov stopped us from studying the collection of fired clay 'altars' from the site of Sapareva Banja; see above, p. 146.

like of which we had never seen before. Burcin and Rabia followed the example of other Turkish archaeologists in dating the sites to the Iron Age, on the grounds that, although there was very little associated, datable material, they were megalithic monuments and local megalithic burials were indeed dated to the Iron Age in both European Turkey and over the border in south-east Bulgaria. I was very impressed by the Turkish monuments but, not being over-interested in the Iron Age, I didn't do anything more about this.

The next summer, we were searching for salt sources in the region when we encountered the megaliths for the first time in Bulgaria. On this trip, we were staying in the town of Targovishte, some 20 km away from Omurtag, because it had one of the best restaurants with a huge menu of traditional Bulgarian dishes which we visited each evening. Each morning, we would drive around local villages to check salt sources. One day, the main road to Omurtag was completely blocked and we were forced to take a 30 km detour to the south. This was an eye-opener because, as we reached the first village, we found a site with standing stones identical to those we had seen in Turkey. Driving to the next village, we found the same and so on. When we reached the village of *Filaretowo*, there were hundreds of standing stones in a clearing in the middle of the village (Fig. 21). At this point, the name the 'Forest of Stones' came to us and it stuck. The menhirs were the same as the Turkish examples – almost all un-inscribed but worked into long, thin shapes up

Fig. 21. The 'Forest of Stones' grave markers at Filaretowo, north-east Bulgaria

to 3 m high. At Filaretowo, we noticed that the stones were sometimes in rows and occasionally in pairs though we couldn't identify a distinct pattern. When we talked about the stones to our museum colleagues, the local medieval archaeologists dismissed them as 'Ottoman' monuments and were utterly shocked when we said they might date to the Iron Age. We had discovered a strange situation in which the Bulgarian archaeologists ignored the standing stones because they were associated with Muslims and the Turkish archaeologists ignored the standing stones because they were dated to the Iron Age and related to Bulgarian megaliths. Hence, nobody had made any research, with the one exception of the Turkish scholar, Dr Beksaç, who was unknown to us at the time but who subsequently sent us many of his works. What was interesting was that there was a strong Turkish ethnic element in the villages where the standing stones had survived in the Targovishte-Omurtag region.

Gradually, we formulated a plan to complete a 'car survey' in an area 30 km wide, forming a transect from the Danube to the Greek–Bulgarian border in the Eastern Rhodopes. This was an unusual kind of survey – ideally suited to lazy archaeologists – in which we would try to find all the standing stone monuments that survived in the transect. Our method was based upon our observation that most of the standing stone sites we had seen so far were located next to roads in or near a village. We would drive into the centre of a village and then drive out from the village centre at least 3 km on every road that led out of the village. In this way, we would get a good coverage of standing stone sites. This was an ambitious plan and we never sought official permission for the car survey, since we (rightly) assumed that no Bulgarian archaeologist was interested in our visits to upstanding Ottoman field monuments. What it meant was that we collected a mass of data in three summer and two spring field seasons in eastern Bulgaria.

Our car transect surveys in 2004 and 2005 covered a huge area, including hundreds of villages. But we surveyed the region systematically, no matter how hot the weather. Often our base was Targovishte and we would drive out to a new segment of the transect each day. There was one particular stretch of road, from Omurtag west towards Veliko Tarnovo, which had a crucial Shell garage cafe that used to sell pint mugs of '*tarator*' (a cucumber, garlic and yogurt drink) and we stopped for a *tarator* every time we passed. The Shell cafe saved us from dehydration and exhaustion on many hot fieldwork days. In five seasons of fieldwork, we recorded over 500 standing stone sites.

My linguistic and mechanical skills came to my rescue once when I was driving Bisserka's Lada around standing stones sites. The Lada broke down in Zelena Morava, a village with predominantly Turkish inhabitants. I could do little more than point at parts of the engine that I thought had failed and the villagers' level of Bulgarian language was equally low. But, with goodwill and much gesticulation, the village mechanic fixed the Lada, which we celebrated with litres of beer.

When we started to look at the overall patterns, we realised that there was a strong correlation between standing stone sites and villages with extant Turkish ethnic elements. This was particularly obvious in the Eastern Rhodopes, where Turkish ethnic elements strongly predominated. The Turkish party often played a pivotal role in the Parliament, helping minority parties to form a government. The price it extracted was investment in Turkish areas, which included road repairs in the Eastern Rhodopes, which made our travel around the Rhodopes much easier. But there were other areas, such as south of Chirpan, where there were strong Orthodox Christian elements in the population and there was certainly an interesting mixture of funeral monuments. Some of the standing stone sites had Christian graves nearby, while others had Muslim graves and some had a mixture of both. It was challenging to understand what was going on, especially with a monument class with an as yet undated time range.

An obvious aim of our research was to find out the extent to which standing stones had spread in the western part of Bulgaria. We had no time to complete a second car transect and I think this would have been a waste of time, because a spot check of 20 villages conducted in the Vratsa area in 2006 showed not one single standing stone site. The only place in western Bulgaria where we found any records of standing stones was in a traveller's account in the 1880s written by Felix Kanics. One of Kanics's drawings illustrated a cemetery of standing stones from a hill overlooking Sofia (Fig. 22). It is well known that, after Independence in 1878, there were very high

Fig. 22. Standing stones near Sofia, with Mount Vitosha in the background, Bulgaria, 1877

rates of destruction of Muslim monuments – including much larger monuments such as *hans* and mosques – and it is quite possible that the standing stones were used as building material, especially for road-building, or simply destroyed as markers of the Muslim faith. To understand this problem, we needed to find a Bulgarian historian specialising in the Ottoman period. Here we hit a real problem because historians were not interested in a class of monuments with so few inscriptions on the stones. We are still looking for such a person to help us deepen our understanding of the many Forests of Stones.

Our fieldwork led to two opportunities for more intensive, site-based investigations. One was at the site of Bozhurka, where not only was the Forest of Stones located right next to the modern village but there were very recent burials within the perimeter of the standing stones group. When we managed to persuade the villagers to speak Bulgarian, it became clear that this was a long-term village cemetery, whose current use was restricted to the western part of the village but with other, older parts of the cemetery not so closely connected to living members of the community and therefore open for investigation. The medieval archaeologist from the Turgovishte Museum, Angel Konakliev, kindly managed to get the permission of the local *imam* to excavate two or three spaces between paired standing stones in October 2005. By then, we began to believe what local villagers told us in many cases, namely that the space between a pair of standing stones was the place for the grave. In each of her excavations, Bisserka found human bones and also organic material, which she was able to radiocarbon date to the late 18th to mid-19th centuries AD – the latest dates that she as a prehistorian had ever recovered! So at last we had demonstrated that the idea of paired standing stones forming grave markers was indeed correct and at least some of the monuments belonged to the Ottoman period.

Our fragmentation research in the Archaeological Museum in Stara Zagora led us to meet a medieval archaeologist called Dimitur (Mitko) Yankov, who told us about one of the most extraordinary standing stone sites that he'd ever seen. He believed that each grave was dug as a monument to a warrior fallen in battle. Mitko very kindly accompanied us on the 80 km drive to the village of Gorno Novo Selo, in the Sredna Gora hills. There was a 45-minute walk from the village to the site but it was well worth it – there were hundreds of standing stones on one of the ridges stretching up towards the hilltop whose forests concealed a Late Antique fortress and an Early Byzantine basilica. It was these earlier features near the Forest of Stones that gave us the opportunity to start a survey and excavation project with Boyan Dumanov, a great friend of Bisserka's from student days, who now worked in the New Bulgarian University and was researching Late Antique fortresses in the Sredna Gora. Thus, we started an excavation project in which the official paperwork was done through Boyan and we were added in as an extra fieldwork component. We worked for three field seasons at Gorno Novo Selo (2005–7), in which we completed a plan of all of the standing stones, which actually reached over 2,000. We also excavated five spaces between paired standing stones and found the remains of human bodies in each of them. We also managed to radiocarbon date the organic remains of two of the graves, which fell in the late 18th and 19th centuries AD, just as at Bozhurka. This was a very important result.

However, the project started in the worst possible way. On the morning when we were due to drive the minibus and the other vehicles to our base in Chirpan, Bisserka's father Ivan died. This was an incredibly difficult time for Bisserka and I left her in Sofia to begin to make the funeral arrangements and inform family and friends. She joined us later that week, by which time the group of New Bulgarian University and Durham University students had established ourselves in the only hotel in Chirpan, next to a square that boasted a fine pizza restaurant and two or three breakfast kiosks, with a supermarket five minutes' walk away. We stayed in the hotel for all three seasons and got used to its basic waterworks and lumpy beds. We had a large team, with Boyan's students excavating in the Late Antique fortress higher up the hill and the Durham students and other visitors recording and excavating the standing stone site lower down on the ridge. For this reason, it was essential to hire local transport and Boyan found a father-and-son team with an ancient van with hardly any seats apart from the front three. This turned out to be the way that the project students were transported up an appallingly bad mountain road to Gorno Novo Selo that hadn't been repaired for years. Because the site was so far from the village, it was impossible to return to the village for lunch, so we had to carry all the water and food for a team of 25 on our 4 km walk to the site, over three parallel ridges. Each morning, a different group of Bulgarian students or a member of staff would take project money and buy lunch for both teams. We would then carry it up to the famous 'food tree' on the standing stones ridge, at which point the food would be divided between teams. When it was the morning for me to buy the food, I took a large quantity of cheese, buying what Bulgarians call '*kashkaval*' (yellow cheese) instead of '*sirene*' (white cheese with much more salt). The mistake that I had bought large quantities of '*kashkaval*' was discovered only at the food tree and I was strongly criticised for neglecting one of the key elements of Bulgarian field diet.

The standing stones project remains an exciting project that has not been fully published. Indeed, we have presented rather few papers on the Forest of Stones. This is one project for the future, in my retirement, but we still have to find an Ottoman historian to create a fitting narrative.

In one of the many discussions we had with Ana Raduntcheva, she mentioned the site of Orlovo, near Haskovo, in south-east Bulgaria. She told us that the museum had a very rich surface collection from an un-excavated Neolithic or Chalcolithic site and she said that, although all the leading Bulgarian prehistorians knew about the site, nobody was interested in the material because it hadn't been excavated. This seemed like a real challenge so, on the first available opportunity, in summer 2006 Bisserka and I went to Haskovo Museum and met the Curator of Archaeology, Irko Petrov, an Iron Age specialist, and we asked if it would be possible to study the surface material. He was surprised at this request but agreed. Once we saw the remarkable material, we couldn't understand why other archaeologists didn't take the site seriously. We came for a study fortnight in the winter of 2006–7 but there was so much material that we couldn't finish, having to return next spring. In the winter study season, we realised that there were three large concentrations of material. The story was that each concentration of finds came from a different field. There was a concentration of fired clay figurines, a concentration of polished stone axes and a concentration of personal ornaments made of a great variety of materials, including turquoise, *Spondylus*, marble, limestone and other green rocks that were harder to identify. It was essential to bring our friend the gemmologist Ruslan Kostov with us in the spring 2007 season so that he could identify the stone materials. We also brought Elena Georgieva, who had drawn some of the material for the Frag 2 book, and who made more excellent drawings, especially of the *Spondylus*. Since we had no official agreement with the Bulgarian authorities, when we expressed an interest to visit the site, we had to have an escort from the Haskovo police force. Off we went to the site in a police car with a sergeant who extremely patiently sat in the car while we walked around the site. All of this research led to a 2010 book of which I was particularly proud, since it exploited the potential of surface collection – one of my long-term interests.

The next opportunity for small-scale fieldwork came five years later, after the Gorno Novo Selo project with Boyan Dumanov. It came in the form of a new project that Boyan was leading in the Mirkovo basin on the southern edge of the Stara Planina. On top of a hill high above the village was another Late Antique fortress that Boyan was excavating and Bisserka and I had the opportunity to join the project as part of Boyan's 2012 team. This time, we brought along some expert assistance from Northumbria University, with Jane Entwhistle coming to look at soils and surface geology and a remote sensing team – Nigel and Helen King, whose drone photographs allowed GIS landscape reconstructions and detailed mapping of the basin. We also brought Petar Zidarov, a member of the New Bulgarian University, who worked on magnetometry. This amounted to a strong team for a one-month survey. Boyan had found accommodation in the Mirkovo campsite, which had a great cafe that did early morning breakfasts – essential in the cool, early summer mornings – as well as solid dinners. Each morning, Boyan would set out with his team, driving to the Late Antique fortress. There was one morning when the Kings went up with their drone to take aerial coverage of the landscape around the Late Antique fortress. This was a mistake, because, on the very top of the hill was a military outpost manned that day, fortunately for us, by extremely sleepy soldiers who didn't realise that our drone photography covered their base. Our team worked lower down in the basin, where we did gridded surface collection across the most important prehistoric site in the basin – the Mirkovo Neolithic tell. The most interesting thing that we found was the Roman, medieval and post-medieval remains stretching across much of the basin. There was an interesting interplay between the Kings' mapping, which informed our fieldwork, and the results of the fieldwalking, which gave chronological depth to the mapping programme. The fieldwalking programme and the Kings' remote sensing and mapping meant that we had perhaps one of the best covered basins in the whole of Bulgaria. This remains a project that we need to write up fully – another task for my retirement.

Early in the 2010s, I had a great opportunity to write a general synthesis of later Balkan prehistory – a summary statement of everything that I had done in my whole career. I am grateful to Steve Shennan who suggested to Norman Yoffee, the main editor of the Cambridge University Press's Cambridge World Archaeology series, that I should write a Balkan volume in this series. Cambridge and I signed a contract for the volume in 2011 and, on the basis of the contract, I soon won a British Academy Small Research Grant to make two research trips to the Balkans to catch up on recent research – a summer trip in 2011 to the countries of 'former Yugoslavia' and western Bulgaria and a spring 2012 trip to Romania.

Bisserka and I started our car trip in summer 2011 in Slovenia, with a visit to Ljubljana, where I renewed friendships with old colleagues, especially Predrag Novaković, and spent a lot of time in the Department of Archaeology library, looking at reports of the recent motorway rescue excavations. In Zagreb, we met old friends like Stašo Forenbaher and made new friends, such as Jacqueline Balen, Keeper of Archaeology in the National Museum. It was also good to catch up on reports of the recent motorway rescue excavations. We then went on to Osijek, where a former student colleague of mine, Marijana Jukić, who had worked with me in Hungary on the UTP, showed us around the museum and told us much more about the rescue archaeological excavations in her area. This was the first time I had returned to 'former Yugoslavia' since Croatia and Serbia had divided and so the first time that I crossed the border from Croatia into Serbia just east of Osijek. It was a really weird experience, in which we were kept waiting a long time, with our visas checked thoroughly and the car searched. But we were eventually allowed into Serbia and drove on to Novi Sad, where our new colleague Lidja Balj showed us round the materials in the Muzej Vojvodine. We next moved to Beograd, where both of us had colleagues and that was a very pleasant experience to catch up with old friends and make new friends like Miloš Spasić in the Muzej Grada Beograda and Ivana Pantović, who commuted each day from Zemun to her museum in Vršac. She drove us to Vršac one day and took us to see the site of Potporanj, which I had (incorrectly, it transpired) published as a 100 ha Vinča settlement. We left Beograd to drive to Požarevac Museum to see the site and finds of Belovode, when we had a burst tyre on the Beograd motorway. This turned into a six-hour wait and repair job, by which time it was too late to visit Belovode, so we had to be content to look at the materials from Duško Šljivar's excavations.

After this disappointment, we were scheduled to drive to Priština in Kosova but we were told that, if we entered Kosova directly from Serbia, we wouldn't be able to exit Kosova in the south into what was then FYROM.[3] So we had to do the trip the other way around, making a long detour south to Skopje where we met old friends like Goce Naumov and Irina Nasteva in the Skopje Institute. We had never been to the new exhibitions in the National Museum, so we saw a lot of new material and collected lots of new books and journals. But the most striking thing about our visit to Skopje was a visit to the recently reconstructed main square, in which workers were putting the finishing touches to a vast sculpture of Alexander of Macedon – now firmly Macedonian rather than Greek – mounted on a horse in the middle of the square. As Bisserka looked around, she saw sculptures of people with whom she was very familiar from her Bulgarian childhood. There were the two patron saints pivotal to the development of the Bulgarian language – Sveti Kiril and Sveti Methodi, now recast as Macedonian saints. There was Skanderbeg, the great Albanian leader, recast as a Macedonian freedom fighter, and several other leading figures from Bulgarian, Greek and Albanian history, who'd all become Macedonians. This extraordinary piece of open-air monumental propaganda showed that the re-invention of history is still alive and well in the Balkans.

After our heritage trip round Skopje, we drove north to enter Kosova at the southern border and drove on a good two-lane road towards Priština. What we noticed after driving 50 km was that there were many petrol stations on that road but there was only one petrol station for each company – there were no chains of petrol stations. This was a sure sign of a money-laundering operation. When we reached Priština, we were met by the director of the Kosova Museum, Kemajl Luci, a prehistorian whom we'd met twice on the EAA Annual Meetings and who had very warmly invited us to come to Kosovo and look at the Vinča material in the Priština Museum. Unfortunately, Luci had absolutely no intention of showing us the Vinča pottery that I'd failed to see because of Jovan Glišić[4] in 1973, almost 40 years ago. But he did take us to see the new exhibition, which was very informative.

In spring 2012, we flew to Bucureşti and took flights and trains within Romania – a much more comfortable way to travel than it used to be. In Bucureşti, we met several old friends and caught up with new material and new books. I was particularly grateful to Constantin (Costel) Haită, who had prepared an enormous collection of PDFs of recent research in Romanian environmental archaeology and subsistence research, which proved a key element in my Balkan synthesis. This was a successful trip, even though there were no site visits because we had no car. We took the short flight to Cluj, where Gheorghe (Ghiţa) Lazarovici (Fig. 7) and his second wife Magda – formerly Mantu – offered to put us up in their flat. Ghiţa and Magda were very kind and shared lots of recent PDFs from their work. They took us out one night to a local restaurant that specialised in '*mititei*' (usually called '*mici*' – grilled mincemeat

[3] Now known as 'North Macedonia'.

[4] For the story of Jovan Glišić and 'his' Vinča pottery, see above, p. 51.

sausages). The speciality of the house was a metre of *mici*, which I thought Ghiţa had ordered for the three of us, since Bisserka, a vegetarian, was excluded from this game. But, to my absolute horror, Ghiţa had ordered 2 m of *mici* – 1 m for him and Magda and the other metre for me. Of course, consumption of this dish was treated as a matter of honour and I somehow managed it – but I didn't eat *mici* for a long time after. A few days later, we took the train to Alba Iulia, where we met Mihai Gligor for the first time. He was kind enough to show us the materials from a series of quite extraordinary human bone deposits from the site of Alba Iulia-Lumea Nouă, which I knew from earlier excavations as a Vinča site. But in his new excvavations, Mihai had found a Late Neolithic deposit with thousands of human bones placed in several concentrations. Although there were other specialists from Britain working on the physical anthropology, I suggested that Durham could get involved in work on the aDNA and isotopic studies and Mihai gladly agreed. We formulated a sampling strategy and we took some of the material there and then, with other materials sent later. To my lasting shame, the Durham archaeological scientists never really delivered the goods for Mihai. At the time of our first visit, Mihai thought that we were going to embark on a valuable co-operation and so he proposed that I was awarded an honorary doctorate from Alba Iulia. Indeed, in 2014, I went out to a fanfare of trumpets and won my one and only honorary doctorate from a Balkan university (Plate 28).

We then took our last train trip from Alba Iulia to Timişoara, a city that I had not visited since the 1989 uprising against Ceauşescu. As we walked around the main squares and streets of the city, we saw that many of the buildings were still pockmarked with bullet holes and sometimes bomb damage. These buildings were maintained as a memorial to the uprising, which started in Timişoara and led to the overthrow of Ceauşescu in 1990. Our colleague Florin Draşovean was extremely kind and showed us the site of Uivar as well as much material from his recent excavations. He took us around the city and invited us to his home for a wonderful dinner. The only sad thing about the Muzeul Banatului was that the Parţa temple room – for me, the most exciting room of the whole museum – was closed. Although one might disagree with some of the reconstructions, especially the statues inside the temple, it was still an inspiring place for members of the general public and indeed archaeologists to go to give a sense of the scale of high-intensity domestic ritual in the 6th millennium BC.

My overall impression of these two trips in 2011 and 2012 is that I had a lot of catching up to do and not just with vast amounts of new material in museums and institutes arriving from the rescue archaeological projects, especially major infrastructural projects, through the 2000s. These had all been funded either nationally or through EU investments since the Fall of the Wall in 1989. But I also needed to catch up with new colleagues – there was a whole new generation of university and museum colleagues whom I didn't know at all. Although many of my old friends had still not quite retired, the vast majority of people consisted of new colleagues whom we hadn't met before and it was very exciting to hear their views about the different kinds of archaeology they were researching. The biggest change in data sharing on these trips came with the prevalence of digital information. The old days of book exchange were on the way out. While we had collected a car-full of books and journals in 2011, by 2012, the PDF was becoming the currency of exchange and it made travelling (especially without a car) much easier.

Chapter 13

The Ukrainian Trypillia Megasites Project

The genesis of the project

The year 2007 was one of the most disappointing of my career from a funding perspective. I applied for six small grants and was turned down for all of them. I was beginning to think that I was out of touch with modern research. But a project that had been a long time in the making brought welcome success to the last stage of my career.

It was thanks to my friends Dan Monah and Gheorghe Dumitroaia (Ghiocel) (Plate 17) that Bisserka and I were able to attend one of the conferences on Trypillia megasites organised by the Kyiv Institute of Archaeology. The meeting was scheduled for August 2003 in the village of Taljanki, the location of the largest megasite. The trip was complicated and started in Iaşi railway station. In a deserted, ghostly part of the station, we met Dan and Ghiocel at 1.30 am to take our documents to the Customs office for clearance for the 4 am train to Chişinau. The inspection passed easily and we walked to the train, which turned out to be a top-security international sleeping train with grills on the windows and locked main doors. If there was a fire, there was no way that we could have escaped from the train. Indeed, Bisserka knew of several tragic accidents with this kind of overnight sleeper: a former director of the Sofia Institute, Rasho Rashev, had burnt alive in such circumstances. We were deeply unhappy about this train design but there was nothing we could do, so at 4 o'clock the train rumbled off towards the border between Romania and Moldova, where the train had to change railway gauge from the broader European model to the narrower Russian gauge. I'd heard about this procedure but never experienced it personally and, even then, didn't see it in the middle of the night. What happens is that each carriage in turn is lifted off by a huge crane and held up until the narrow gauge wheels and bogeys have replaced the broad gauge wheels and bogeys. This procedure was repeated for each of our six carriages and took over an hour. This enabled us to travel anywhere inside the old Soviet Union. We then trundled onwards through the rolling Moldovan countryside and eventually reached Chişinau, where we were met by a friend of Dan and Ghiocel's – Valentin Dergachev, Moldova's senior prehistorian – who put us on a tram for the bus station.

The temperature was heating up and at noon the bus departed for Uman. This was what you might call an international village bus, with lots of people going from village to village, town to town along the route but, because we were to cross several international borders, the route was classed as 'international'. There were not as many goats, sheep and chickens as on a normal Balkan village bus but the appearance of local wildlife during several parts of the journey made this an entertaining trip.

The first long stop we had was at the border with Trans-Dniestria, which had made a unilateral declaration of independence from Moldova in 1992 and was run by a bunch of ex-Red Army colonels who didn't like the idea of democracy. Since it was hardly recognised by any other country in the world, the only foreign income that Trans-Dniestria earned came from the two dollars each person paid for entering into the country and the two dollars paid for going out. Dan and Ghiocel had warned us in advance about this payment and we had small dollar bills with us. That was not the problem at the border – the problem was Chapman, as Chapman had a British passport – which the Trans-Dniestrian border guards had never seen before. It took an age for them to check with their 'foreign office' to find out if this was a legal document. Eventually, the guards accepted the document but they questioned me for another half an hour. Since all of the international conferences I'd ever been to in Eastern Europe were extremely hospitable, I knew I should need very little money, so I had only $10 with me. When I said I was going to Ukraine for five days with $10, they accused me of being an extremely bad capitalist but eventually let me go. The bus sped onwards, reaching Uman at 8 pm. There, Alexei Korvin-Piotrovskiy, the Secretary of the Kyiv Institute of Archaeology, met us with a project minibus – the first comfortable piece of transport in the whole trip. He drove us some 30 km to Taljanki for a great feast to start off the conference in the right spirit. There was an enormously long table, laden with food and drink, and Alexei's hospitality was the best way to recover from the trip from Iaşi.

We had all been given accommodation in the Taljanki Agricultural College. Bisserka and I had a room in the local college, with a single bed with a profile resembling that of a polished stone axe; whenever we lay in the bed together, we slipped down into the middle of the deepest part of the bed, which impeded our beauty sleep. My legs stuck out too! However, we were given filling breakfasts – mostly dumpling-based – with vodka available on tap. We were rarely in great shape when we arrived at the conference for the 9 am start. On the first day, we met Volodymir Kruts (Fig. 23), the doyen of Trypillia megasite archaeology, who was an extremely friendly colleague who spoke Russian to Bisserka and showed us around the Taljanki megasite. The conference organizer, Alexei Korvin-Piotrovskiy, organised a visit to Dobrovodi – another megasite that stretched seemingly endlessly to both the north and south of the road. It was at Dobrovodi that we began to understand the scale of the Trypillia megasites, which were bigger than anything

Fig. 23. Vladimir Kruts with Bisserka Gaydarska at Tuljanki, Ukraine

we'd ever seen before. The megasites certainly piqued our curiosity to see how such large sites had ever formed.

I have to admit that the conference facilities at the Agricultural College were not up to Western standards. Although we brought a PowerPoint with us on our laptop, there was no PowerPoint projector at the conference, so everyone had to sit around our laptop and look at the pictures on the screen, which worked reasonably well. By far the brightest spark in the conference from the Ukrainian side was Mykhailo Videiko (Fig. 24), a senior Kyiv prehistorian who spoke fluent English and had some very interesting ideas about Trypillia megasites. We recognised that this was the person with whom we'd like to collaborate and we indeed did speak in general terms about a future project. Ever since the collapse of the Soviet Union, funding for excavations in Ukraine had decreased dramatically, so this would be a great opportunity to return to solid funding.

Finding a megasite

With other pressing research, the Trypillia project slipped into the long grass until 2007, when Durham invited Roland Fletcher to be an Institute of Advanced Study Fellow for a term's research on low-density urbanism. Roland reiterated the global importance of the Trypillia megasites, which we had already realised from his

Fig. 24. Mykhailo Yurgevich Videiko with the author, Mega-structure, Nebelivka, Ukraine

1995 book on *The Limits to Settlement Growth*. When he heard about our contacts in Kyiv, Roland did all he could to persuade us that it was worth trying to set up a megasite project so, at this juncture, we got back in touch with Mykhailo (Misha) Videiko and organised a low-budget visit to Ukraine in the summer of 2008.

When we arrived in Kyiv, we stayed with Misha and his wife Natasha in their little wooden house surrounded by vast Soviet style high-rise blocks. There were perhaps 10 or 15 of these blocks along the main street and, tucked away between them, was Misha and Natasha's house, populated by cats and with a lovely garden full of flowers and even a couple of tiny ponds. This was a real oasis in a Soviet-style housing desert, in the middle of Kyiv but at the same time out of Kyiv. We stayed there three days while we looked around the city, visited museums with Misha and then visited the eponymous site of Trypillia, with its own village museum full of Trypillia finds.

During this time in Kyiv, Bisserka re-discovered her long-buried Russian language. As a Bulgarian child growing up in the 1970s and 80s, she had had to learn Russian but, after 1989, she never spoke it at all and it sat passively in her mind for another 20 years. When she came to Kyiv, Natasha didn't speak any English at all, so the *lingua franca* was Russian. Bisserka understood what our hosts were discussing but she couldn't speak the language for several days. On the third day, her ability to speak Russian returned.

One of Misha's friends was a hunter who prided himself on his backwoods skills. He owned a well-equipped jeep with a portable barbecue. He agreed to take the four of us on a trip to south-central Ukraine to visit Trypillia sites and see if we could identify one as the basis for a long-term project. We drove off down the Kyiv–Odessa motorway but we found that, as soon as we left the motorways, the B roads, C roads and tracks were uniformly appalling. Our hunter had a SatNav but the Ukrainian coverage was patchy. On the way to the village of Mogylna, the SatNav directed us to the middle of a grassy field. It was only with the help of local informants that we managed to get to Mogylna, where we visited two of the three Trypillia sites. We visited a couple more Trypillia sites before ending a long day in the town of Gayvoron. We looked around the town and could find only one place to stay – a sad hotel with two beds in one room and three beds in the other. The food in town was fairly non-descript. We were slowly realising that this was par for the course in rural Ukraine.

We persisted and visited three more megasites on the next day, which included Nebelivka. Although the megasite was largely overgrown with maize, it was extremely rich in surface pottery. We were very impressed with Nebelivka and pencilled it in as *the* project site. The last port of call was the site of Volodymyrivka. Under a little grove of trees next to the River Synusha, our hunter had his greatest triumph – a barbecue lunch with the best food of the trip.

After our visit to Ukraine in 2008, we thought that it would be best to have a short trial season at Nebelivka in 2009 to see if we could work together with the Ukrainian side. We managed to obtain a British Academy Small Research Grant for the three-week season and, on the basis of some very successful results, applied for a much bigger grant. We put a big effort into a grant application to the AHRC for a six-figure sum for a four-year project with three major field seasons and an international travelling exhibition. We also proposed two international conferences – one in Ukraine and one in Durham. Although we found out in May 2010 that our application had been rejected, we were invited to re-apply next year. This time, we succeeded. This was the largest AHRC grant that anybody in Durham had won up to that point and it remained the largest AHRC grant for another 10 years.

Travelling to Ukraine

The basic project transport was the red Transit van nicknamed 'Jupi' (short for 'Jupiter', since it was once owned by a Romanist!) (Fig. 25). For the 2009 trip, we met the team of Durham University students and drove to Dover for the ferry trip to Calais. As soon as we reached Belgium, torrential rain slowed us down, especially on the infamous ring-road around Brussels. We arrived late in the town of Merchelen, where we'd reserved 12 beds in a youth hostel. The youth hostel was close to an all-night cafe bar, so we had street food on our first night in Europe. We set off bright and early for what would be a long drive and we managed to reach our hostel in Bavaria. On the third morning, we were singing Goran Bregović songs in Jupi and driving up

Fig. 25. Jupi the Project Transit van with his driver, Nebelivka excavations, Ukraine

towards the German–Austrian border south of Passau, when a German police car signalled us to pull over and stop. Bisserka opened the (wrong) window and the motorway policeman asked who was in the van and she said 10 British students. We'd already worked out that passports would be needed, so I passed the policeman the 12 passports. The cop was utterly amazed when we came up with the passports immediately, since he was absolutely sure we were people-smuggling. When Bisserka asked him how we could possibly be gypsies with a right-wheel van, he said, 'Oh, you'd be surprised what people are using.' We escaped and drove into Austria and on into Hungary, to a small hotel near Nyíregyháza, at the end of the Hungarian motorway. We had a good breakfast on the fourth day and drove off to the Ukrainian border. Since we had more passengers than excavation kit, we managed to get through the passenger side rather than the commercial side of the border – the last time we managed to do that. Driving off into Ukraine, it soon became clear that motorways were a much-lamented thing of the past. We had a stunning drive over the Trans-Carpathian mountains and drove on past Lviv. When we reached the fledgling motorway system, there were many road repairs and many 60 km/h speed limits. I was too impatient and was fined three times, with successively higher fines; perhaps the police phoned ahead and were told to watch out for easy money from a red Transit van? The drive through Ukraine was so slow that we couldn't possibly reach our hostel booked in Kyiv by the end of the fourth day. We had to spend the night in a motel near Lviv, with good food and a sauna that we did not use. We reached Kyiv by Saturday noon on the fifth day. I dropped the students off at their hostel in the centre and drove Bisserka and Jupi to the Videikos' house. We had a day to recover from the trip and, on Sunday, we would go south to Nebelivka by minibus or by bus. We spent most of the Saturday buying extra kit for the excavation.

Coming back to the UK was a fraught affair. At the end of the 2009 season, Bisserka returned to Bulgaria to meet her son Boyan and then rendezvous with me in Budapest. After the teams dispersed from Nebelivka, I took eight students with me in Jupi. We had one night in Kyiv and then we set out the next day for Lviv, where I had booked nine beds in a hostel in a converted industrial building. We set out bright and early the next morning, with the aim of getting into Hungary – possibly even close to Budapest. We had just started on the two-lane motorway out of Lviv when, some 12 km out of Lviv, a tyre blew when I was driving at 100 km/h. This was a section of the motorway in which there was a grass verge going down a bank into a field. I was certain that, if I let Jupi slip down onto the grass verge, it would turn over and that would lead to student carnage. I steered Jupi hard into the central reservation, turning through 180° and smashing the right-hand side and back of the vehicle against the barrier. The successful part of the manoeuvre was that I had managed to avoid falling down the slope and turning the van. In this way, none of the students were injured. This was not the case with Jupi, however, who was in a terrible state. I couldn't really move Jupi at all and somebody driving back to Lviv on the other side of the motorway clearly realised that we needed to be towed back to a garage and that kind person contacted a towing organisation who came out and took €500 for a 10 km tow back into Lviv. At this point, the students loyally bade me farewell, took a bus into the centre and caught the first train to Budapest. While Jupi was at the garage, the mechanics confirmed that, amazingly, there was no mechanical damage to the van. They seemed very confident that they could repair the bodywork even though in a terrible state. Over the next four days, the garage found spare parts, turning Jupi into a thoroughly international van, with parts from Ukraine, Poland, Slovakia, Czech Republic, Germany and even Malaysia (the back door). I had found a nearby hotel attached to the Lviv racecourse, with a pleasant room and a beautiful restaurant. There was little that I could do but look around Lviv. I visited the wonderful Archaeological Museum several times and also looked at many of those places that were mentioned by the Jewish author Bruno Schulz, who had written movingly about Lviv in his novels The Street of Crocodiles and Sanatorium Under the Sign of the Hourglass. Once I'd met a mightily relieved Bisserka and Boyan in Budapest, we had no problems driving back to the UK.

In 2012, Bisserka and I drove the minibus across Europe to Ukraine, using the same route as in 2009. We didn't take students this time because of the quantity of geophysics and surveying equipment. This meant that, instead of going down the passenger route at the Ukrainian customs, we had to go down the commercial route with all the lorries. Even though we had all our paperwork in order, the Customs procedure was glacially slow, for the Customs man had never encountered a load like ours before, so every few minutes he would telephone his superiors in Kyiv to ask what he had to do. Eventually, we managed to get through the border with the requisite permit and drove straight off towards Kyiv. All of the staff and students arrived in Kyiv that weekend and we put them on the bus and drove down to Nebelivka ready for the second week of the season.

For the 2013 trip, Bisserka, myself, our project PhD Marco Nebbia and our student Stuart Johnston travelled in Jupi, with all the geophysics and surveying kit. We made our usual ferry crossing from Hull to Rotterdam. This time, the ferry crossing was enlivened by the presence of over 40 veteran bikers. We had no need to worry how we would sleep, since the bikers didn't party long into the night. When we arrived at Rotterdam, there was a breathalyser test for all drivers. But the canny bikers were experienced and not one of them tested positive. The same could not be said for a smartly dressed man in an open-topped sports car, who tested positive and had to leave his car at the Customs. I was driving Jupi, sitting on the right-hand side, with Stuart sitting next to the left-hand window. When we came to the breathalyser point, the policewoman took one look at us, passed the breathalyser tube to Stuart, who, keeping a straight face, blew down it and tested negative and we drove off. This caused great amusement amongst the other policeman, who were watching the lady policewoman testing the wrong person. We could hardly contain ourselves.

When we arrived at the commercial part of the Hungarian–Ukrainian border, we met the same Ukrainian Customs man who had processed us in 2012. He recognised these troublesome foreigners immediately and asked if we were carrying the same kit. I explained that we had more or less the same kit. He found the record of our 2012 visit was still on his machine, so he had to make only a small number of alterations. We managed to get through the border in two hours but we still couldn't reach Kyiv in four days.

Our 2014 drive with Jupi began with three of us – Bisserka, our student Tom and me, with Dan Miller driving his own car. We had our usual long first day's drive across European motorways and reached a village somewhere near Regensburg in Bavaria. This was the year of the World Cup and that evening there was a quarter-final match between Brazil and Germany. The first guesthouse we happened to find also had the largest public room with a giant TV screen in the village and most of the men came to watch the match in the bar. We thought it would be a close-run thing and sat there supporting Germany, who took 11 minutes to score and then proceeded to rattle in another six goals and win the match 7–1. Every time the Germans scored, the villagers jumped up with their full glasses of beer and an enormous amount of beer went up in the air and came down and soaked everyone to the skin – a true beer shampoo. It was particularly special for the village because six members of the German national team came from their 'local' team, Bayern Munich.

On the third day, we reached the commercial route of our favourite border. When we arrived in the office, there was the same Customs man! Suspecting that this might happen, I had brought him a present of the complete geophysics plan of Nebelivka to show him what we'd been doing in Ukraine. The Customs man's boss was in his room when we were making the presentation. He expressed total amazement at how four strangers came to give his Customs officer such a magnificent plan. We did our best to explain that these Ukrainian sites were probably the earliest cities in the world and the Customs team showed a quiet glow of reflected national glory. Our 'friend' managed to process our documents in record time – only an hour and a half – and we left for Kyiv, which we did manage to reach on the fourth evening for the first time.

Accommodation in Nebelivka

In 2009, the only accommodation big enough for our team was the infamous Brygantina children's summer camp, which had occasional visits from the Communist Party to instil proper discipline into the lives of unruly children in their Wild East capitalist country. Brygantina had all kinds of issues. There was a curfew and no alcohol on sale. There were strict eating times and, if you didn't turn up for breakfast by 7.30 am or for dinner at 6.30 pm, you wouldn't get any food. The only concession that the camp made to our group was that we were able to eat in a room separate from the 300 children. There were also strict time limits on the showers, with the women in our group allocated 30 minutes and the men a different 30 minutes. I don't think the students had expected to see a naked Chapman having a shower with them! The biggest issue for me was the transport to and from Nebelivka, since not all of the team could fit into Jupi. Novo'arkhangelsk District Council supplied a bus and a driver and the only time we could work was when the driver had picked us up at Brygantina and dropped us off at the site. We didn't have that much contact with the villagers of Nebelivka that year because we lived in Brygantina. The most helpful person was Mayor Bobko, who was very welcoming and provided storage space for our excavation kit in the village school. Apart from Bobko, our main contact was with the shopkeepers where we bought alcohol, which, like teenagers, we smuggled back into Brygantina to drink at night.

After the deprivations our team had suffered with Brygantina, Misha Videiko managed to arrange second-season accommodation in the Nebelivka school during their six-week summer holidays. But there was a serious logistical problem with a team of 25 staying in a school with only two loos – a male loo and a female loo in wooden huts at the end of the football field 50 m from the school. The plan was hatched to build a shower and loo block next to the school. The first idea was to build a freestanding block but the Kirovograd architects suggested that we attach a loo and shower block onto the end of the school and this was what we did. The new block was built in the first couple of weeks. I had made rather general plans of the shower and toilet block to show friends who were builders in England and they came up with a ballpark estimate of the costs. I had to put this new plan to the AHRC and managed to persuade them that this would save a lot of project money. The AHRC recognised that we would be saving £20,000 in each of the three major seasons, which was eligible to be ploughed back into general project expenditure. After receiving the AHRC's permission to build the 'Chapman Block' (as it was called[1]), we were faced with a bill from Kirovograd County Council for £50,000. A set of invoices had been prepared which purported to show how much money had been spent on the block. When we came to look in detail at the invoices, it became clear that these had been grossly inflated and it was only because of a grant for rural projects from one of the

[1] This block was said by some to be my principal contribution to Ukrainian archaeology – indeed perhaps to the archaeology of Central and Eastern Europe.

national political parties that the block was affordable. To give you one example of the financial arrangements: a sum of money was set aside for a JCB to drive from Uman 40 km to the village, excavate the foundation trenches for the shower and toilet block and then drive back to Uman – a total of three days' work. In fact, we knew very well that this service was performed by a local farmer who owned a JCB and it took him precisely half a day to do the work. A lot of creative accounting was used to inflate the size of the grant from the political party, to be paid to somebody (to whom?). When I stated that £10,000 was the sum in my estimates for the block, Kirovograd County Council eventually accepted this was the British contribution and they made up the rest. The result was that Nebelivka school became one of the best equipped schools in the whole of the county, with showers available for staff, toilets available for children and a washing machine available for anyone who needed it. Also, because we paid the school in kind for the rent for each six-week occupation of the school, we repaired floors, windows and ceilings and gradually provided the school with a satellite dish, new televisions and computers. Whenever officials came to visit the Nebelivka excavations, they were taken into the Mayor's office for a drink and then straight to the school to show off the main beneficiary of the project. A minority of the visitors even visited the excavations.

One major health and safety incident in 2013 seriously tested our nerves and patience. This took place on a Friday night after the usual Friday evening village disco. Unusually, all of the students had returned to the school by midnight and we'd kept the main door shut with a large wooden beam. There was a great commotion in the night and a huge crash woke up the students, although I have to confess that I remained fast asleep. The students went to the entrance of the school without opening the door and saw a red Ukrainian Volkswagen Golf, which had broken some of the school benches in the yard. The driver then tried to smash his way into the school, which failed for two reasons: first, the car was wider than the school door and, secondly, there were three concrete steps in front of the school door and the car couldn't climb up the steps. At this point, the drunken driver realised that this would not work, so he drove off into the night. The students checked the front door's wooden beam and went to bed. An hour later, the Ukrainians came back to smash their way into the school again. This time, one of the Ukrainian students – Volodya – managed to take note of the Ukrainian car number plate. I had still not woken up and I hadn't even woken up at the time of the third attack, when the drunken teenager really did make mincemeat of his own car and I don't know how he managed to drive it away.

When I woke up in the morning, the students briefed me on what had happened. It was obvious that we had to inform the police and also Mayor Bobko. By the time the police arrived, I was out on site and was called back to give a full statement to the police for use in court, even though I didn't see anything at all of the attack. The police promised to look into the matter and find the driver. After all, it was a serious, criminal offence to destroy Government property – viz., the school benches. But it was Mayor Bobko who identified the owner of the car within two days.

Bobko convened a meeting without the police in the school yard after we returned from our morning excavations. In front of the whole team, there was an embarrassed middle-aged man and a sullen youth. Bobko chaired the meeting and it was clear that the man was the owner of the car and the father of the teenager who drove the car. Although the youth never apologised directly for what he did, he promised he would never attack the school again. Bobko put to the meeting a choice of punishments: either the teenager would work on community service for the village for three weeks, cleaning ditches, or we would report the matter to the police, in which case he would be brought to trial and undoubtedly serve a jail sentence of six months or even a year. Almost everyone was in favour of the community service punishment, apart from one right-wing student who felt that the youth should be made an example. Bobko also negotiated with the father, who owned a JCB, to backfill all of our excavation trenches at the end of the 2013 season without charge.

What remained a mystery was why this youth had committed the attack. What was most important for Bobko was that the family did not come from Nebelivka but from the next village of Oksanina. We concluded that this was not an 'ethnic' attack on British students but rather an attack on the village of Nebelivka, which had become famous and prosperous from the project. By contrast, Oksanina had not received any national or regional TV coverage and we spent little money there. This suggested that the attack was an act of jealousy on behalf of another village. Bobko and I were extremely relieved that locals had not carried out the attack, which would have been very hard for him to bear.

Project logistics

One of the great kindnesses of Mayor Bobko was to offer us a room above the village kindergarten, which we turned into a project finds lab. Bobko was very aware that, because we were living in Nebelivka, we spent a large amount of money in the village, benefitting the two food-and-drink shops. Larisa and her family, who ran an eco-hotel near Novo'arkhangelsk, did a fine job as organisers of the catering in the school for the students. We had three meals per day in the school, which were announced by Svetlana, the project admin lady, in her beautiful Russian accent with the phrase 'dinner is ready', the thought of which warms Nebelivka students' hearts to this day.

The major plank of the 2012 season was the excavation of the 30 m × 20 m building we called the 'mega-structure', identified in the 2009 geophysical plot and the largest building known in the Trypillia world. We needed a strong project team to complete this huge job in seven weeks and hired six professional archaeologists for the summer season to complement the students. The point that Misha made very firmly was that we really had to excavate this building in one summer season, for the price for not completing the dig would be that looters would remove the rest of the material when we left in August. Misha's argument was very persuasive, so we made it our aim to excavate all of the mega-structure in 2012.

We had an 'integrated' excavation with all finds and structures recorded on the Total Station. In practice, there were different zones of this enormous trench – some areas excavated by the Ukrainians and different zones for our professional archaeologists and students. What we hadn't realised from the 2009 trial season was the mistrust with which Misha and Natasha held students in general. This dislike became a serious problem because Natasha would criticise the students openly in Russian for most of the excavation and the brunt of these endless complaints fell on the ears of the only member of the British side who understood Russian well – Bisserka. We managed to control things up to a point but the poor relationship between the teams spilled over into problems within the British team. In week three, two of the British professional archaeologists decided they couldn't work on a site under such extreme conditions, so they left in the middle of the project. This really made a big hole in our professional digging team but we still had four diggers who loyally stayed on to the end. I have to say that I was immensely grateful to them, for at one point, it seemed possible that three of them would leave too.

The side-effects of the 2012 mega-structure excavation were that we had to process, analyse and publish very large quantities of finds, which we had not anticipated. This led us to plan two extra post-excavation seasons, which we financed by the savings we made on accommodation at Nebelivka school. We had a one-week winter season in January 2013, when a team of four – Sofia Arbeiter, Ed Caswell, Bisserka and myself – rented a flat in the centre of Kyiv and took the tram each day to the Kyiv Institute of Archaeology. The Institute is in a 10-storey Soviet block on the outskirts of Kyiv, overlooking the river Dnieper. One of the great moments each day was to go out onto the seventh-floor balcony overlooking the Dnieper and watch the fishermen digging fishing holes in the frozen river.

The trickiest incident in 2013 concerned public health. One day, three of the British students came down with food poisoning, with 10 more students falling ill in the next two days. The head of the village medical centre came to inspect the students and said that there was a danger that this would be declared an epidemic, resulting in the closure of the school and a big accommodation problem. She was duty bound to report this incident to the district hospital in Novo'arkhangelsk. A team of doctors from Novo'arkhangelsk came to the school and inspected every single staff member and student. All of us had to give an anal sample for hospital analysis, which caused much entertainment for the female doctor and nurse. The doctors repeated the threat that they would really have to close down the school as the site of a major infection. But we explained that, since there was nowhere else to stay in the village, closing the school would spread the infection into a number of different village houses or indeed to a hotel in Uman. The doctors re-considered and agreed that it would be better to contain the infection in one place – namely the Nebelivka school. The most important task was to find the source of the problem, which turned out to be food poisoning.

The illegal Russian invasion of the Crimea in February–March 2014 meant that Durham University was extremely concerned about the situation in Ukraine, not least because there was a build-up of Russian troops on Ukraine's south-eastern border and a threat of further invasion. Before the 2014 season could go ahead, I had to get insurance cover for the Durham University students. Although cover for the staff was important, we were really of secondary concern to the university; students and especially litigious parents were really what gave the university nightmares. I had to devise a detailed plan explaining how the team could leave safely in the event of a second Russian invasion, despite the fact that (a) Nebelivka was 600 km from the focus of Russian forces; (b) Nebelivka had no strategic value at all; and (c) Nebelivka had no concentration of wealth to attract the Russians (in fact, the main concentration of wealth was inside Mayor Bobko's mouth in the form of his gold teeth). Nonetheless, the University insisted on the provision of a detailed escape route in case of invasion, in which I had to specify road names, distances and the time it would take to escape from Nebelivka into Romania. The university accepted my escape plan and gave our students and staff insurance cover for our 2014 season.

Time off

The project had one day off per week and, apart from a sleeping day off, our free time was divided between three different activities. We had a favourite beach not far from Novo'arkhangelsk on the River Synukha, where we would go swimming and play football and cricket. Near the beach, there was a restaurant that did barbecue meals. Another place that we'd found in the second year was a Veterans' Military Museum, 130 km south-west of Nebelivka, where discharged veterans of the Afghan Soviet campaign had bought up as much spare Soviet military equipment as they could and set up a military museum in the Ukrainian countryside. When we arrived for the first time, this is when we realised that the political education of our students was not quite up to scratch. When we asked the students the identities of the two statues of Marx and Lenin flanking the museum entrance, most of the students couldn't identify both minor celebrities. We had quite a long way to go in political indoctrination. For the modest price of the entrance, we had a very rough ride on a personnel carrier through a steep, wooded area. This ride was absolutely terrifying – you had to hold on for dear life, otherwise you'd be thrown off the personnel carrier. The second ride in the back of an army lorry was much more sedate. Each visitor had two bullets to fire from rifles in the woods, where we were aiming at trees rather than people. There was also the possibility, for an extra charge, for students to rent sub-machine-guns to shoot a lot of bullets at the trees in the forest and quite a few students enjoyed doing this. Some of the students were terrified by the museum but others liked it so much that we visited it once a year. The third place we really enjoyed going to was Sofiyivsky Park in Uman, a 19th-century landscape park given as a gift by the Ruthenian *voivode* Stanisław Szczęsny Potocki to his Greek wife Zofia Wittowa. Potocki landscaped the area all around the palace and turned the whole area into a fabulous landscape of lakes, Classical Greek temples, gazebos and caves with underground boat trips and 2,000 different tree species (Plate 29). This was a lovely place on a sunny afternoon, where there was also the possibility of hiring 19th-century costumes, pedal boats and bicycles. There were different things to do for lots of people all of the afternoon, with the opportunity to go for a good meal in Uman centre after enjoying the landscape park. In 2013, we discovered an additional treat – a visit to Larissa and Igor's eco hotel – further from Novo'arkhangelsk than Brygantina – where we ate wonderful Larissa food and went swimming in the Synukha river.

Excavation, fieldwork and the house experiment[2]

We managed to complete the excavation of the mega-structure in the eight-week 2012 season. While the structure was impressive, it was curious that the finds in the mega-structure were not particularly special. We had gained funding for the excavation from the National Geographic Society on the basis that we were excavating a major Trypillia 'temple' and we genuinely expected large concentrations of ritual finds and probably prestige goods as well. Yet we simply didn't find them! There was only one spectacular find – the first piece of gold jewellery (a hair ornament) that had ever been found in the Trypillia group. But apart from the concentration of 22 miniature vessels, we found no other significant concentrations of finds and this was deeply puzzling. It gave us a clue about Trypillia communities which were perhaps not as hierarchical as had been assumed.

The geophysics research had progressed well in 2009, 2012 and 2013 but the sheer size of the megasite and an unlucky set of crop conditions prevented the team from completing the survey in summer 2013. We were within 70 ha of completing the plan and it seemed worthwhile to hold a second geophysics season in autumn 2013 to finish off the job. A small group of geophysicists went out to Nebelivka in October, accompanied by Bisserka for translation and negotiation. The result was the completion of the first and so far only complete geophysics plan of a Trypillia megasite.

The two real innovations of the 2014 season concerned the Ukrainians' excavation of what they thought was a pottery kiln and the experimental programme. The Ukrainians targeted the excavation of a high-intensity circular anomaly on the geophysics plan. This was a broadly circular feature with three grooves cut into the clay. We had certainly come upon nothing like this before and, although the feature had general similarities with the Taljanki kilns, the Nebelivka grooves were very shallow and there was no sign of any ceramic wasters as by-products of failed kiln firings. There remains to this day a disagreement over the interpretation of this feature. While the Ukrainians remain convinced that this was an early form of kiln,

[2] A full account of the excavations and fieldwalking programmes can be found in the project monograph (Gaydarska 2020).

the British interpretation was of a cooking facility for communal roasting of bread and meat.

The aims of the experimental programme were to build two 'Neolithic' houses, burn them down and excavated the ruins. The construction season was run by Stuart Johnston with a team of village helpers. The house-building programme was a great joint achievement between the village and the project and made a big difference to our social relations (Plate 30). The preparations for the Nebelivka house-burning experiment were going well in terms of the quantity of timber needed for the burning. But Mayor Bobko had come to love the two experimental houses in the centre of the village and wanted to keep both of them to develop heritage tourism in the village. I explained that we needed to burn both houses down to make a comparative, scientific study. We eventually reached an Anglo–Ukrainian compromise whereby we would burn down only one house – the two-storey house. The house-burning was integrated into the project's Kirovograd Conference and proved an enormous social success for the delegates, the Nebelivkans and other neighbouring villages. There was also that essential safety component – the Novo'arkhangelsk Fire Brigade, who turned up in an ancient fire engine staffed by two extremely large, round and jolly firemen. The fire continued to burn really well for the next five hours (Plate 30). Two years later, a small team met to excavate the burnt house remains produced in 2015. We excavated half of the remains, showing that the structural remains of genuine Trypillia houses could be interpreted with the help of a modern experiment.

Outreach

Roland Fletcher's important role in the genesis of the project made it important that Bisserka and I attended the first major Society for American Archaeolgy (SAA) session on 'Great Anomalous Sites' (aka 'Big Weird Sites') which Roland, Nam Kim and Kirrily White had organised in April 2013 in Hawaii. This was not only a great opportunity to talk low-density massive sites but also to visit part of the world we had never visited before. Roland had assembled a group which included Nam Kim who was working on Co Loa, Tom Emerson who was working on Cahokia, the Brazilian archaeologist Eddie Neves who was working on huge Amazonian sites that nobody had heard of before and one of my earliest Newcastle graduates, Adam Rogers, who was working on Iron Age *oppida* in Europe. This impressive session introduced the rest of archaeology to low-density anomalous sites.

The most exciting project event in spring 2014 was the Tucson Amerind workshop, held in the remote Dragoon ranch in Arizona. The idea behind the workshops was to assemble a group of specialists for four or five days to thrash out important conclusions for a key theme in anthropology and archaeology. Roland Fletcher had persuaded the Amerind Foundation to host a workshop on huge, anomalous, low-density settlements, to which we were invited. The other British colleagues were Tom Moore, an Iron Age specialist from Durham, and Mike Parker Pearson, a professor of Archaeology in UCL. The ranch provided not only three beautiful meals a day but also fine wines. Since there were no other distractions, talks went on long into the night. There were opportunities for early morning walks or runs round the ranch, with minor risks of rattlesnake attack. We had four days of really relaxed discussions with many of the low-density, 'anomalous giants' crowd who came to Hawaii as well as one discussant – Trish McEnaney – who added much clarity to the debate. We marked the end of the workshop with a pot-smashing ceremony. I'd bought a recent Amerindian pot from the nearby village and I broke it on the stone flags and gave one sherd to each of the participants. Some people, including Innocent Piriyaki, told me years later that he still had his Amerind sherd from John's fragmentation experiment. It simply underlines how enchainment works.

At the EAA Annual Meeting in September 2014 in Istanbul, Bisserka and I organised a session on European urbanism, which included Tim Taylor talking about the Iron Age site of Bil'sk in Ukraine, Anthony Harding talking about the Romanian Bronze Age site of Corneşti and Tom Moore talking about Iron Age *oppida* in Europe. Slowly, a gap was opening up between the German and Ukrainian maximalist view of megasites and that of the British side, who were thinking increasingly about minimalist interpretations of megasites. It was at this meeting that our interpretational differences showed up in public for the first time and it was important to cope with these differences in a creative and positive way. The urbanism session led to the production of two completely different books. Johannes Müller, with Misha and Knut Rassmann, a geophysicist from Frankfurt, co-edited an EAA Special Monograph on the Trypillia megasite phenomenon – very data-rich and focusing on the recent excavations at Nebelivka, Taljanki and Majdanetske. Bisserka was the guest editor of a special edition on urbanism for the *Journal of World Prehistory*, focusing on the conceptual problems of what is urbanism, how to define it, whether Trypillia megasites could indeed be considered as 'urban' and, if so, what kind of urban. This set the tone for the divergent directions of our future investigations.

The project's Kirovograd Conference in 2015 lasted two evenings and one full day of papers, with our group presenting six papers on our Nebelivka research. It was at Kirovograd that we launched our travelling exhibition – a small affair based upon pop-up stands with replaceable display panels with texts in five different languages apart from English. This was a clever exhibition design by Chris Unwin, using materials from Alphagraphics North East, and combining each of six translated versions of the standard text with the same graphic materials. The logistical issue was how to move the stands from venue to venue, while at the same time bringing the new panels with different languages from the UK. This involved more flights than I wanted, as well as relying on a Moldovan colleague to transport the stands from Varna to the National Museum of Moldovan History in Chişinau (Plate 31). Evetually the exhibition returned to the UK, where we set up the six-week exhibition in Durham University's Museum on Palace Green, with several school visits and lots of interest from the general public.

The exhibition made its last outing to the Theoretical Archaeology Group (TAG) conference in Southampton – a placement that Josh Pollard had kindly organised for us. The exhibition was displayed in seven locations, involving six different languages, and we were extremely pleased with the results of this outreach.

The Durham Conference in 2016 was the project's second international meeting and focused on early urbanism. We had invited David Wengrow, who had been a staunch project supporter and made a major contribution with his comparative research on early urbanism but, at the last minute, he couldn't come. All of the other leading Anglophone specialists on Trypillia and Cucuteni had been invited and they all came, except for Stas Ţerna. Unfortunately, the Moldovan postal service lets Stas down very badly and he never received his train ticket by registered mail. This meeting was the first time in which the interpretational gap between the 'maximalists' and the 'minimalists' was publicly very obvious. This was displayed in no more pronounced a way than with the German palaeo-environmentalist Wiebke Kirleis' hostile comments on Bruce Albert's presentation of the Nebelivka pollen diagram, which was crucial in demonstrating that there was very little human impact on the local environment from the megasite. The battle lines were being drawn.

The greatest surprise for the project came about in the autumn of 2015, when we were invited to the second Shanghai Archaeological Forum (SAF). The Forum was the brainchild of Professor Wang Wei, of the Chinese Academy of Sciences in Beijing, who wanted to expand the Western connections of Chinese archaeology and realised that the best way to do this was to bring world archaeology to China. So Wang Wei set up the SAF, organised through the Chinese Academy of Sciences Shanghai Branch and, to our great delight, we were nominated for an award for the period 2013 to 2015. We had to wait until November to receive confirmation that we had indeed been awarded one of the Top Ten Fieldwork Project prizes.

The SAF was an archaeological version of Hollywood – extremely glitzy and glittery, with two stunningly dressed *compères* – one male and one female – making all the announcements in English and Chinese. There was a lifetime achievement award, that year awarded to Colin Renfrew, 10 fieldwork prizes and 10 archaeological project prizes for analysis and publication. Since, perhaps unsurprisingly, there were very few female archaeologists who would receive SAF gold medals, I suggested to Bisserka that she was the person to receive the award. She duly collected the award (Plate 32) in a ceremony dominated by flashing strobe lights and rock music.

Most of 2016 was spent writing up the Trypillia project for publication. There was a twin-track approach to publication, with all of the material being available for free download from the web. The first part was the basic information, including a huge number of site and finds photographs, hosted by the Archaeological Data Service in York, in which Ray Moore and Louisa Matthews created the basic archive structure for the project. The other part of the publication was the interpretation of the basic data in an open access monograph published by De Gruyter through their editorial team in Poland and particularly Katarżyna Michalak.

Our last major project activity was a second visit to the SAF for the third forum, which took place in December 2017. We hadn't realised that previous prize winners would be invited onto the organising committee of the next forum and asked to return to Shanghai. This was another great opportunity to meet many of the world archaeologists whom we'd met in 2015, with Brian Fagan this time receiving a Lifetime Achievement Award.

I wish to pay tribute to Kirovograd County Council, and especially the boss, Andrei Nikolaenko, who was a strong supporter of the project, Nadia Lishnjak, the chief of the Heritage Section of the County Council and Valentin Sobchuk in the Heritage Section. The site reports in the Kirovograd county newspapers and the Kirovograd regional TV programmes drew the attention of the Ukrainian national TV, so Nebelivka featured in two programmes on regional TV and a 20-minute feature on Ukrainian national TV.

Holidays

While we were in Honolulu, we took the chance to look around the war museum explaining the role of Hawaii in the Second World War and how the Japanese came to attack Pearl Harbor. One boat took us to see part of one of their boats sunk in the attack – the USS Missouri, where we could see the main deck and were shown a dramatic video of the Japanese attack. Since Boyan came to Hawaii with us, he had a lot of free time on the beach and was able to check out lots of places to visit. After the conference, we decided to take a short flight to one of the other islands – the Big Island – where there were still active volcanoes. Indeed, Kilauea had erupted so recently that no one could make the trip up to the volcano's rim so we had to be content with walking around at lower altitudes. One day, we drove down and parked near the Pu'u Loa Petroglyph field and walked on along the tarmac Chain of Craters Road. We turned a corner to find a huge lava flow across the road. The lava flow, which had descended from Kilauea in 1983 continued for another 2 km, putting the road out of action for ever. We had the chance to climb a small, thoroughly extinct volcano up steep wooden steps. Boyan flew up the steps and had to wait 20 minutes at the top for Bisserka and another 20 minutes for me. But the next day, neither of them could walk at all, whereas my legs were still in good shape. There were some stunning places to see – especially the tropical valleys, which one could walk to over steep terrain to see some of the most amazing vegetation on the island. The 2013 SAAs were memorable for many different reasons.

Boyan joined us for the last week of the 2013 season, after which we spent a three-week family holiday in the Crimea. Although we didn't know this at the time, this was our last opportunity to visit the Crimea. We had rented a flat in Yalta and visited the palace where the Yalta Conference took place at the end of the Second World War. We spent a blissful afternoon in Chekhov's summer house, which he bought after his first visit to the house. He spent most of his later summers there, writing *The Cherry Orchard* and *Three Sisters*. Not only was there a wonderful garden but the house itself was a monument to Chekhov's writing career – the most evocative place for us in the whole of Yalta. Yalta also had a great range of restaurants, featuring Turkish, Georgian and Armenian cuisine.

Since it seemed foolish to go all the way to China for the Shanghai Archaeological Forum and not tour around, we first flew to Zhengzhou, where our Hungarian friends Alice and Laci had put us in touch with a local heritage chief, who persuaded Kaifeng University to invite us to give a research seminar on the Trypillia megasites. We had two days of trips around local sites and cultural monuments and saw the Yellow River – about as yellow as the Danube is blue. The Kaifeng seminar was extremely revealing in that, although the archaeology students had never heard of Trypillia megasites, they asked some of the most penetrating questions that we'd ever faced. In comparison with this intellectual potential, the sites that the heritage chief showed us in the countryside outside Zhengzhou revealed how backward Chinese archaeology was in remote sensing. The current method to detect the buried layers of sites in 2015 was coring by bamboo rod. Although the archaeologists were extremely keen to find out about the archaeological world beyond China, they had not even heard of some of the most important global sites, such as *Çatalhöyük*. There was a very long way to go for Chinese archaeology to catch up with what was happening in the world and this really underlined the importance of the SAF.

On the next leg of our trip, we took a bullet train with a top speed of 262 km per hour from Zhengzhou to Xian – in the medieval period the starting point of the Silk Road. The train moved so fast you could hardly see the landscape but the speeds were necessary to cover the vast distances.[3] We had expected to be met at Xian station by a Chinese archaeologist called Janice Li, who had a part-time job in UCL Archaeology. Xian railway station was more like a secular cathedral – an impressive building with different shades of marble and ceilings 50 m high. But we could not detect a word of English and Janice was nowhere to be seen. After half an hour's wait, we had no idea what to do, since there was no way to contact Janice. It turned out that she'd been delayed in traffic and was profusely apologetic for keeping us waiting so long. Janice drove us to a hotel in the hills on the south side of Xian, with thermal pools and saunas. The next day, Janice took us to see the Terracotta Army. She was researching the soldiers' equipment with a UCL colleague, Andy Bevan. Janice spent half her year in Xian and half in UCL, truly having the best of both worlds. She was an inspired guide and took us to the lowest, ground-floor level of the Terracotta Army burial place. While the tourists looked down from two levels above, we could walk to within a few metres of the soldiers. It was the individualisation of each soldier that was such a surprise – they truly were 'all individuals'.[4] Janice also took us around other parts of the royal burial complex, showing us how much more remained for future excavation. We also had time to look around the city of Xian, with its 17th- and 18th-century

[3] Compare the speed of the train from Novorossisk to Skt.-Petersburg, p. 86.

[4] With apologies to *Monty Python's Life of Brian*.

Fig. 26. Xian mosque, China

Chinese temples and pagodas. In the main market for the Silk Road was a sign for a mosque and we saw the most Chinese-looking mosque we had ever seen, complete with dragons and pagoda terminals (Fig. 26). We asked to see the famous Chinese Neolithic site of Banpo, which appears as a small village with a cluster of houses in Chris Scarre's *The Human Past*. In fact, Banpo had been excavated over a much larger scale and turned out to be a major triple-ditched enclosure with over a dozen houses. Janice explained that the Chinese custom whenever archaeologists excavated a remarkable site was to build a site museum over the top of the excavations and this is what they'd done with Banpo. This was an appropriately Chinese, impressive approach to cultural heritage.

The final leg of our trip involved an evening flight from Xian to Beijing, where we stayed in a small hotel in a quiet Chinese street whose staff spoke not a word of English – in fact, the only way we could communicate in the hotel was by Google Translate. We saw the main tourist attractions, including a walk through Tiananmen Square, the Forbidden City and the National Museum with its endless rooms of treasures, which we could have returned to see for three or four days. We also took a coach trip to the Great Wall of China. Here, we were reminded of the scale of Chinese ambition. We were told that, two years ago, the village at the foot of the most visited stretch of the Wall simply had not enough facilities for the tourist flow. In the next year, three new hotels were built, together with six new restaurants and a large number of tourist shops. The village was completely transformed within a year to provide the infrastructure for Chinese-style mass tourism.

We made two more memorable visits in Beijing. The first was located at the very outskirts of Beijing – beyond the 10th motorway ring. A kind Russian archaeologist we'd met at the SAF put us in touch with colleagues in the Geological Institute in Beijing, who offered us a guided tour of the Choukoutien Caves – a huge Palaeolithic complex of many cave sites, which had produced human fossil remains of what was first known as 'Peking man' but now was recognised as a *Homo erectus* population dating to 400,000 years ago. Our guide for this trip was a retired geologist who was extremely vivid and enthusiastic, spoke excellent English and gave us a wonderful tour around the sites. There was an immense new exhibition, whose most impressive feature was a 'wall' of flint tools, including thousands of pieces of flint displayed on a glass background 25 m high and 30 m wide. At the end of the tour, we were invited to a special reception, where the museum bosses sat with us at a perpetually replenishing round table. There was also the challenging Chinese custom, which we'd met in Zhengzhou, of offering extremely hard liquor in tiny thimble-cups that you had to down in one after a short toast, invariably in Chinese. We didn't meet local expectations when we downed only a few thimble-cups of rice whisky!

Perhaps the most interesting visit that we made in Beijing was to the Ethnic Minorities Museum – an extended ethnographic city with a village for each of the 56 ethnic minorities found in China. Our only regret was that, because this was the winter season, the southern half of the complex was closed. But it took us a whole day to look around the northern part of the city. This astonishing ethnographic display belied the harsh Chinese treatment of the Uighur minority, since the local minority was very well represented in the ethnographic park. Perhaps the ethnographic city has changed in the last few years.

The 2017 SAA meetings provided an opportunity to visit Vancouver – a part of the west coast we'd never been to before. We went for a five-day trip to Vancouver Island before the conference. The best collection of north-west coast ethnography for us was in the Victoria Museum, with its amazing collection of totem poles. They had a wonderful designer of exhibitions who drew you completely into the Indian mentality. We also had amazing times on the beaches, looking around Indian sites. We had missed by three days the giant whale migration route of 20,000 whales heading north past Vancouver Island to their summer grounds. On the west side of the island, we tried to book a commercial whale-watching trip but we cancelled the visit because we had to sign an insurance waiver that if anything happened on the boat it was entirely our fault. I was not prepared to sign such a waiver and instead found a local Indian – a former tribal chief who had a much smaller boat that he wouldn't take out into the open sea because it was too rough but he would take us around the more sheltered parts of the harbour and show us some of the Indian sites on the shores. Although we didn't see any whales, we didn't get seasick and had a great time looking at Indian sites instead. When we returned to Vancouver, we rented an attic flat in a house in a modest suburb in east Vancouver and took the tram in each day to the conference centre. The nicest social occasion was meeting Marg de Guzman, who took a Masters degree from Durham and who came out to Hungary to work with me on the Tiszagyulaháza project in 2002. By now, Marg was running her own commercial archaeological unit and she took us out to a lovely bay-side restaurant to swap stories about old and new times.

We had a week of holiday before the third SAF, looking around Shanghai and a few days after the meeting in Hong Kong with Isla Brown, the daughter of our Spennymoor friends, who had a placement there from Lancaster University. Our trips around Shanghai were more relaxed than the first time because we had more time to look at some of the infrequently visited shrines and temples and indeed museums that we hadn't managed to visit before. The one thing that we really wanted to do was to see one of the Bronze Age megasites not so far from Shanghai. I did some basic web research on the site, booked a train ticket to the nearby Chinese city of Zhejiang and we took a bullet train there. When we got to the station, we asked the taxi-drivers how to get to the site of Liangzhu and we were very puzzled that they had not heard of the site. The taxi-drivers suggested we went to the Tourist Office inside the station. The tourist agents were equally puzzled by our request and didn't recognise the site. One member of staff asked if we perhaps meant the city of Zheijang; there was only one letter difference between the name of their city and the name of the city where the site was to be found. I'd got it wrong! Since we were in a major Chinese city that was unknown to us, we asked the tourist board to recommend anything worth seeing in their city. One of the saddest moments of our entire Chinese experience was when the tourist lady looked at us mournfully and confessed that they didn't really have anything worth seeing at all. There was nothing for it but to take the bullet train back to Shanghai.

Two days later, we took another bullet train to the correct city and asked in the station tourist office how to get to the site. We were told that there was a bus that went from the station to the north-west suburb, from which we should take another bus to the site. We managed to take the two buses very close to the site but we didn't quite manage to reach the site. We admitted defeat and took a taxi for the last 3 km. Sadly, the site museum was closed for repairs, so there was no one who could show us the site. But there were many signs to the 'ancient ruins' which we followed. The signs went on south of the museum until we got to a motorway, at which point the signs disappeared and we had no idea of the location of the ruins. We walked on south into what was clearly a new suburb that had presumably been constructed in the middle of the megasite but we could find no archaeological remains. On the tourist map, a Metro station was marked and I thought that, if we walked to the Metro station, we would be able to take the Metro straight back to the main railway station. Unfortunately, when we got to the Metro station, it was only partly completed. We had to walk back and get another bus to the same suburb where we'd arrived, so we managed to get the bus from the suburb to the railway station and catch the bullet train home to Shanghai. We were proud of getting close to the site and back on our own steam. However, it was frustrating to have been within the perimeter of a Chinese Bronze Age megasite without seeing any archaeology. When we eventually got to the third SAF and talked to an old Chinese hand, Jessica Rawson, she said that it's actually impossible to visit Chinese sites without a local guide because they were never properly signposted (for security reasons) and no one knows what's going on there in the local community. On the latter point, she was surely right. We were unaware that there was a post-SAF trip to this site.

After the conference, Isla showed us around Hong Kong for two or three days, after which we looked around ourselves for a few days. We had one great day with a Macao family, whose daughter Fan was studying with our musician friend Toni in Durham. Our hotel was right next to the main Hong Kong racecourse, so we went for an evening of horse-racing. There was a terrific atmosphere, which swept us up and it felt impossible not to bet on the races. I hadn't bet since my teenage years[5] but I bet small sums, which I lost immediately. Isla had developed a good sense of local cuisine and she took us to several of the local food outlets near her hall of residence. We had a real insider's experience of Hong Kong cuisine in those days. After one late-evening dinner, we walked back along the north side of the bay and crossed the bridge to 'our' side, soaking up the illuminations and the warm night air. This visit came just before the huge student and citizen protests in Hong Kong and the subsequent Chinese crack-down. It's hard to imagine what those peaceful streets have since become.

Summing up

The Trypillia megasites project helped us to join the global debate on low-density anomalous sites and on urbanism with some of the most thoughtful archaeologists in the world, while at the same time bringing us down to earth in forcing us to deal with the most basic, mundane issues that recurred on a daily basis in any rural Ukrainian village. It was this stretching over all the scales of interaction that made the project the most challenging that I have ever faced in my career. My limited linguistic abilities were exposed in Ukraine and I had to rely a lot on Bisserka to keep the project afloat. By the end of the project, the provincial officials used to address Bisserka in Ukrainian!

In all of my other major projects, there was a dominant element of fieldwalking, in which the team kept moving around the landscape and gained insights from the constant new perspectives and new scenery. Although the Nebelivka project incorporated some fieldwalking, this was a minor component and most of the fieldwork involved 'sedentary' on-site work, with close contact between the teams. The peak of proximity came with the 2012 excavation of the mega-structure, when the teams were in the same trench for six weeks.

The social relations in a project with up to 50 people in the field at the same time were necessarily heterogeneous. All kinds of unexpected relations developed – not only between UK students and village pet dogs. There was great camaraderie between UK diggers and our Ukrainian driver Sergei, who often brought watermelons for the hot, sticky students after their six hours of fieldwalking and tried to add to his meagre English knowledge each year. A friendship developed between Bisserka and a village lady called Alina, who was very bright and a natural excavator, who would surely have benefitted from a university education if she had had the chance. Alina often brought home-cooked food to the trench where she was digging and shared it with the UK team. Stuart Johnston got on famously with the village building team, sharing beers rather than food with them. And all the students had a love-hate relationship with Sasha, who fed them *samohon* in the evenings and at the village disco. Our friendship with Mayor Bobko was of a different kind, partly diplomatic,

[5] I once lost some money on a horse called 'Chapman's Peak'!

partly based on mutual self-interest. But who could not warm to such a kind-hearted rogue who loved his village and wanted the best for the villagers. I hope that Nebelivka village, and especially the school, benefitted long-term from our project, in parallel to the ways in which the teams benefitted from our understanding of the third largest Trypillia megasite.

It was a poignant moment when we left Nebelivka for the last time in summer 2017. We may go back perhaps but we haven't managed it yet.

Chapter 14

Looking back – looking forward

Looking back

If you have read thus far, you will have realised several essential traits about me. I was amazingly lucky to have loving parents – especially my mother, who gave me the kind of unconditional love that enabled me to deal with most problems. I have never pushed myself to those extremes which may have given me more enlightenment than the middle way. I have had remarkably good health, with no broken bones, one minor operation in my childhood and two minor operations in my 60s – both stupidly self-inflicted by trying to impress a woman, as well as a period of mental pain after my second marriage broke up. I have been moderately well-off except for brief periods after the collapse of each of my first two marriages. I have fully paid-up membership of what J. K. Galbraith called the 'contented classes'. I have never seen warfare at first hand and I have never put my life on the line, although friends in the West Balkans have fought in battle and villagers from Nebelivka have died fighting the Russians in the Donbass region. In a curious way, I have suffered from none of the events or processes which are central to the dramatic tensions of life and literature. I believe in the emotional and social value of laughter and have always tried to lighten the mood in both departments where I worked and in all three families in which I shared. If you consider this memoir lacking in emotional tension, it is because of this essential stability from which I have benefitted and which has so often suppressed high emotional tension. Even with my two divorces, I was able to survive because of other friends who supported me in black times. My gratitude to them is palpable, even if I have not expressed it consistently.

I have become an archaeologist, which I take to be the person whom I really am. This came about through a series of chances and decisions. It is an irony that someone who made such a catastrophic start to public speaking at school ended up in a career filled to overflowing with public speaking. Overcoming my shyness was perhaps my greatest single challenge and one in which I was helped enormously by the tolerance and supportiveness of my University of London Extra-Mural students during my first two sessions of lecturing. One of the reasons for being a prehistorian was political – in the 1960s and increasingly onwards, I felt a low probability of being able to influence wider political movements in the UK; making a difference to the interpretation of Balkan societies in the 5th millennium BC gave me a sense of social power, albeit limited.

There is an element of selfishness in surviving the good times which have been overwhelmingly dominant in my life. It is easy for an academic working in high-quality British universities to become isolated from the humdrum – the sheer tedium of everyday work in factories, fields, supermarkets or banks. I have been incredibly fortunate in never having had to work at what David Graeber has called 'bullshit jobs', where creativity and the potential for self-development are routinely excluded or sucked out of your life. The focus on one's own research is the lifeblood of one's career – a reward for completing teaching and university admin in time. When I chose not to go down the contorted path of Durham university politics, I was giving up with open eyes the possibilities of power over other people and scarce resources in favour of my selfish career research. I have worked hard at teaching and admin but few senior academics in their 50s and 60s, except research professors, have published as much as I have in those decades.

What has been the central part of my research is the academic equivalent of the childlike desire for 'Let's pretend!'. So many archaeological ideas have so little positive, evidential support that I often feel that we begin from a 'Let's pretend!' starting-point and move on to more concrete formulations of an idea, perhaps even dignified by the term 'hypothesis'. For psychoanalysts such as Donald Winnicott, many of the malaises of adult life stem from the inability to keep pretending. As Josh Cohen says, 'if we've not known what it is to pretend, we cannot feel properly alive'.[1] Likewise, there is an element of play in intellectual enquiry, which I have always felt as part of the process of constant rejuvenation in university life. My planned contribution to a future Zoom workshop is a pretend dialogue between a forager (played by Bisserka) and a farmer (played by myself), whose content was true if not real.

What I have also firmly believed and tried to put into practice was the idea that a university teacher needs to help their students to develop a critical attitude to their studies and also to life – to well-camouflaged marketing lies, right-wing articles in the *Spectator* and, most recently, Trumpian falsehoods on Fox News and the maelstrom of fake news. The citizen's duty to be critical is one of the most important aspects of modern life and resistance – in fact, it is foundational to a functioning democracy. Without such guidance from university teachers, the primary social duty of a university can easily fail.

Do I have regrets? Of course .... in many different ways. My body tells me that it would have been much happier if I had started yoga when I was in my 20s, since it now lacks suppleness and flexibility. My mind tells me that I could have caused less sadness and rancour during the break-up of two marriages. My social and familial

[1] 2021, Guardian Reviews, 20th March 2021.

sense tells me that I wish my daughter Eleanor had had more of a life - with happier times outweighing hard times. And my professional sense tells me that I should have compromised more in order to write final project reports with my partners rather than going it alone. Do these regrets keep me awake at night? Not very often ... I wonder what that means? It suggests that I have made a habit of insulating myself from feelings of guilt.

I once wrote in the concluding chapter of the Balkan prehistoric synthesis:

> By far the majority of the individuals who lived and died in later Balkan prehistory did so in relative anonymity, loved, respected, feared or hated by their families, occasionally known beyond their home settlement for a feat of skill or daring and, at death, mourned by an increasingly dwindling stock of seniors. In that sense, they resembled the great mass of humanity now, for how many of us will rate an obituary in the *Guardian* newspaper? We are indebted to the vast prehistoric silent majority for their contributions to changing patterns of social practices in the past (Chapman 2020, 386).

I neither expect a *Guardian* obituary nor deserve one but am happy that I have contributed something to the minor field of Balkan–Carpathian prehistory and to the wider field of archaeological theory through an appreciation of fragmentation. My deepest hope is that I have helped my students to develop a critical awareness that will make them good citizens.

Looking forward

I retired from Durham University in September 2017 and have never looked back. I remember several people saying to me that they were busier than ever when they retired but I haven't found that - probably because I have refused most requests for extra writing and reviews of ESF applications. Apart from the two major projects, I've written relatively little apart from contributions to my friends' *Festschriften* or memorial volumes. I have ignored the requests for writing for people I don't much like and so I have written only a few chapters - hopefully making these as original as possible and tailoring them to the interests of my good friends. I have been persuaded to do a module of online teaching in archaeological theory for a Masters course at the New Bulgarian University (Sofia), which proved not to be too taxing.

The main project has been finishing the publication of the Ukrainian Trypillia project with Bisserka. The first strand was the preparation of the materials for the ADS York archive, which opened in early 2020. The second strand was the publication of an online monograph with De Gruyter, which met its publication date of 27 August 2020.

My second major project for something that's been going on for almost 10 years now is a major synthesis of later Balkan prehistory.[2] I was sad that I fell out with Cambridge University Press over misunderstandings with Norman Yoffee and Beatrice

[2] For the start of this book project, see p. 189.

Fig. 27. Fur Tor, Dartmoor

Rehl over word limits, the number of figures and the possibilities of a book website that I would organise with additional material that was not in the published book. All of these were serious matters and so I felt I had to break my contract with CUP and move on to another publisher. There were two front-runners – Oxbow Books and Sidestone Press. I was sorry not to be able to work with Julie Gardiner, since we had spent such a long time in the Prehistoric Society working together but the Sidestone offer was substantially better and so I'm happy to say that the book was published in December 2020. This is one of the last major archaeological projects that I plan to complete in retirement. If there are further books in the pipeline, I am hoping that Bisserka will be the principal author – a long article on the Mirkovo Survey and a book on the Forest of Stones. If I live that long, a minor article would mark the centenary in 2027 of the publication of the first article I know of in Balkan prehistory, by Hortensia Dumitrescu, in which deliberate object fragmentation is mooted.

I have several other projects in mind at the moment, which should keep me going for a few more years. The first one is this book, when I have finally been able to work with Julie Gardiner at Oxbow. My second project is a Dartmoor guidebook. As a Plymouth lad, I still have close emotional connections to the moor (Fig. 27) and it gives me great pleasure to visit it at any time. I am working on a framework for a guide which can be accessed online, by smartphone, while taking in prehistoric and historic remains, the many tors and other rock formations and new recreation sites signposted on the famous 'Brown Signs'. It is amazing to discover so many details of Dartmoor landscapes that I missed entirely when I was a teenager.

The third project is musical. My main retirement present from the Durham Department of Archaeology was the Sibelius Version 7 composing software. This version is more advanced than the Sibelius Version 2 programme that my friend Duncan gave me some years ago and which I learnt to use for a series of simple arrangements for Tom Lehrer and Mony Python songs (Fig. 28). I need to learn Version 7 and try it out on small-scale pieces. I have recently written two Covid-19 songs – one for the UK and one for America – and I am looking forward to arranging music for the

Fishburn Academy brass band as well. In the slightly longer term, I should very much like to write something rather *recherché* – a Tuba Quartet – but I've still got to get started on that. There so many more possibilities for music in the next few years.

In January 2021, I reached 70. I still see my daughter Eleanor, who lives in Gateshead now. We have lots of things to do together, although she is still not in the best of mental health, with some mobility problems too, so I can't really go too far or too long from the north-east. We see each other twice a month and we hope to go on some more short breaks soon.

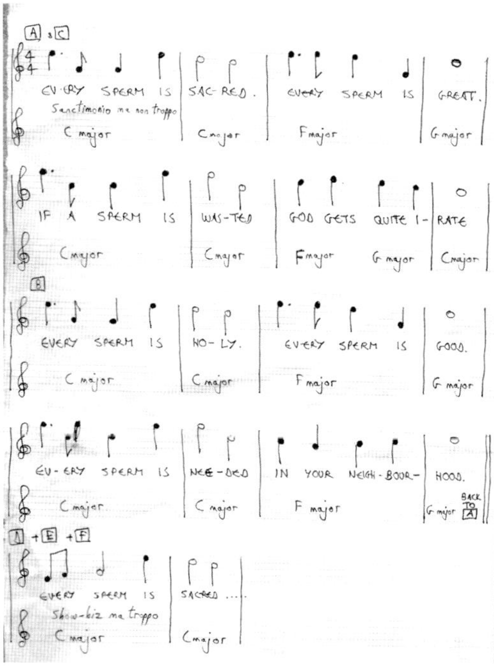

Fig. 28. *Author's music arrangement of Monty Python's 'Sperm Song', from* Monty Python's Life of Brian

I am still doing yoga classes with Bisserka and, during Covid-19, we are still walking round the village most mornings. Bisserka is on the hunt for a further post-doc at Manchester University and has been working as a consultant for Historic England. She has been offered a visiting fellowship in the Römisch-Germanisch Institute in Frankfurt and will take this up if Covid-19 outbreaks are controlled in 2021 or 2022. As for myself, my own health is not too bad. I caught Covid-19 and suffered from the symptoms for two weeks, with an 18 hour spell in hospital at the peak of the symptoms. I have high blood pressure and a high cholesterol level, for which I take tablets every day. I am resisting Type 2 diabetes through a combination of healthier diet and more exercise, with the support of a Weight Watchers programme. But, apart from that, I haven't really been showing too many signs of slowing down. Fingers crossed for a bright future.

Further reading

Chapter 1

Crossing, William (1912) *Guide to Dartmoor* (re-printed in 1965, with an introduction by Brian Le Messurier). Dawlish: David & Charles (more than a century after its publication, still the most enlightening introduction to Dartmoor).

Gerrard, Sandy (1997) *Book of Dartmoor. Landscapes through time.* London: Batsford (a wide-ranging survey of prehistory and history on the moor).

Whitfield, Henry (1987) *Torch in Flame: History of Devonport High School for Boys, Plymouth.* Exeter: Devon Books (the only available history of Devonport High School for Boys).

Woods, Stephen (1988) *Dartmoor Stone.* Exeter: Devon Books (a magnificent, illustrated tour of Dartmoor).

Chapter 5

https://www.ncl.ac.uk/who-we-are/history (an informative website with details of the history of the University of Newcastle upon Tyne).

Chapman, John (1981) *The Vinča Culture of South-east Europe.* 2 vols. Oxford: BAR (the book that emerged out of my PhD).

Chapter 6

Chapman, John, Shiel, Robert & Batović, Šime (1996) *The Changing Face of Dalmatia.* London: Society of Antiquaries of London (the principal publication of the Neothermal Dalmatia Project).

Chapter 7

Chapman, John (1994) Destruction of a common heritage: the archaeology of war in Croatia, Bosnia and Hercegovina. *Antiquity* 68: 120–126 (my article on the archaeology of the war).

Perica, Vjekoslav (2002) *Balkan Idols. Religion and nationalism in Balkan states.* Oxford: Oxford University Press (a general history of the Third Balkan Wars, with a grim summary of damage to all of the various cultural heritages involved).

Chapter 8

Chapman, John *et al.* (2010) *The Upper Tisza Project. Studies in Hungarian landscape archaeology.* International Series 2087–2090. Oxford: BAR (the detailed project reports for the Upper Tisza Project can be found in one e-book and four volumes) http://archaeologydataservice.ac.uk/catalogue/uppertisza_ba_2003/html/home.htm.

Raczky, Pál (2018) A Complex Monument in the Making at the Late Neolithic Site of Polgár-Csőszhalom (Hungary). In T. A. Bács, Á. Bollók & T. Vida (eds.) *Across the Mediterranean - along the Nile.* Budapest: Archaeolingua, 15–60 (a re-interpretation of the Csőszhalom mound and flat site).

Raczky, Pál & Füzesi, András (2018) Unusual clay artefacts and their imagery from the Late Neolithic settlement of Öcsöd-Kováshalom on the Great Hungarian Plain. In S. Ţurcanu & C.-E. Ursu (eds.)

Materiality and identity in pre- and proto-historic Europe. Homage to Cornelia-Madga Lazarovici. Suceava: Karl Romstorfer, 145–170 (an account of special deposition and object fragmentation at Öcsöd).
Raczky, Pál, Kovács, Tibor & Anders, Alexandra (1997) *Paths into the Past. Rescue excavations on the M3 Motorway.* Budapest: Hungarian National Museum & ELTE (a general account of rescue archaeology in north-east Hungary).

Chapter 9

Chapman, John (2000) *Fragmentation in Archaeology: People, places and broken objects in the prehistory of South Eastern Europe.* London: Routledge
Chapman, John & Gaydarska, Bisserka (2007) *Parts and Wholes. Fragmentation in prehistoric context.* Oxford: Oxbow Books (the two main products of the fragmentation research programme).

Chapter 10

Chapman, John (2001) Editorial. *European Journal of Archaeology* 4/1: 5 – 6 (my final Editorial).
Novaković, Predrag (2013) 'The EAA is up and running': behind the scenes of the Inaugural Meeting of the European Association of Archaeologists. In Bergebrant, Sophie & Sabatini, Serena (eds) *Counterpoint: essays in archaeology and heritage studies in honour of Professor Kritisian Kristiansen.* International Series 2508. Oxford: BAR, 21 – 25 (the account of the preparations for the Inaugural Meeting of the EAA).

Chapter 11

Draper, Simon, Gerrard, Chris & Graves, Pam (2014) *Archaeology at Durham. A short history.* 2nd edition. Durham: Durham University (a history of the Durham Department of Archaeology was produced for its 75th anniversary).

Chapter 12

Chapman, John (ed.) (2010) *From surface collection to prehistoric lifeways. Making sense of the multi-period site of Orlovo, South East Bulgaria.* Oxford: Oxbow Books (a study of one of the richest surface collections from a prehistoric Bulgarian multi-level site).
Harding, Anthony (2013) *Salt in Prehistoric Europe.* Leiden: Sidestone Press (the most impressive volume on prehistoric salt research came later than our early salt forays).

Chapter 13

Chapman, John, Nebbia, Marco & Gaydarska, Bisserka (2020) Trypillia megasites in context: independent urban development in Chalcolithic Eastern Europe. *Cambridge Archaeological Journal* 30/1: 97 – 121. http://dx.doi.org/10.1017/S0959774319000301 (a summary of the project)
Gaydarska, Bisserka (ed.) (2020) *Early Urbanism in Europe: The Trypillia mega-sites of the Ukrainian forest-steppe.* Berlin: De Gruyter (the project monograph). The open-access Project Archive is held by the Archaeology Data Service, York at: https://doi.org/10.5284/1047599.

Chapter 14

Chapman, John (2020) *Forging Identities in the Prehistory of Old Europe.* Leiden: Sidestone Press (a synthesis of my career research on Old Europe).